WINTER
DREAMS

Books by Jay Martin

Conrad Aiken: *A Life of His Art*
Harvests of Change: *American Literature 1865–1914*
Nathanael West: *The Art of His Life*
Robert Lowell
Always Merry and Bright: *The Life of Henry Miller*
Winter Dreams: *An American in Moscow*

JAY MARTIN

WINTER DREAMS

An American in Moscow

Houghton Mifflin Company   Boston 1979

Copyright © 1979 by Jay Martin

Library of Congress Cataloging in Publication Data
Martin, Jay.
    Winter dreams.

      1.   Russia—Social life and customs—1970–
2.   Russia—Social conditions—1970–   3.   Martin,
Jay.   I.   Title.
DK276.M35   947.085   78-26653
ISBN 0-395-27589-X

Printed in the United States of America
V 10 9 8 7 6 5 4 3 2 1

To Laura and Jay
— perfect comrades

You dream: that you are not asleep,
but only dreaming that you yearn for sleep, that
   someone is dozing;
and two black suns throbbing under his eyelids
are singeing his lashes as he sleeps.

— Boris Pasternak, "In a Wood"

Preface

I SPENT FIVE MONTHS in the Soviet Union as Visiting Professor of American Literature at Moscow State University (MGU). This book concerns that time.

Many other Americans — diplomats and journalists and businessmen — were in the capital while I was there, living in foreigners' ghettos, carefully guarded by Russian police. I lived among the Russians, occupying a small apartment on the fifth floor of Building B, a wing of MGU.

On my floor lived several families of workers in the university; I often met with friendly grandmothers, serious-looking married couples, and bumptious children in the hallway or rode the elevator with these neighbors. At first I could hear them whisper about the "Профессор калифорнийского университета," and I understood that the arrival of a professor from the University of California had caused a ripple of curiosity. But soon I became a familiar, accepted sight, and talk in the elevator naturally returned to speculations about the temperature and whether oranges might be found at a reasonable price in the farmers' market on Lomonosovsky Prospect. (Here, where farmers sold their products privately, I once paid six dollars for a pomegranate from Samarkand.)

I had no diplomatic passport. Unlike many of my countrymen, I hadn't brought over an American automobile or several cases of Skippy Peanut Butter. An official in the United States Embassy once explained to me that there were six categories of Americans in the Soviet Union — and I was in the lowest.

So, I took my place with my colleagues and fellow workers at MGU and lined up at the university payroll window once a month to sign my name in indelible ink and collect my salary of 240 roubles. I wasn't permitted to purchase frozen bologna at the Embassy commissary, but the Soviet Ministry of Education authorized me to lecture in Central Asia, Georgia, the Caucasus, and Leningrad. In Moscow I learned to ride the Metro and I studied the intricate bus system until the day arrived when a muddled Russian from the provinces begged my aid outside the Kievskaya railroad station and I gave him directions like an old-time Muscovite.

I hadn't thought about writing a book concerning my experiences until one of my nicest Russian friends, a member of the Journalists Union, took me to lunch at the Hotel Tsentralny, ordered fish hors d'oeuvres with vodka, and then got to the point.

"Perhaps you will write about Russia some day. Many of your countrymen have done so — and they all write the same things."

"And those are —?"

"That we have no freedom; that the bureaucracy is awful; that food is scarce, our goods old-fashioned, and service terrible; that one is followed everywhere."

All true, I thought to myself — *but not all of the truth*. And I promised him that I would try to tell about the rest of the Russian reality.

Then when I began to write I found that I couldn't write an American book, a book of reportage. Instead, I found myself writing a very Russian book. The spirit of the great nineteenth-century authors, especially of Gogol and Turgenev, still lives in Russia and it fused with my lines and made me understand that the Russian reality, though often bleak enough in itself, can be understood only through dreams, fantasies, enduring faiths, and quixotic passions.

For a long time I worried about my title — but then suddenly it came to me fully formed. I wanted "Winter" to point to the hard realities of Russian life and "Dreams" to point to its mysteries. Only later did one of my friends remark to me that "Winter Dreams" was also Tchaikovsky's subtitle for his first symphony, the most purely national of his works. So my title also had its Russian roots.

Anyone who has lived in the Soviet Union, even for a short time, understands how close truth and deception, actuality and make-believe, can become. In my book, the facts are all true. The fantasies are true too, but for different reasons, in different ways.

Without my Russian acquaintances and friends, I could not have understood enough to write these adventures. All their names are changed to protect the guilty.

Contents

WINTER
DREAMS

I

The Hotel Peking

The first time I went to the Hotel Peking I thought I would never go back. But I did go back, many times.

On my second day in Moscow I called on Tatjana Efimovna, one of the graduate students in literature who had been assigned by the Foreign Office to help me out — and keep watch on me. In her tiny dormitory room we sat on her bed and talked.

"I want to become familiar with the city as soon as possible," I told her. "What do you suggest?"

"I had the very same problem when I first moved here from Krasnodar," she said brightly. "You have a map?"

"Yes." I showed her my city map.

"No, I mean a map of the bus routes. You could purchase one at any newsstand. We'll walk up to the Metro, if you're ready. One can be gotten there. I'll put you on the Metro. Be sure to get some five-kopeck pieces. Then, this is what you will do. Get off at the Park of Culture. Upstairs, find the stop for the 5 bus. You can ride this around the Sadovoye ring road, which encircles the inner city, and follow the streets on your map. Everything goes from there into the Kremlin, of course."

Tatjana seemed to be efficient in everything; even she believed herself to be utterly serious, and she meticulously executed her official obligations toward me. She was, anyone could see, a loyal Party member. When I first met her I realized that I might easily learn to rely upon her help, but I hardly anticipated how much I would come to like her, really like her. And neither of us, I'm sure, realized what a change my casual Americanness would work in her, and how fully and rapidly her natural merriment would emerge.

But I did recognize at once how pretty she was. She had long blond hair which she usually wore in a ponytail, but when she had time to give to it, she wove it into soft braids and piled them in great coils high on her head. Her skin was very white and she wore the reddest lipstick I saw in Russia. Somehow her eyes gave harmony to her face. They were grayish-green and too large to be perfect, but they were so clear and luminous that when she blinked, as she often did, they almost flashed. Her face was full of life, always changing. I saw her fall asleep, but I never saw her look tired. She was short, and her hands and feet were really tiny, but her figure was full and she had beautiful, round breasts.

But here, I'm getting far ahead in telling about my relation to Tatjana. At the time I'm talking about I simply wanted to learn from her how to get around Moscow. And her notion about riding the city's outer circle by bus seemed like a splendid idea. It would be a start anyway, though it made me feel like a lone Indian planning to surround a wagon train of settlers.

Actually, it didn't work. The bus was so crowded I couldn't get close to a window. Besides, the windows were glazed with ice. I could only look upward, over the heads of the other straphangers and see the tops of buildings. And that was how I first saw the Hotel Peking.

It looked like a miniature duplicate of the university. Both were built in a soaring style that I came to think of as "totalitarian Gothic." Stalin's idea of grandeur was perfectly conveyed in the architecture.

At first glance there seemed to be nothing about the Hotel Peking to seize the attention of a Visiting Professor of American Literature. But my dreams that night told me I was wrong, for the place had gotten caught in some crevice in my mind. Maybe it was the architecture, maybe the political incongruity, maybe that the hotel seemed as much out of place in Moscow as I was. I don't know. But my dreams made me single it out.

My room at the university looked upon a field that had been flooded for outdoor skating. I could see some people careening around the perimeter, others improvising hockey games with jackets for goals, and lovers and groups of young girls skating hand in hand.

I watched this from my desk while I finished the notes for my first lecture. I felt sleepy and laid my head on my arms for a moment at the desk. Then I dug my own skates out of my trunk, pulled on a jacket, took the elevator downstairs, and found a way through the fence.

I skated until my ankles ached, dodging hockey players, following linked couples. The air was so cold that inhaling was like breathing flakes of marble. But it was a happy time, there among the skaters.

I felt irresponsibly glad, and that made me think that instead of taking off my skates in the frozen air, I would just pick up my boots and skate back across the street into my building and clank up to my room in my skates.

But somehow when I slipped through the fence, I made a wrong turn. I lost sight of my building and found myself skating on the ice-covered streets, down Vernadskovo Prospect toward the river.

I am going fast now. My ankles must have become

numb because they no longer hurt. Everything seems easy. The marble balustrade overlooking the river whizzes by, and like a skier I slide down the long embankment under the shadow of the ski jump until I flash out onto the Moskva itself. I can feel my blades slice into the grainy surface.

Keep to the middle, I warn myself, remembering my father's caution about the treacherous ice on rivers. I skate a hundred feet from either shore. The wind is at my back and the skating is fine. Sights reflect dully on the dark blue ice. I am enclosed by granite walls, holding the river — and me — to our course. Beyond these loom the Lenin Hills on one side and the lighted buildings of the city on the other. My shirt balloons in the wind like a sail and I fly along, past the Lenin Sports Stadium, past the Novo-Devichy Convent, past the Kiev Station.

Finally, I arrive at Kalinin Prospect, its modern skyscrapers rising like towers over me and the giant globe of the world spinning around beneath the word AEROFLOT. Just before I would pass under the bridge I take a ramp that runs up from the river. I notice a yellow sign with a squiggly arrow on it, just as on my own freeway exit in California, and I slow automatically.

Then, on the street again, I sweep under the Hotel Mir and cut across back streets and frozen fields toward the zoo. Even in this cold, a congealed odor from the apes hangs over the animal park.

Now I am working hard, swinging my arms. I think for a moment that I too must look like a singular sort of ape. The ice beneath my blades is bumpy. I feel I am pushing my way over wet cobblestones.

Toiling, I pass under a statue of the great Georgian poet Rustaveli, then take a fork to the right. Above me is a large building that casts a deep shadow across my path. When I finally burst out from beneath it onto Gorky Street and look back, I am struck dumb. There, in the middle of Moscow, in the heart of Russia, I see a legend on this building written in letters that are ten feet high and look as if they were copied from the fake Chinese calligraphy of Johnny Kam's menu in Newport Beach —

— The Hotel Peking!

The next morning, the lead-colored sun filtered through my double-paned windows making sun spots on the notes for my first lecture. My books lay open just as I had left them before pushing back my chair and dropping into bed.

I tried to think about the mainstreams of the American literary tradition, but my dream kept calling me back. I had gone through enormous labor in my dream just to arrive at the doorstep of the Hotel Peking! Yet, what could be easier than to take the Metro downtown and walk right into the hotel itself? Naturally, I planned to do so.

My whole experience of Russia would have been different had I not dreamed my way to the Hotel Peking, or not followed my dreams there.

2

I followed them as soon as possible. My second week in Moscow I started a series of Wednesday lectures at MGU's downtown campus, the original Lomonosov University, which dates from the time of the czars. Before the time came for the first lecture, I consulted my guide.

"Tatjana Efimovna," I said to her, "I thought I'd go out to dinner next Wednesday after my lecture downtown. Do you know anything about the restaurant in the Peking? Would I need to make a reservation?"

"Yes, certainly. Oh, Professor dear, it is one of the finest dining rooms in the world!"

She seemed lost in a vision of innumerable dishes sent steaming out of the kitchen.

"And is *Chinese* food really served there?"

She was hurt. "Of course! Better than in China, certainly. My sister Elena went there once. As you know she studies in the Institute of Nutrition. For weeks afterward she sang the praises of the famous Friendship Salad."

I must have looked dubious still. She had saved her clinching words of praise for the last.

"*And,*" she said in a tone of glorious triumph, "they have thousand-year-old eggs!"

Wednesday at 1 P.M. I sat down beneath a large portrait of Lenin and lectured for eighty minutes on American novels about business, by Dreiser and Norris and Howells, up to Norman Mailer and Louis Auchincloss, a predictable group. But all during my talk I was thinking less about the Robber Barons and their minions and victims than about thousand-year-old eggs.

At the conclusion there were a few questions and then Viktor Bukovsky, one of the members of the Journalists Union, came up. "A wonderful lecture," Bukovsky said. "Let me take you to the Professors Cafeteria for a coffee."

He talked as he guided me through the hallways.

"You certainly tell us many interesting things. But what about Arthur Haley? You didn't mention him. I think he is wonderful, don't you? We like him very much in our country. He is your proletarian novelist, isn't he? It's marvelous how he shows the workings of your factories."

We sat in the cafeteria talking of the delicatessens in New York City, where he had spent a year at Columbia doing research on *Fortune.* After we finished our glasses of sweet, bluish-brown coffee, he offered to drive me back to the Lenin Hills.

"Thanks, but I'm staying downtown. I'm going to have dinner at the Hotel Peking."

"What an excellent idea," he answered. "I will drive you there."

"It's very nice of you. But I think I'll just walk up."

He looked blankly uncertain at this idea.

"I have a map," I assured him.

"But, dear fellow, it's freezing out — not like your California."

"I don't mind."

"Ah, it isn't in your bones yet. You still are filled with the sun."

We walked down to the checkroom, then stood between the classical columns near the entrance putting on our coats. A squadron of noisy journalism students pressed into the doorway. They were coming from military exercises and were wearing khaki fatigues. A nimbus of frozen air clung to their jackets. They beat their arms against their chests vigorously, shaking off the cold like sheets of ice.

"It's a real Russian winter," Bukovsky said. "You're lucky. A good hard freeze."

"I just go to the left here, and then walk up Gorky Street, right?" I asked.

"Yes, that's it. Just keep going."

As I started to pull the door open he stood aside and winked. "And don't forget to have the famous Friendship Salad!"

3

I walked outside into the shadow of the Kremlin. The sky had the thick color of bloodstone. The walk was much longer than I had expected. I tightened my scarf around my neck at the first block, and after the second I let my earflaps down.

Finally, I saw the ring road coming up. I crossed over into Mayakovsky Square. Rising up behind Mayakovsky's statue, the hotel looked dismal and poor.

The lobby had a self-effacing woebegone look. Here was a hotel so poor, so ashamed of its disgraceful Chinese connections, so admittedly second-class and declassé that it didn't even possess a dollar bar or a hard-currency souvenir store, only a commonplace newsstand.

But the restaurant was amazing. In the little circular foyer four large, elaborately painted statues of Kuan Yin were set in niches. Even though I could hear the unmistakable gurgle of toilets just to the side of the foyer, I was impressed.

In the early fifties, when the hotel was built, its architects must have been convinced that Sino-Soviet relations would always be happy, and they had set out to create a glorious image of China. They created what they adored: the lacquered elegance of imperial China, an atmosphere of silk robes, embroidered slippers and rich gilding.

The far wall was covered by a stained-glass window, rich in oriental designs. Columns ran down the room. Large Chinese lanterns hung from the carved ceiling. All this tacky elegance was reflected in the mirrored walls. It looked like a set for a Fu Manchu film. Luise Rainer or Rita Hayworth could have been sitting at a far table.

Instead, the room was deserted. Someone, probably the maître d', popped his head out of a door and, seeing me, closed it like a clamshell.

I took the simplest way of attracting attention to myself by walking into the room and sitting down at a central table.

Immediately a waiter appeared in great alarm. He came at me sideways, like a crab on roller skates.

"Sir, dear sir," he breathed, "are you with a group?"

"No, I'm alone."

"That must not be, for you see this is a group table. It is all set up. It is all paid for, the meal. You must be in a group."

"I simply wish to have dinner. Any table will do."

"Ah, may I see your confirmation, your schedule? Do you have Intourist coupons? No? No written reservation? No group? Sir, this is unthinkable. You must leave at once. In our Peking restaurant here we serve only groups. You are alone."

He paused and then brightly said, as he edged me out of my chair, "You may eat your fill in our cafeteria upstairs. I will show you."

He urged me back, past the musical latrines and peeling Kuan Yins, to a staircase.

Was I still dreaming about the Hotel Peking?

"Up," he grumbled now that he had me safely out of the dining room. He jerked a stiff thumb toward the stairs, dimly lighted by one bare bulb. I followed his directions.

At the head of the stairs I passed into an empty bar. Hollywood again. It had the submerged, watery look of the bars on all those sinister cruise ships that Mary Astor,

Peter Lorre, and Tyrone Power rode across the sound stages of Warner Brothers.

At the other end of this murky room I took another flight of stairs and came out — in the cafeteria of the Hotel Peking.

4

It looked quite horrible, thoroughly Russian, not a trace of Chinese. Though about sixty people were in the room, hardly a murmur could be heard. Everyone looked shabby, beaten. Most hunched over their plates, picking at pieces of white fish covered with wrinkled yellowish skin, or toying with lumps of meat in a brown, gluey sauce. Others seemed engrossed in moving mounds of mushy *kasha* around their plates. The rest had pushed their food aside and sat vacantly, staring into space and rolling beads of black bread between their fingers.

At one end of the room a partition was set up to conceal the food counter. A line of people waited at one end, while at the other a similar group carried trays to a cash counter where an enormous woman hovered over an abacus. I followed the line to the food and when I got in back of the partition the odors came at me as if they were greasy slugs with wings.

Three women, their hair tied up in bandannas, stood behind the steam table. Once white, their jackets had acquired an antique brownish-yellow patina, like a fine old skull.

These dragonish Rhine maidens, these three fates of the Peking, were all engaged in a hissing argument with a customer. He stood there holding a plate of bouillon in one hand and gesturing toward a soggy meat dumpling lying on the floor. With utter conviction he insisted that the accident had been the woman's fault. This *pirozhole* had slid off the plate before she had relinquished her hold on it. Her eyes flashed a gray leaden fire as she maintained that he had accepted the plate from her.

As I watched, he picked up the *pirozhole*. A few buttons of grease remained on the grimy floor near the base of the table. Gesturing with the bit of food, he continued to berate all three women. They proposed to ignore him and waved him away with a string of oxlike *nyets*. But he wouldn't budge.

Suddenly the argument was over. One woman seized a fresh dumpling from the steam tray and tossed it onto his plate. Then, imperiously silent and bent upon putting him in the wrong, she thrust her hand out, palm upward, and scowled at him, as if to say, "Well, do you intend to take away the food about which you've just raised an unholy fuss?" Shamed, he placed it in her hand, carefully, as if it were an egg.

Until he passed out of sight of the counter area she glared at his back. At the end of her rodlike outstretched arm her upturned palm was stiff and immobile. A meat dumpling sat on it as if it had been entered into the scales of justice. When he disappeared she relaxed, and in plain sight of all of us, she defiantly tossed the manhandled dumpling back into the steam tray. It happened so quickly that no one could tell which was the soiled one.

And I had already decided to order bouillon and *pirogi*! I settled for *soljanka* stew instead.

I sat by a window overlooking Mayakovskoro Square and stared at the blank faces of buildings. I tried to imagine all the walls removed. In one apartment after another families were eating their evening meal, fried meat, potatoes, semolina balls, cheese and mayonnaise, cucumber with *smetana*, a little pasty rice. The way I imagined it, no one talked, no one opened his mouth except to stuff some chewy morsel into it.

Then I did imagine I heard them talk, a few mumbled conversations. All talk finally came around to one subject, not sex, as in my own country. Here, it was food. The theme was the same: were you getting enough? Had you found a café where the lines weren't long? Were there Samarkand pomegranates this week at the big farmers' cooperative market on Lomonosovsky Prospect? Do you have a piece of chocolate in your pocket? Mothers leaned over to toddlers and taught them this maxim: eat whenever possible, eat all you can.

I invented all this, of course. Because I was terribly lonely I invented these people and their conversations to keep me company. I imagined that when dinner was over the families pulled on ice skates and rushed down to the Moskva River, sailing on skates before the ice-splintered wind, laughing and shouting to each other and calling into the deep night to lost friends and children who had skated and skated so far and fast they had not come out until they reached the other side of their dreams, in the gulf of Finland — or Timbuctu.

For a long time I dawdled by the window. The soup tasted like ocean water flavored with kidneys. I let it sit until it congealed into a lavender paste.

5

Mentally I was already pushing myself away from the table to leave when I caught sight of a figure half rising from a table, half bowing and half turning aside, half beckoning toward me and half concealing his face, as if to provide for every eventuality.

I knew that I had seen him before, but at first I couldn't place him. Then I did place him distinctly — in the third row, fourth seat from the left, in my classroom at the university. Twice after class he had approached me with some obscure questions about American art. In the absence of anyone else I had become his expert, and he asked for information of the most strange, improbable sort concerning Benjamin West and other early American painters. Now, when he saw that I did recognize him, he became incredibly agitated. He behaved like a paint-mixing machine trembling to a halt in a series of convulsive jerks.

I rose and started toward the table to join him. While I was still some distance away he stuck out his arm stiffly, as if to shake my hand in greeting. Then he pulled it back and began to wring his hands. Next he wiped them briskly on the flaps of his jacket.

He was tall and pitifully thin, and this was exaggerated by the fact that years before he had outgrown his jacket. His arms stuck out of the sleeves like oars from a galley. His face operated completely independently of his body. While his arms and hands went through their sequence of motions, he gave me a smile, a look of abstraction, a wink, and a grimace. At the last he bit his tongue.

By the time I actually arrived at the table his two companions were also standing. Having come full circle he again stuck out his hand. In haste, before he should go through the same cycle again, I seized his hand. It felt like a mummy's. He looked at me, his eyes wild. I thought he might faint if I let his hand go. His face had lost all color. I could see the tracings of veins, like blue spider webs, under his skin.

"Professor! Dear me, how good to see you," he mur-

mured in a surprisingly deep voice. "Kavelin, Andrei Nikolaivich," he added in a dead tone as if pronouncing a
sentence. "This is wonderful, wonderful, this chance
meeting," he said, stressing the last phrase for the benefit
of his companions.

"Professor!" he said again, giving a special upbeat
stress to the word, emphasizing its ceremonial character.
"Allow me to introduce my wife, Flora Tursunovna, and
my good friend, Lev Alexandrovich."

The woman was short, so short I was amazed to hear
that she was Andrei's wife. The top of her head barely
reached his chest. She said nothing and did not offer to
shake hands. She simply looked at me with a desire not to
flinch, the way a very sick person does.

Lev Alexandrovich behaved very differently. He shook
my hand cordially and while Andrei and his wife stood
there like frozen marble pillars he waved me into a chair.
Except for very bad teeth he was a handsome, graceful
man with wavy white hair, a man who took good care of
himself. He smiled at me as if we were old friends and
though I was sure he hadn't been to my classes, under the
charm of his smile I began to feel that I had met him before. Even the voice sounded vaguely familiar.

He started right in to talk.

"It's fine, simply fine, that you have come to Moscow to
teach our students about America. Andrei here has told
me that you've been an enormous help to him already. He
says you know the most astonishing things, he says you're
a marvel, an American font of wisdom — just like the famous baths at Palm Springs where your president goes for
refreshment, eh? Andrei sings your praises, I can tell
you."

Andrei, meanwhile, seemed to be trying to pull his long
neck into his wrinkled shirt collar.

"I don't count myself among the fortunate ones," Lev

continued, "who have been to your lectures. They talk about you in the Journalism School too, I'm sure. 'Uptown, downtown, all around the town' — isn't that one of your famous American songs? But I have promised myself that on the very first opportunity I shall be sitting in the front row to hear you. You'll allow me, I hope — thanks awfully — we *are* very busy in Moscow, we workers."

When he paused I said a little lamely, "I'm glad to meet you both. What luck to find you here, Andrei."

At the word "find" he looked at me as if I had struck him between the eyes with an ax. "Quite an accidental meeting," I added to soften the blow.

"For my own part," Lev interjected, "this is a miracle. I never eat here. But it is an amusing spot to take a glass of tea and chat with friends and smoke a friendly cigarette."

He pulled out a vermeil cigarette case.

"Have one, will you? They're Turkish. At my age I can't tolerate Georgian tobacco — and certainly not the Cuban. These were given to me by one of my friends who is allowed to travel abroad."

I took one to fill in the gap in the conversation. He had a disposable lighter too, which he held out to me.

He chatted on in a bubbling, lively way, not asking questions. Or, if he did ask them, he was ready to answer them himself. Perhaps I would like to meet some Soviet writers? Or visit Pasternak's grave? He'd be glad to accompany me to Mamontov's house out in the country at Abramtsevo, where Gogol and Turgenev and other writers had stayed as guests. What about Chekhov's apartment? Did I like my own apartment? Had I as yet received an invitation to meet with the editors of the *Journal of Foreign Literature*? A most charming woman was the editor.

As he spoke he often nodded to Andrei and Flora as if he were simply phrasing their questions for them. Sometimes he'd interject something like, "Ah, yes, Dostoevsky's apartment too — Andrei will happily take you there." But generally he spoke for all of us.

The more he talked the more I felt I had met him. But Andrei had botched the introduction, hadn't given me Lev's last name, though perhaps that wouldn't have been a clue either.

The feeling grew as Lev switched to talk about Hollywood. He wanted to know all about the costumes in *Chinatown* — were they wonderful? And the special effects in *The Towering Inferno*. And had I seen *Deep Throat?* — all Americans had been to see that movie, hadn't they? And *The Godfather, Part Two* — he had read the reviews. Did it really show that the Mafia were the heroes of America?

"Your own book on Nathanael West," he said. "I believe it has appeared already. I haven't read it. I'm sure it's in great demand at the Lenin Library. I'm pleased to tell you that at long last Progress Publishers is putting out a translation of *The Day of the Locust*."

Before he finished, I remembered when we had met.

"Yes, my biography has come out," I said. "When was it, nineteen sixty-seven, that we talked about West? At a party at Michael Blankfort's, if I remember."

"A splendid fellow. I taught him how to serve vodka the Russian way — freezing a good bottle of Starka in a block of ice with just the spout showing."

Then I remembered all the details of that meeting. Leo Dahl — that was how I had gotten his name on that night. Mike had told him that I was in Hollywood interviewing people who knew West for a biography, and Dahl had said at once,

"Pep West? I myself met him in Hollywood in nineteen thirty-three. Columbia Studios, yes. He complained he was grinding out dog stories. And I — I was doing something with cameras, stranded, just as he was, in Hollywood after my dear master Sergei Eisenstein had gone back. I had heard about his book *Miss Lonelyhearts* and I wanted to see more of him. He had a sad Russian look, and he talked like Dostoevsky. But I only met him that once. He was gone. I was gone."

Dahl wasn't the main Russian figure at Blankfort's party; he appeared to be the interpreter and guide for the well-known writer for whom the party was given. But he had done most of the talking that night.

I believed his story about meeting West until later the same evening when I heard him tell another story that seemed obviously a lie.

"Here's how things were in those days, in the thirties," he said. "I myself was in love with Svetlana Stalin and she returned my love. We had no thought of getting married — it was too much to expect. But we considered ourselves married. What is marriage anyway but a promise, a sign, between two lovers?

"One day, however, I am summoned to the Kremlin and ushered into Stalin's office. The conversation lasted only a minute.

" 'I wish you to stop seeing my daughter, comrade. I have other plans for Svetlana,' he says.

" 'We are in love. I cannot do as you ask.'

" 'Very well.' Nothing more. His eyes moved me to the door.

"The next day I was arrested and sent to a labor camp for four years. Some political deviation had been discovered in my camera work. All that time I received no letters, not a word. Then when I returned to Moscow, I received a message from Svetlana: 'I am still your wife.'

"We resumed. These were the happiest days I had ever known.

"Then came the same summons from the Kremlin.

" 'I wish you to leave my daughter alone, comrade. You are interfering with my plans for Svetlana.'

" 'We consider ourselves as one, Comrade Stalin.'

" 'You are mistaken.'

"The next week I am taken to a labor camp in the Urals for seven years. I was released early only when the war came. No message from Svetlana greeted me this time. That broke my heart."

As I say, that story had seemed so obviously contrived to give Dahl center stage, to play upon the fantasies of Americans, that I thought he might add on the end that he was the last of the Romanovs too.

So I believed until the following year when I actually dipped into Svetlana Stalin's autobiography and found the same story there — told from her side and differing in details, but essentially the same. Then I believed him. Later I doubted him again. The story might be true, but he need not be the man. And finally I just forgot him because I decided I never would know the truth about him. Ten years' time had all but erased my memory of that evening. Now I was as perplexed as ever.

"Well," I said after the conversation ran out, "I have to go home. There's always a lecture to prepare. Let's have lunch one day. Do you have a phone? Why not write it here?" I offered my address book.

"Lunch? It's impossible," he sighed, refusing the book gently. "But I'm here often in the afternoons. Come see me. This is a good place to meet. Downstairs is full of CIA. Here is the only place in Moscow at the moment where one can talk freely. You must come back — you must. You'll meet people here, I'll see to it. Why, if you didn't have to go, there are at least a dozen people in the room that you would find it amusing to meet. How very unfortunate that you must leave. Come back! I'll prepare the way for you. Yes, you *must* come. Andrei will bring you."

We were standing, edging toward the door while he pinched my sleeve. At Lev's last words Andrei nodded his head vigorously on his poor thin neck.

I thanked them all, made exaggerated gestures of hurry, and made for the door. At the exit I turned to make a formal salute of goodbye. But none of them looked my way. Among the other diners there they sat, staring into space, like three cadavers.

My dreams had prodded me to this Hotel Peking. The hotel was like a Chinese box. Beyond its rooms were vaster secrets, one inside another. Skating, the mythical Friendship Salad, the university, Lev, the murky cafeteria, all of these seemed no more substantial than images flashed against a blank wall, one succeeding another without leaving a trace. These too were like dreams, each contained in the next.

But you always come out on the other side of your dreams.

Outside the hotel I looked back once before diving into the Metro. On top of the spire a red star burned against the blue-black sky, like fiery ice dropped into a bottomless sea.

II
I Become the Head
of the Party

My dream of skating was not the only dream I had during the months I spent in the U.S.S.R. But to tell about another I first have to tell about Marya Fyodorovna. She was, and I suppose she still is, an office manager in the Ministry of Defense. Despite all the things that might have stood in our way, we became lovers quite easily and naturally soon after we met at a university dance recital.

I liked Marya Fyodorovna. I was dazzled by the vast range of her emotions, though I was never sure how deep they went. Sometimes I thought they went very deep. In any event, a great many superficial things also amused her, and so she made an excellent companion. Moreover, she had connections of all kinds. No one else I knew in Moscow could get fresh Iranian caviar on a day's notice. Not another soul in my acquaintance could bypass the long lines at the Pushkin Museum by speaking discreetly to one of the guards at the entrance.

Like my other friend, Tatjana Efimovna, Marya was as accomplished as a ballerina when operating in her own particular sphere of life. Tatjana arranged all sorts of complicated excursions and helped me cut through impossible bureaucratic tangles, while Marya Fyodorovna understood the intricacies of Soviet courtesies and was an endless source of gossip. She instructed me in Russian social relations as few others could have done.

A few years older than Tatjana, Marya was even prettier and she certainly had more style. Her apartment was full of snapshots and studio portraits of herself, and I thought it was a significant sign of her singularity that in none of them did she wear her hair in bangs like most of her contemporaries. She had fine, thin bones and a wide brow which was traced with delicate lines when she was thoughtful; and she cleverly framed her face against a circle of dark, softly curled hair, cut shoulder length. Her voice was much softer, much more wistful, than Tatjana's and she always spoke to me, barely moving her lips, as if we two shared some really splendid intimacy, some perfect accord, that must remain secret from everyone else in the world. I liked her voice; it had no edges on it.

I liked her, too, because of the way she regarded her body. She treated herself as if she were a fine thing. Of the few women I came to know in Moscow she was the only one, for instance, who had nice underwear. The others had regulation white synthetic bloomers, usually coming apart at the seams. But Marya wore nothing but satin bikini panties, in mauve and taupe and black. They fit so perfectly that when she walked around my bedroom wearing only them (and always staying close to the electric heaters), all her little rounded contours and even her silky mound were sheathed in perfect visibility. She had other fine, delicate clothes, too, which she brought out when I went to her rooms: negligees, robes, camisoles, little short slips, all manner of undergarments. She'd reach into her big bureau and pull them out, these bright and colorful things, as one would haul exotic fish from a tropical aquarium.

For anyone else this stress on clothes would have been

absurd, but it was right for her: she made it seem proper because it was not a matter of vanity — it was simply the way that one should treat such a body, a body like hers. To do any less for it would have been a sacrilege, like draping filthy rags over the Easter altar. That was it: she looked at herself, if I may put it this way, sacramentally. Or, still more accurately, she saw herself as a veritable piece of history. Her soul was like the eternal flames burning outside the Kremlin to commemorate the hero cities. And the clothes in which she dressed herself were like flowers laid on a monument.

I learned this about her just before the first time we made love. She lay back on the bed, her head propped up by pillows so that she could see herself, and placed her hand reverently on her pussy.

"Do you see," she whispered, "this is a wonderful thing for an American." She rubbed two fingers over her mound so that I could hear the hair crackle under the silk. "There's nothing else like this in all of Russia, nothing at all."

She was so wrapped up in wonder of herself that she was like a guide giving a tour of the Taj Mahal.

"Yes, here between my smooth thighs, the most wonderful man in Russia, the greatest man in all the world, found his pleasure. Isn't it wonderful," she cooed as she slipped her pants off, "isn't it marvelous?"

"Yes, I can tell you, Nikita Sergeevich Khrushchev found solace — *here!* I was nothing, just a teen-ager, just a translator on General Malinovsky's staff. But he saw something in me, he brought me presents whenever he came back — from London, Camp David, Paris, Vienna. He made me a great person."

But for all the honor she accorded her body, she never treated it as sacred, untouchable. She was like a mu-

seum. And despite the ravages, she wanted people to visit it. And she made me feel that for her to make love to me, an American, was a special honor. She told many stories about Nikita Sergeevich, always in the most affectionate terms. The day this sixty-odd-year-old man caught sight of her, a girl of eighteen or nineteen, and took her, must have been the greatest day of her life. The only trouble was that she never really seemed able to connect herself personally with the event. It was her body he had taken, and she was the custodian of this treasure.

Still, she did, as I say, talk about Khrushchev. She told me once of the heart-rending moment when Nikita Sergeevich began to speak of his early days, in Yuzovka, working for the Party. As a boy he had worked in the Yuzovka mines, owned by foreign capitalists. But now, after the triumph of the Bolsheviks, he returned there as assistant manager. There were no foreign capitalists anymore. He understood in a dim way that there were no capitalists at all: he was one of the bosses now. He was a respected functionary for the Party. Someone named him secretary of the Party cell in Yuzovka. Who had selected him? Why had he, not long ago a laborer, been singled out? He tried to think what talents he had. Perhaps it was because he *was* a laborer, the kind of guy, he was told by Party members above him, who made the revolution: *proletary*. But there were plenty of laborers. Lots of them were starving. He had had only three years of school. He could barely read his letters.

He went to a Cheka school to learn something. He believed whatever he was told. Otherwise, how could one be sure of anything? He learned that Russia needed electrification; electrification needed coal. Everything else was confusion. The Cheka often shot people, men who knew how to read. Marya said he wanted to make her under-

stand how confusing this was to him — it really was a revolution when men who knew how to read were shot, and the likes of him were made Party functionaries, secretaries.

He didn't want to be shot. What was the answer? From a long distance away the answer came: *coal, the revolution is coal.* He could understand that, he could cling to that. He had been born in Kalinovka: he knew coal.

So he would line up the workers before they were allowed to go into the pit, and harangue them: "Listen to me. I have a message from our dear Vladimir Ilyich Lenin for you. Coal is the revolution. Yesterday you produced so much. Today you must do better. Look how easy your lot is. Vladimir Ilyich has much to worry about, shoes and shirts and light bulbs, hundreds of things. He worries about you. He worries that you will not take your job seriously. All he asks is that you worry about coal. Nothing else. He will send you boots and medicine and tinned meats, just as if they dropped from the hand of God. You must forget about these things. He sends you picks, too. Take them and beat them with all your might against the stones."

Because he was confused he said this slowly, deliberately, very loudly, as if he were in a dream. People respected him. The Cheka listened to him, even though he was a pupil in the school, even though he could barely read. Sometimes he banged the table with his books. He was the real *proletary*, a valuable guy.

But production in the mine went down. One day he had two of the miners taken out of line suddenly. It was the morning shift. He told the Cheka to take them around the other side of a shed, where the workers couldn't see them. But the miners could hear the shots. Coal. He couldn't remember why he had selected these particular workers. They had a hurt look in their eyes as they stood in line. Perhaps this was enough. He remembered that look.

He worked night and day. Did he sleep or eat? He couldn't remember. Then, one time when he came home, an old grandmother was serving soup to his two little children. His wife was dead. They said she died of starvation. How could it happen that she was dead? She was a worker too.

The Revolution was changing. Someone told him he was to leave the mines. Coal was not so important after all. Politics were important. The Anarchists were important. And the Social Revolutionaries and the Mensheviks. The GPU was important. He was to enroll at the Donets Mining Technical School, he was to be a *politrook* there.

When his wife died, he told Marya, he had moaned and cried, but he had also learned something. Coal was important. Potatoes and grain were also important. To stiffen the resolution of the Party at Donets was crucial. Most important of all was not to starve. Yes, and to care for the little ones. Not to starve — yes, to get power. Use power. The power of Coal: the power of Grain. The power of the Party. Things weren't so confusing after all.

Marya said that often when he told her such things she thought he was going to cry. But by the time he finished his little eyes were glittering. He gave her one of the large beaming smiles that only he could give, and he reached out his arms to her like a great panda and exclaimed, "Dear little *devochka*, I do believe in having you give me another vodka — yes? — and coming over here to sit on my lap!"

She told me many stories about the times before he fell from power. Naturally he never really spoke about politics to her. He told her little comic stories about pompous men like Bulganin and Shepilov. And he made fun of Malenkov whose brains, he said, suffocated in his rolls of lard.

For her benefit he drew charts of Soviet power on the tablecloth. "Here, watch this. Take this pepper shaker: that is me. And the salt is Mikoyan: this fork is Suslov, the knife is head of the secret police, Beria. That is a joke, my dear. Let us say that this dish of butter is poor Georgi Malenkov. Here, take the sugar bowl — that's Molotov. This napkin ring — that's my darling Yekaterina Furtseva."

He made it all so vivid as he moved the utensils and dishes around the table, Marya said, that she felt he should have been a stage manager: he would have done splendidly with Chekhov. As a film director he could have brought *War and Peace* to the screen. Anyway, he kept knocking candlesticks down or turning dishes over and saying things like: "Now Kaganovich is done for, the old fox!" When he took the butter dish and with a grand stroke dumped it into a pitcher of ice water, he shouted with glee: "Here goes little Georgi to his power station in Siberia!" He removed the sugar and said, "All the way to outer Mongolia! Serves Vyacheslav Mikhail right!" Yes, Marya said, he could have been the head of M.G.M.

During Khrushchev's very last days, he took a good-will trip to Simferopol and then went vacationing in Sochi, suspecting nothing. Then she began to hear the rumors going around Marshal Malinovsky's offices that Khrushchev's own men, Brezhnev and Kosygin, were forming an alliance with Suslov, which was supported by Shelepin's KGB connections and confirmed by Malinovsky himself. Certainly in the Ministry of Defense it had never been a secret that the Marshal was unhappy over Khrushchev's fixation on rockets, ICBMs, sputniks, nuclear warfare. Like all the senior staff — those who had fought in the great armored battles at Leningrad or the Kursk salient — Malinovsky wanted to know: what about tanks? Tanks, bigger and bigger tanks, were the necessary ingredients in their idea of combat. Khrushchev had forgotten about tanks, and so the Ministry of Defense wanted him replaced. Khrushchev had lost the army. The pepper shaker was empty.

Rumors flew all about Moscow. In the offices of the Ministry of Defense, they had a special intensity. Little work was done. The Plan was ignored.

Perhaps the Presidium had gathered in an unusual session. Perhaps the industrialist Ustinov had flown to Sochi to ask Khrushchev to return to Moscow. Perhaps Malinovsky was ready to encircle the city with his tanks — as Marshal Zhukov had done for Khrushchev seven years before. Only now, this would separate the master from his supporters in the Ukraine and the Crimea. She had no way to warn him. It never occurred to her that to do so was possible or even desirable. She had her job, she was only in her early twenties by this time, and who knew how such manipulations would all come out? She was doing a lot of dancing those days in a restaurant where several young army officers often took her. They often asked her if she had had any letters from the head of state. What kind of spirits was he in? Was he enjoying his vacation? It was almost mid-October. The first snow of winter would soon fall on Moscow. No one could do anything about it. Everything came to an end.

She really told her stories well; it was apparent that she had read something like Alexei Tolstoy's "How We Write" attentively, for she had an excellent sense of style. That and the very strangeness of hearing about these matters directly from her — especially, often, after lovemaking and before we went to sleep — gave her and her tales a dreamy power. Every time we made love she treated it as a special — almost historic — occasion. She was, perhaps, the last woman alive to have slept with N. S.

Khrushchev, and I was an American. She invested our lovemaking with an aura that made it like another Summit Meeting — as if in us, somehow, Khrushchev and Kennedy met.

I'm telling about Marya because my affair with her was intimately connected with one of my dreams in Russia. Perhaps without success, I'm trying to describe the intense effect that her stories had on me. That's the only way I can explain a dream I had following an evening of her tales.

I am sitting at my desk, contemplating the amazingly rapid accumulation of snow. Five floors below me students dressed in dark clothes and, in some cases, in military uniforms hurry across already obliterated paths, but paths their feet know well. Old women, their heads wound all about in long gray scarfs, shovel snow or chop ice. I cannot hear the sounds through my double windows. But then as I watch I do hear what the sounds must be like. No, I hear exactly what the sounds are.

The phone begins to ring shrilly. In a moment I step into the little hall and pick it up. As usual, the line crackles with static.

"El-loo? El-loo? Professor Martin?"

"Yes. That's right."

"Good. This is the Kremlin secretariat. I am calling for First Secretary V. I. Lenin."

This does not seem so unusual. But it is certainly exciting. I feel, literally feel, a shiver run down my left side.

"I understand."

"Yes, Mr. Lenin has asked me to invite you to a party here."

He names a date and a time and gives other trivial details, but I have no recollection of what these are.

"Can you come?"

"Certainly, I'm honored. Yes, certainly. I'll be glad to do so."

"You understand, the time is a matter of the utmost importance. You must arrive early, before the other guests do. First Secretary Lenin wishes you to act as, shall we say, a receptionist, to help out with the guests. Is that clear?"

"Yes, I'll be there," I answer. But I'm not at all clear just what it is intended I should do, what it would mean to be a receptionist at a fête given by Lenin.

For some reason the man on the other end of the line senses my confusion and so he goes on to explain: "When the ladies and gentlemen arrive, you will greet them at the door and see that their wraps are taken. The servants will be under your command. It is most important that you should give the ladies your arm and lead them into the main hall, the ballroom. Once there, you will please transmit their orders for drinks to the staff of butlers. In short, you will be essential to the success of everything."

While this seems a very curious request to make of me, it is not, after all, so thoroughly outlandish as to cause me to reject an invitation by Lenin.

As it happens, moreover, when I arrive, dressed in the tuxedo for which I haven't found earlier use in Moscow, Lenin himself is waiting for me. We have a chance for a talk together. He looks exactly as he does in the motion pictures that are shown every hour on the hour in the Lenin Museum on Prospect Marksa.

I am actually in the presence of Lenin. Everywhere in Moscow on holidays big portraits of Lenin are posted. Statues of Lenin are in every city square from Minsk to Irkutsk. He's so nice, so down to earth that I have to remind myself he's really a famous guy.

But Lenin is doing his best, I see, to put me at ease, giving me that boyish smile of his, a smile that goes right from his lips to his cheeks and even enters his eyes. Everything is concentrated in his eyes — the lids around them are crinkled, giving him a merry look, and the light in them is sharp and piercing. He is almost laughing, he is certainly ready to laugh. Any little thing might start him going — that's the impression he gives. Besides, he is giving me the salute that one often sees in his pictures, a little wave of his uplifted arm.

As he draws me with him across the room to a window seat he speaks in the most cordial manner possible, without really saying much. It is a rare view we have, looking out over the Kremlin grounds, across the walls and toward the city. Quickly, as if a drape has been pulled, the night comes on and makes the yellow and gray and red buildings vanish.

"Well, tell me what you think about the Twenty-fifth Congress," I ask him. I'm really interested in his views. The Congress is in session at this time. Delegates have come from all over the world, and the city is filled with many foreigners, all important Communists. Indeed, there are so many official visitors here, Moscow is closed to tourists: there is simply no room in the hotels except for *delegatsiya*. The phrase has a splendid ring to it: Moscow is a "closed city." This makes it sound like ancient China or Japan. I feel very special being inside it. I myself am often mistaken for a member of the American Communist Party.

Besides, the Congress is also on my mind because every time I turn on the television, the same speech seems to be on all four channels; yet no progress seems to be made, nothing seems to be happening at the Congress.

Others apparently feel the same way. I tell Lenin: the

only real joke I have heard during my stay in Moscow is about the Congress. A Soviet citizen turns on his TV. Channel One: a speech by Comrade Brezhnev. Quickly he flips to Channel Two: Brezhnev, speaking from another camera angle. In haste, he snaps the dial to Channel Three: Brezhnev again! One last chance. Quickly he goes to Channel Four. There, in an empty room sits a man staring sternly at him, wagging his finger at him and clucking: *tsk, tsk, tsk*. At once the abashed citizen switches back to Channel One and watches attentively to the end of the five-hour speech.

Lenin likes the joke. I can see that. He says nothing, but he keeps smiling in a hazy way, like a face floating on a silent movie screen.

Still, I feel certain that behind the scenes at the Party Congress something really significant is occurring, and that is why I seize the opportunity to ask Lenin about it. I believe he is about to tell me the answer to my question.

But before he has the chance to offer his observations the doorbell rings. Not a single servant is about. And, though he is wearing his cap, Lenin is attired only in his shirt-sleeves and vest. In the little space between his vest and his pants one can see that he is wearing suspenders. He has soft, backless slippers on his feet. No discussion is necessary. I take up my part for the evening and go to answer the door, long before the guests are expected.

Standing in the doorway is a beautiful middle-aged woman; she may be in her early fifties, but she stands erect and moves with grace. As soon as he sees her, Lenin flies across the room in the greatest of agitation, quite in contrast to the easiness of his manner just a few minutes earlier. He embraces her, and she him, with genuine enthusiasm.

It develops that these two old comrades have not seen

each other for years. Once they had been very close —
not as lovers, I guessed, but sheerly in their devotion to
the destiny of the Party, the achievement of world socialism. Perhaps they had even grown up together. Yes, they
played together as children. For a long time, while Lenin
has presided over Russia, she has been elsewhere, fo-
menting revolutions. She is a kind of universal secret
agent, the very spirit of rebellious change. Now the winds
of history have blown her by the Kremlin and, quite simply, she has "dropped in" to see Lenin. Without a doubt
she is the only person in the world who would have been
permitted to do so.

"Why, this is perfect. I am giving a great party tonight.
You must be present!" Lenin says with joy.

"Look at me," she says, making him see that under her
flowing hooded cape she wears a green peasant blouse,
belted, and battleship-gray pants tucked into black riding
boots. "This is not the costume for a party. I have come
at the wrong time, Comrade Lenin. I see you have many
things to keep you busy."

Has Lenin become too accustomed to being an administrator — has he forgotten the Revolution itself? That
seems to be the accusing implication of her hard, unyielding answer; and, in any event, it is what he infers. It
stings him a little.

"Let's not fight about it, comrade. We each have our
own ways." Then he gives her his astonishing smile. "But
tonight, let me have *my* way. You must go to your hotel
and dress. Dress for me, won't you? Why, I won't have
anything else. You must!"

She looks dubious. She will not bend under pressure,
obviously.

"Let us both have our ways, then. We *shall* talk. We'll
go together to your apartment in my car, and we will talk

of the Revolution as we go and while you dress and on the way back. Marya Fyodorovna, I simply won't lose this rare opportunity."

This moment is the first time that either of them has noticed me since her arrival. Lenin turns my way.

"I'm leaving for a while. Now you are in charge of my party."

"But do you know what you are saying?" I ask, talking only to myself. Nonetheless, I promise to manage the party for him until he returns.

But as soon as he leaves, everything starts to happen. The doorbell begins to ring like crazy. All the servants decide to take a holiday. The whole place falls into a shambles. First off, a very large group arrives, an African delegation. Their dress is perfectly splendid. Cab Calloway is among them, but all of the others outdo him in finery. Big-lapeled yellow and lavender suits on the men and floor-length sequined dresses on the women glitter and dance. All by myself I have to take their coats, greet them in the name of V. I. Lenin, make drinks for them, show them the way to the ballroom, and make small talk. I feel like a single-handed Mack Sennett cast.

At last, in frustration I give up and go into the ballroom to ask the orchestra leader to prepare some music for a dance, just to keep the guests occupied. Fortunately, the band is sitting in its place, eating sliced sturgeon sandwiches. I tell them to await my signal before playing.

By the time I get back to the entrance room, the place is mobbed. I realize that unless I establish some kind of order chaos will ensue. When the band starts to play everyone will make a frenzied rush toward the door of the ballroom just the way thousands of people push a hundred deep at the cloakrooms after the ballet at the Palace of Congress.

With hardly a thought I form a plan and act on it immediately. I gain attention and order everyone to get into line so that I can march them into the ballroom in an orderly way. On the chance that Lenin will return I tell them that this is a reception line. Everyone must wait patiently to pay respects to the master. More than anyone else, Russians are accustomed to waiting in line, so they obey me readily, naturally, and form a thick phalanx, starting at the entry door and ending just at the door to the ballroom.

I feel that at least I have gotten them calmed down, so I can plan my next move. But, as luck will have it, just at that moment Lenin slips in the door. He too is a Russian and even though he is more powerful than a czar, he forgets who he is and, seeing a line, meekly joins it.

I, however, get so excited that just like the secretary in Tikhon Khrennikov's opera *In the Storm*, I cry out: "ВОТ Ленин "—(behold Lenin!) and start to applaud his entrance. And everyone else starts to applaud also.

To my horror, the band apparently takes this as my signal and swings into a rollicking "Cu-ca-ra-cha."

My god! Each person grabs the comrade in front of him and, four abreast, the lines sway and kick into the ballroom.

"So," I say to myself, "this is the way I lead the Party!"

Marya rolled over in bed that morning and threw her leg over mine. After a few minutes she said quietly, "Are you awake?"

I hoped to stay in my dream and discover what would happen next. But her words had opened a black hole in my head. And besides, by her tone I knew that she had been dreaming her own dreams, dreams she perhaps wanted to keep awake from. She wished to talk them away.

"He was a great man, Nikita Sergeevich," she said, just

as if our last night's conversation had lasted all night for her, while for me it had been transformed.

"But," she added with surprising ferocity, "he was a peasant, the son and grandson of a peasant."

She paused for a while. I gathered she felt she had gone too far and wanted to pull back. But it was not that at all.

"I was a friend of Irina, and her mother, Olga Ivinskaya," she said dreamily after a long time.

After another pause she asked, "Don't you read Pasternak? I'm talking about the real Lara and her daughter — the woman, Olga Ivinskaya, who was Pasternak's great love, the real Lara."

The anguish of the end of *Dr. Zhivago* came back: *One day Larisa Feodorovna went out and did not come back. She must have been arrested in the street at that time. She vanished without a trace and probably died somewhere, forgotten as a nameless number on the list that afterwards got mislaid, in one of the innumerable mixed or women's concentration camps in the north.*

"Yes," I said. "I remember."

"She was lost, she did go to the camps, Stalin sent her there. Oh, she suffered horrors, unspeakable things . . .

"But she didn't die. She came back after the death of Stalin. They were close again, she and Boris Pasternak, but not lovers. She began to do translations from the French for the journal *Novy Mir*, she and her daughter Irina, a girl my own age. In official circles it was rumored that Olga Ivinskaya herself typed the manuscript that Pasternak smuggled to Italy for Feltrinelli to publish.

"And then, of course, the storm over the novel and the Nobel Prize broke and Pasternak was called — everything. Nikita Sergeevich hated him. Pasternak confused him. He wanted to have Pasternak taken out and shot behind some shed. He once said to me, 'If I had to pull the trigger myself, my hand wouldn't tremble.' But Kosygin and Podgorny had their way — Malinovsky, too, of all people — and Pasternak was simply hounded to death by his triumph.

"But Olga and Irina had no protection. Not long after Pasternak's death they were accused of submitting the translations of others as their own. A great crime!

"It was the only time I asked anything of Khrushchev. But he didn't understand what I was saying; he believed I was just asking for information.

" 'A trumped-up charge, you say? Of course it is. Of course it is! I invented it myself — I passed the word to Shelepin: I want those women to have the fate our fine novelist provided for them in his wonderful book. I want them sent to some nameless camp in the North. I assume the list on which their names are written *will* be misplaced.'

"He sent them back to prison," Marya whispered. "Back to the horrors from which they had escaped. Now they'd have to go through them all, all over again."

She stared at the ceiling.

After a time she said, "Well, people are lost, even one's friends, even one's classmates."

She waited again.

"He never got beyond the solution of coal and potatoes. He clung to what he learned there. It was the only thing that never confused him. That and the shot behind the shed. He was a peasant always."

Then, she blurted out quickly,

"He made love to me, to this body, many times. And he never once said he loved me. All he ever understood was coal!"

III

Krupskaya and St. Cecilia

I spent many afternoons at the cafeteria of the Hotel Peking, sitting by the window reading the newspapers, drinking weak tea and smoking cigarettes made with Tashkent tobacco.

I liked the way the afternoon sun washed through the dirty windows, dappling the tables and age-spotted hands and illuminating the edges of rough wool jackets or glancing off steel-rimmed glasses. The sun fully lighted up the poverty of the place. It reminded me exactly of the Bickford's Cafeteria near the Bowery where I once sat many Saturday afternoons looking over the treasures I had collected in the secondhand bookstores on Fourth Avenue. Both places had the same depressed, washed, fiery look that nothing could change. Whatever they contained, poverty or duplicity or misery, they remained the same.

I liked to watch the people in the Hotel Peking. They gave off the aroma of my youth in New York. And they looked just like the figures in the etchings and paintings of Reginald Marsh, Martin Lewis, and Moses Soyer. I wrote many of my lectures among these people, while my earliest associations flooded back on me.

Lev Dahl had misled me, though, when he said I could find him there in the afternoons. I met others there, but it was a long time before I saw him again in the same place.

One afternoon just after a lecture I sat by the window eating a dish of potato salad when I saw an old man carrying a glass of tea with the utmost delicacy between thumb and middle finger and coming straight toward my table.

"I am a great admirer of your lectures," he said hurriedly as he came up. "May I sit down?"

No one in Moscow ever introduced himself by name, I'd noticed, and so I'd formed the habit of asking, "Of course. And you are — ?"

"An actor, a journalist, a pensioner, a person of no importance, a one-time musician, a superannuated man. Shall we say: simply one of your audience. Ah, of course, let me present myself: Yuri Ivanovich Telgrin."

"You were at the talk today," I said, not really sure that he was, since for most of the time I had been showing slides in the dark.

"Of course, I come invariably to hear you at the Journalism School. Today, especially, your readings from *All the President's Men* and the examples you showed of the Watergate cartoonists were especially impressive to me, to us all. And this made me bold to come here today, where we are aware you come, and drink a glass of tea to your health."

"You knew I come here after my talks?" I was taken aback and asked more than I meant to. "How?"

"Forgive me, my English is rusty. I haven't spoken it for years. Someone said you came here. It is a thing one knows simply. How is impossible to say. And of course I could not be certain you would be here. I simply strolled down Gorky Street on the chance of meeting you."

"It's a very long walk in this cold," I remarked, to try to set him at ease after the interrogation implied in my question had all but driven him away.

"Yes, personally I'm freezing. But I have not bought

my transport pass for this month, and I refuse to pay five kopecks for an individual ride."

He didn't have to say anything of the sort to point out to me how poor he must have been. Like the men and women sitting at the other tables, he was dressed neatly, even fastidiously, in old clothes that were once good. He wore a thick woolen jacket, with a cardigan sweater beneath that and a once-white, now tan shirt with a greasy silk tie. His outfit gave the impression of being truly ancient, of prewar vintage, patiently brushed and skillfully mended. It must have been years since he had rested his wrists on a table for fear of wearing out his cuffs. He would always have to be on guard against rubbing his jacket front against the edge of a table. For fear of wearing out the seat of his pants he barely settled his full weight on his chair. So his coat and pants seemed equally worn and brushed all around, equally shiny in every inch, all ready to fall into a little dust pile of threads at the same instant.

We talked very pleasantly for a little while about political cartoons. He showed a rapidity of association and a particularity of knowledge that surprised me as he moved the conversation from Washington politics and Paul Conrad, to Florence and Dante, to Giotto, Baroque grotesques, Pompeian graffitti, Russian joke books, and the popular puppet shows of the city. What was more, he knew something of the scholarship on all these subjects; for he occasionally referred to obscure old European texts as well as to modern studies — up to about 1925 — with perfect ease, sometimes even quoting from memory an author I had nearly forgotten. He gave the impression, without any intervention of arrogance, that he would have been equally erudite on any of a dozen other subjects. He was the first person I had ever met who appeared to have read all of the novels of James Fenimore Cooper.

When I finished my tea he immediately leaped up, saying, "Please do me the favor to allow me to buy you another!"

"Oh, let me get it," I started in my foolish American way, thinking first of his poverty, and not of his pride.

"No, dear friend, it's good of you, you know. You suppose I am poor — and so I am" — here he looked miserably about — "I am a poor wretch, but I do have plenty of money."

I didn't know what to say. I had expected to hear him complete his sentence by saying that though he didn't have money he had integrity. I supposed that was really what he meant, anyway; he didn't fool me into believing that he actually had a pocketful of roubles.

I was embarrassed at having struck an unfair blow at him, and so I said what I could, looking up at him steadily. "Of course. I'd be delighted to have you buy me another tea."

I gathered at once that he probably wanted to talk to me about a particular matter and that he leaped to his feet so abruptly when I drained my glass because he was afraid I would hurry off precipitously and he would lose me, lose the chance he had so elaborately prepared.

I guessed right. As soon as he had carefully deposited two new glasses of tea on the table and gingerly seated himself he started right in.

"You know, sir, it often happens that one finds it easier to speak, to unburden himself, if I may put it so, to an almost complete stranger — a person, of course, that one had reason for respecting and even admiring — than to speak to a relative or a friend of many years. In Russia, it is often better not to speak to one's friends of personal matters: it puts too much weight on their heads. Each of us knows almost to the kopeck how much he can sell his information for. To know anything is to know that one might become an informer should the price for information increase. In my own case, even these choices have been obviated for me. If I may speak directly, I am the last member of my family alive, though a collateral branch survives — I cannot say flourishes — in Leningrad. As for close friends, they too are mostly gone, or silenced by time or distance. I alone have endured, as they say, from Ilyich to Ilyich.

"Therefore I followed you here today to speak to you — oh, not about *The Last of the Mohicans* or Assyrian monumental sculptures, believe me. How can I be concerned about art when I am burning up inside!

"Sir!" he cried in real anguish and reached his hand out as if he were going to grasp mine, but he paused in mid motion and held his arm stiffly thrust upward, suspended in air.

"Sir! I cannot expose myself here. I beg you, will you accompany me to my flat where we can speak. Believe me, it is not far. Save a soul that is in torment, won't you?"

We walked in the direction of the Byelorussian Railway Station. All the while I cursed myself for letting him drag me along, particularly since once we had got our coats and come out of the hotel he fell into a morose silence and simply slid his feet sullenly over the icy sidewalks. Finally, after ten minutes of rapid walking, he turned off into a little street, hardly more than an alley, that came to a dead end at the tracks.

Around the middle of the block we turned into a house, like all the others on the street four stories high, made of broken gray and white stucco. It was an old place — probably going as far back as 1900 — and from all appearances had the style of houses once owned by wealthy families

and later converted into apartment dwellings by the Soviets. Part of the first floor front was occupied by a small
meat market and once we were inside the hallway the
smell of dried blood and rotten intestines was over-
powering.

We walked to the back of the building and ascended the
rear stairs. The hall was so dark that I could barely see
him on the stairs in front of me, but I could hear him muttering angrily to himself all the way up to the top floor.

Despite the dimness, I peered closely enough to see
that four doors opened onto the landing. The space between the wall and the balustrade was just wide enough
for one person at a time to squeeze his way to the proper
door. Telgrin proceeded directly to the one at the far rear,
seized a large padlock and thrust an iron key into it, snap-
ping the lock off and opening the hasp. Then he turned a
regular door key in a lock and swung the old scarred,
soiled door open. All this while he was saying under his
breath, like a litany, "Just a moment, only an instant now,
here we are, yes, just in a moment . . ."

He flung the door open and without so much as a word
rushed into the room. Uninvited I followed him.

It was a tiny cubicle, hardly bigger than a closet. The
only light came from the electric wall fixture. I could see
that a heavy velvet drape had been nailed where a window
must have been; some pinpoints of light filtered through
the material where it had worn or rotted to a gauze. Finally, he flipped the switch on a brass floor lamp. In the
low light his eyes seemed to burn as he stood there defiant
and helpless. I felt that for him bringing a guest to his
room was like laying his heart bare.

I had to look away, it made me so uncomfortable to look
at him. One glance took in the whole room. On one side
of the cell a sink stuck out of the wall, suspended by a
stained, sweating zinc pipe; beside it a rough wooden shelf

was nailed onto the wall, its splintering wood showing through the streaked paint. A glass was turned upside down on it to dry. In the corner stood a lumpy-looking barrel-like chair. Its upholstery must have been worn through long ago; even the fringed woolen shawl that had been spread over it was threadbare. A little Chippendale type of table stood next to it on spindly legs, like a thin brown heron.

But what filled the room so completely that it was a wonder that anything else at all could have been crammed into it — chair or sink or Yuri or me — was a grand piano, black and enormous as some antediluvian beast. Tucked beneath it against the wall was a thin pallet. To sleep there would indeed have been like crawling into one's coffin.

Meanwhile, he threw himself into the chair, leaving me standing, and covered his head with his hands. Of all the surprises of this afternoon, none was so jolting as the sudden sight I had of his fingers as I saw them outlined sharply against his hair. They were perfectly, beautifully formed, long and thin and supple, completely unaged.

I heard him utter a deep sigh and then he looked up and said, hopelessly but without a quiver, "This is where I live. Welcome to my lodgings.

"Please pardon me!" he exclaimed when he saw me standing while he sat. In haste he leaped out of the chair and motioned me into it. His distress was so acute that I took his seat without a protest, while he pulled a three-legged stool from under the sink and settled himself upon it.

Suddenly he jumped up again; he could not sit still.

"Look at me," he demanded. "Do you see a man who could inspire passion, uncontrollable passion, in a woman?" He waved his hands over his body as if to point out how poor and thin he was. He hadn't yet removed his outer garments. He stood there, his shoulders sloping under the weight of his oversized woolen coat, his neck and sunken chest muffled, his head topped by a beaver hat with flaps hanging over his ears, and he certainly did not seem to be a man who hypnotized women.

"I know what you are thinking," he said. "You need make no answer. For my whole life I held the same opinion of my attractiveness. Perhaps that is one of the chief reasons why I have remained a bachelor.

"Certainly, when I was a young man in those few, few years before the Revolution, I assumed I would marry someday. I knew many women — and not always of the most virtuous kind, I can assure you. It's the way of a young dog who fancies himself an artist, in my case, a musician." With his eyes he gestured slightly toward the piano.

"But this girl's bangs were cut in a foolish fashion, that female spoke with a lisp, another cared to talk about nothing but the cultivation of tea, another could not speak French even passably. And so I went, finding fault with all of the females of my set. Of course, perhaps they weren't as bad as I made them out, since other young fellows found them attractive enough to pick them off the vine — you follow my meaning? — to marry them.

"And so the result was that what with this fault-finding and the many hours that I gave up to piano practice and lessons — for I was truly passionate about my playing at this time — I did not get married. One fine day I found that all of the girls were gone.

"Besides, in my late twenties, when a man should be seriously looking for a wife, I was living abroad, fluttering between Paris and Capri. Certainly, I was still a fervent socialist and I used to say that I had two wives, Krupskaya and St. Cecilia, Socialism and Music. Fortunately for me, I had served with distinction against the White forces that were led by Admiral Kolchak. And my father was still a trusted military adviser to Vladimir Ilyich, so I was let alone. Or pretty much. I was rebuked in print only once by Anatoli Vasilevich — Lunacharsky, you know? — and pretty much ignored by the others. I had concert engagements and was always 'on the wing.'

"Then, in the thirties when I returned, who would have thought of marriage? There were plenty of girls about who would call me 'comrade, dear' and spend the night. There were still parties after my performances at the Conservatory. Certainly opportunities for entering upon the state of marital bliss came my way. I was tempted — a little — only once. I had a chance to marry the daughter of General Surkov, and she was a real beauty too, but I delayed, I'll never be sure why. Suddenly my father disappeared. Our dear leader no longer valued his advice. Certain other inevitable consequences followed. Our dacha was 'no longer available.' Before the Revolution we had owned this entire house, and afterward we continued to occupy it for our services to the state. At this time, however, my mother and I were moved into the top floor of the house so that some comrades, recently arrived from Georgia, could be accommodated. Like Nadezhda Stalin, my mother, in a fit of melancholy, committed suicide. Needless to say, my style of playing went out of fashion around the same time."

He stopped, as if he had said all he wished to say, or needed to say. Or perhaps he supposed I knew enough to piece out the rest. But when I looked at his face, the skin seemed tightened around his fine cheekbones and in the soft light it glowed, his eyelids dropped — he seemed younger. He was living in his dreams of lost times.

"And now," he said, rousing himself to misery, "she's back again. My dear fellow, do you know what it is like to be pursued by a beautiful woman? She never leaves me alone. She is always after me. Often when I come home I find a note slipped under my door. I don't have to look! I know it's going to be written in her neat little hand. It will say nothing, just a trifle, like 'Do wrap yourself up carefully when you go out, Yuri Ivanovich. This is a real Moscow winter we're having.' Or 'Here is a ticket for a concert of chamber music which I can't use. Do me the favor of taking it, won't you?' And I haven't been to the Conservatory in twenty years! Yes, there's a real sweetness to her every action. She herself has climbed up three flights of stairs in the dark just to place such notes under my door and hurry off. It gives me the shivers. I see her removing her glove to slide the envelope carefully under the crack. Perhaps a roach will run over her fingers as she puts them near the floor — isn't it a horrible thought, that roach running over her white fingers?

"So, when I go out, with coat flying as I let it do sometimes, having heard that in back of the Central Cinema some guy is selling tomatoes from Georgia, I feel guilty because I am not properly buttoned. I remember her note. I go back to my room and get my scarf and mittens. I may take so much time remembering to do all that she has advised — it's the least I can do when she takes such pains — that when I arrive the tomatoes are all gone. Perhaps, though, it was only a rumor. When did you ever hear of us poor folks being able to buy tomatoes, at any price, in the dead of winter?

"Once I did accept the ticket that she offered me and actually went to the concert. I had held out for a long time. But when I saw the announcement of a performance of Bach's Klavier pieces, that conquered all my scruples. I fully expected to find her there, sitting at my right elbow, smiling a little all during the performance and offering to buy me some smoked salmon at intermission. I was fully prepared for that. I was ready to go through with it all. But she was too delicate. I should have known it. The seat at my right simply remained unoccupied all evening, silently reminding me that she wouldn't think of coming unless I asked her to accompany me.

"All that night I cursed her for her insidious decency. But in my dreams she comes to me saying things like 'Yuri Ivanovich, eat more oranges.' Where could I find an orange in Moscow? And then, lo and behold, the next day I come home to find some crude fellow standing in front of my door, doffing his cap and holding out a package to me while he mumbles about the 'directions of a lady.' And what does it contain? You guessed it — a dozen oranges, brought all the way from Istanbul.

"At first I didn't understand. When she first wrote me a little note, nearly a year ago it was, and asked me to come to tea, I was excited to see her again. You're wondering who she is? Didn't I say? Why, General Surkov's daughter, of course.

"I was fully prepared for the house, for I knew well the district where she lived. Instantly I recognized the very number of the house to which she invited me. I had been in the house many times, naturally. Who, in the days before the Revolution, *didn't* know the house of Pyotr Sempronovich Khurzov, the merchant? I perceived that she had taste, I knew how fine she was and I believed she would have maintained . . . standards. But, well, in these days, who could expect more than a decent standard of luxury?

"But how could I have anticipated that she should have kept the house exactly as it had been? From my earliest youth, when I used to visit this house with my uncle when he went on Sundays to play patience with Khurzov, I remembered those malachite urns that stood on each side of the fireplace in the drawing room — those Bohemian chandeliers, the Kazak carpet, the panels. All, all was un-

touched. Everything was so authentic that I almost giggled in her face when I had the thought that to complete
the picture she might have placed a stuffed Khurzov in
the library — holding a hand with three queens!

"She saw what I was thinking — she is very clever and
she sees everything.

" 'Of course,' she said, 'there was nothing easy about
restoring this house to its former grandeur. But it is fine,
it is good, don't you think? Permit a poor woman her little
smile of satisfaction. Let me brag to you how I did it.

" 'My father, of course, had a high position. And my
first husband, as you know, had won the eternal gratitude
of our nation for the part he played in the victory over
Denikin.

" 'I know I am talking in a roundabout fashion, like
running around the whole Kremlin just to get in at one of
its gates. All I mean to say is that, certainly, we were not
wealthy. From my father I had a position. My husband
added to my position. In 1942, when they died — died together, I might say, in the bombing of staff headquarters — I too was crushed. But being simultaneously
orphaned and widowed by war heroes completed the solid-
ification of my standing in the state. I was "solid," you
might say. To put it nakedly, though I didn't see it myself,
I could be useful to some man of wealth who needed a
wife to cover him with her umbrella of respect.

" 'Hardly two months had passed before Nikifor Yefremovich Berman came around to bring his condolences.
Everyone knew how wealthy he was. He had a pleasant,
breezy manner about him, too. "You must not stay in the
house like this and mourn," he said cheerily. "I am placing my car and a driver here to stand ready to take you out
whenever you've a mind." You must understand that my
father and husband had bade me to go to one of our
dachas, in Sovmin, away from the danger I might be ex-

posed to in the city. But it was still scary enough to be alone, I can tell you. Did Daddy suppose that the brick wall around Sovmin would deter Nazi Panzers?

" 'It was no easy matter, in any event, for Nikifor Yefremovich to ride out from Moscow to this country place. I appreciated the effort he had made, just for a few minutes' visit. I could see by it that he had serious things on his mind. It didn't take me long to guess what these were, and I prepared myself to give him an answer.

" 'A few months before, my father had said in a casual way, "Anyone who supplies materials to the army in the way that Nikifor Berman does will either end up in a labor camp or as a millionaire." He had a quick mind, a lot of money already — enough for bribes to keep the tracks greased — what he needed to keep the train rolling was a connection, a source of respectability, a little bit of protection, like the iron fence around our dacha.

" 'Not to mince words, I saw that I could be useful to him in making it likely that he would become rich.

" 'I'll say this for him, he gave me the credit of assuming that I would soon figure out exactly why he had come. In a month's time when he came back to see if I needed anything, he came to the point at once.

" 'I gave him no trouble. Indeed, before he got out a word, I told him, "I have recovered my health rapidly due to your thoughtfulness." At that he beamed broadly. He spoke of the way that the war effort required all of us to put aside our personal woes. Conventions — say of mourning — which were completely proper, even necessary, in peacetime would appear ridiculous when battles were raging and men were "dropping like flies." That was his phrase — he excused himself profusely, alarmed at speaking with such complete insensitivity to me, still mourning two war heroes, afraid that such a slip could spoil everything.

" 'But I was barely listening. I had already anticipated and discounted such probable grossness in him. I knew he was not fine. I was ready for everything.

" 'In short, we were soon married. Certainly, I did not become a bride again without some concessions — well, they could hardly be called that, really, since they were granted so freely. Berman knew my worth. He was never a miser.

" 'A word from me concerning the furnishings of Khurzov's house, which had been stored in the Armory since the merchant's departure, and a tidy sum which Nikifor Yefremovich distributed in the right places, and the house was furnished, just as you see it. What did the custodians of the Armory care about some malachite urns and a few dozen Louis Quatorze chairs? They had a ton of trash from the czars.

" 'Besides a fine house was useful to my husband's operations. And a clever wife who knew whom to invite and how to see that they all came. Generals and ministers and Politburo members, friends of mine through my father and husband, came and went in a perfectly natural way. Everything went as it should have. My husband, you may rest assured, never went to a labor camp; indeed, he got a lucrative contract to supply blankets and bedding to the camps after the war, when they sprang up like mushrooms. When he was a boy he had a dream, he told me, that he would become very, very wealthy. He died happy.

" 'So,' she concluded, 'you see to where it has led. I have position and money.' Her eyes burned. 'But I am a wretched woman, a woman without shame. Still, before I was twice widowed, I learned the virtue of plain speech.

" 'Yuri! I must tell you, then, that all these years I have loved you. I ask myself, when you came to my father's house, why did I not clutch you by the knees and beg you to marry me? Instead I threw out sly hints that my father's offer of my hand to you would not make me unhappy. Yuri! I have loved you, and never anyone else, all these years. Now I *will* clutch you around the legs and never let you go!'

"Never have I been so astonished. True to her word she did fall down before me and try to embrace my legs — I, who had not seen her for fifteen years. And these legs, which are so spindly they give me the shivers. Involuntarily — but to my shame — I leaped back, which made her come at me, waddling, on her knees like some old crone crawling up to the iconostasis. Thump, thump, thump — her knees went on the floor, and she didn't even notice — but I was humiliated for causing this." In misery he struck his head with his fist. "I hear the sound in my dreams.

" 'Olga Sergeeva, dear woman, do not kneel before me,' " I cried in horror, and I reached out my hands to lift her up — but she seized them and kissed them passionately. She was a lioness, I can tell you. Now she haunts me."

"I don't fully understand. This was General Surkov's daughter, then," I said stupidly. I was simply talking aloud, to get the fragments straight in my mind.

"Yes. I rejected, to be sure, the offer of her hand. I never really did consider her, you know."

No sooner had he uttered these words than the color drained out of his face. He leaped up, scuttled to the door and listened intently. Then, wide-eyed, he flung the door open. The hallway was empty.

He came back to pace the room, shaking his head.

"For a moment I felt she was standing outside the door. Never would I have her hear me speak ill of her. She adores me — it is driving me crazy."

"And she asks of you —?"

"Yes, to marry her. To move in with her. To share her life. What shall I do?"

"Do?" I couldn't help staring at this room, with its meager furnishings. "Why, you should marry her, of course."

He was tormented. Perhaps he really felt that he didn't deserve this good fortune. Perhaps he was afraid of being deceived. I don't know why, exactly. Is it possible to fear happiness? At any rate, he certainly fought against her proposal.

"Am I an Onegin capable of sending a woman into ecstasy merely by a letter or a look? Why does she want me?"

"She says she loves you. Why not accept her at her word? Certainly, you care for her?"

Swept up by the rhythm of the conversation and a sense of rightness in the drama of the moment, he was about to say something extravagant about his passion. If only he could have brought himself to say, "Care for her? Why, she's a saint. I worship her" — then he could have taken her position, her money, her passion — he could have had everything, he could have been *saved* by her without feeling the doubts and hesitations that so obviously beset him.

Instead he gaped, let down by the moment, and staring sightlessly at the tips of his delicate fingers, murmured, "I don't know. I don't know."

We talked on, like sailors rolling in a trough of waves. I felt increasingly in a false position. He had caught me up in his story, and so I had somehow, subtly, been forced into agreeing to give him advice, see him through. I knew nothing of him. I felt that perhaps I would never know anything of him, that he would always keep himself cloaked in mystery.

Yet I was being required to decide his fate. It seemed as if he had chosen me precisely because I could not see into the depths of his problem; he himself was all too skillful at recognizing its ambiguities. He needed help in seeing the surface of his situation. "If this American can be persuasive enough," he must have told himself, "then I can simply follow his advice and give up responsibility for encountering the complexity which he'll never see."

He relied on my simplicity and thus he kept me ignorant. While he absolved himself of responsibility, he made me responsible. I felt this, I resented it a little, but I didn't know how to get out of the trap.

For an hour we continued the most boring of conversations. He kept encouraging me, indirectly, to tell him to marry her, while he resisted the idea forcefully but then urged me to reassert it. Of course, he never gave me any facts to make it reasonable for him to repel her offer.

I suggested that we go out for a drink. I had the Arbat Bar in mind, the closest to an American bar in Moscow. There, at least, I'd be, as much as I could be, on solid American ground. And besides, to ride the "5" bus around the ring to the Kalinin Prospect stop would clear the air, break the flow of our talk. We'd be forced to reassume the true, impersonal character of our relations.

But he deflected my plans again. Had there been any doubt about his having money he dispelled it decisively, as he pulled out a wad of ten-rouble notes. "I shall send out for a bottle of cognac," he said. "Yes, and champagne." He gave me a wry smile. "The condemned man should at least have a last drink, eh?"

He skipped out of his door and banged on another door leading from the landing.

"Marta Ivanova," he said in Russian when the door opened, "send your son out for a bottle of cognac and a few liters of champagne, will you? And have him get something to ease your cold too!"

Eventually we did drink the two bottles of champagne. I'm afraid we even got to the stage of drunkenness at which I showed him how to make a champagne cocktail by mixing the Armenian brandy with the champagne and a slice of orange. By the end of the bottle of cognac he was proposing toasts "to fate" and beaming broadly. And I was saying confidently, "Why, if you don't marry her, I'll do so myself!"

At last, he sent out for a fellow who moonlighted as a taxi driver and who took me back to my apartment in his private car. Once there, I forgot everything — the preparation for my next day's lecture, Yuri, the Hotel Peking — everything. I had a splendid sleep, and no hangover.

Although I continued to lecture at Lomonosov I didn't see Yuri at the next four or five sessions, nor did he show up in my cafeteria. I was glad, really, because not knowing what happened to him, I had no knowledge of his decisions and thus no responsibility for them. And so I simply forgot about him.

2

In March, when the American composer Boris Chankin made a visit to Moscow, naturally there was a reception for him at Spaso House. Certainly, the Russians were unlikely to allow performances of any of Chankin's electronic compositions (though, in truth, he was regarded as rather old-fashioned in the States, like his colleagues Ussachevsky and Luening). The Russians hated his modernism but they liked his presence and they knew how to make propaganda out of it since he was a world-renowned figure who had been born in Russia and brought to the United States as a child. He had even expressed a long-distance love of Russia and was a prominent supporter of the student side during the Columbia University riots. So the Russians were making much of his visit.

And just as naturally, the Americans were outdoing the Russians in making much of Chankin, and reminding them by the way they guided him about that he was, after all, an American, who didn't know ten words of Russian.

Walter Stoessel, who was ambassador in Moscow at that time, caught my eye as I came up the stairs in the official residence for the biggest party given in Chankin's honor.

"Professor Martin, glad you could come," he said, shaking my hand in his straightforward Midwestern way. "Mr. Chankin is here — you've met him, haven't you? He looks exhausted. And there's someone else here who's also been waiting for your arrival. He keeps asking about you. A Russian pianist, a famous old guy, Yuri Telgrin. *I* never heard of him, but Chankin says his parents used to talk about him. He was performing back in the thirties. All the Soviets here pay him a lot of respect. How come I never heard of him? And Matlock and Lynn Noah haven't heard of him either. So how do *you* know him?"

I didn't take the last part of his question unkindly. After all, ambassadors spend thousand of dollars of government money on experts and informants in order to be kept current on just such inconsequential matters. I simply replied; "Oh, he comes to my lectures. *You* ought to come sometime."

"Of course, I'd love to. But, you know, I just couldn't walk into Lomonosov, past the guards, the way you can. It would be an incident. I'm really a prisoner in the Embassy."

We were walking through the large central room of

Spaso House. Waiters in white jackets darted about like fish, carrying silver trays with assortments of American cocktails and crystal vials of vodka. I sent one off for a glass of orange juice.

"Here's Telgrin now. Imagine, he asked *me* to bring you to him when you arrived. He takes a high tone."

This was high comedy for me, Stoessel's perplexity, though I didn't meditate very long on the fact that Yuri Ivanovich had also mystified me. Besides, he was already shaking my hand vigorously.

"It's wonderful to see you," he exclaimed even as he lightly touched a woman's elbow to signal her to turn away from the conversation in which she was engaged. She lifted her face and smiled a little at me and stood there prettily, like an empty champagne glass waiting to be filled.

"Allow me, my friend, to introduce my wife, Olga Sergeeva. Dear woman, this is Professor Martin, about whom you've heard so much."

"Of course," she responded in a charmingly old-fashioned British accent, "I'm really delighted. I believe I am in part indebted to you for my present happiness." So far as I could tell she said this warmly, too, without a trace of irony.

"Not at all," I said. "Mr. Telgrin is very lucky."

Now she did show a flicker of ambiguity. "I am not sure that he is entirely convinced. But" — she brightened — "I shall convince him. I shall, shan't I, Yuri?"

He had obviously been the subject of a great deal of convincing already. The old clothes were gone. He stood there in a tweed suit with vest that had unquestionably been made on Savile Row. In his buttonhole was the ribbon of some old decoration. His tie was silk, handmade, and his shoes were new and highly polished — probably Italian, and certainly not suited to anyone who had to walk a Moscow street in winter. Chauffeurs and black cars, tailors and bootmakers had all been required to bring him to this fortunate state.

"You have already done so, my dear," he said pleasantly.

We strolled into the dining room, chatting cordially, and came to a halt before the enormous fireplace. When he noticed us, Chankin detached himself from his group and came over to us. He and I had served on a National Endowment for the Arts panel a few years before and we shook hands distantly. But it was Yuri he wanted to see.

"So, I have heard that you are going to give a recital again," he said — rather boyishly, I thought. "I'd love to hear it."

"Why, I wish you could. I remember your father well. Technically he was an excellent pianist, with a fine attack. I heard him play often when I was in my teens."

I said, aside, to Olga Sergeeva, "Is it true? He's going to give a performance?"

"Yes," she replied breathlessly, "at the Small Hall in the Conservatory. It's all scheduled, the program is announced. The same program he gave his very last time there, in nineteen thirty-six: Bach *seulement* — the most demanding pieces."

She saw my amazement, and not just over the program. But she didn't take it amiss. "Astonishing isn't it? He's kept up his talent all these years, he's better than ever. He's plainly a genius! Really. Every day he's practiced on that massive piano in his room. He's allowed me to see it there, to hear him play. It will be a triumph. What a reckoning!"

The president of Moscow State University was there and Matlock, the United States minister, introduced me to him and to the director of the Conservatory and a Soviet historian of music, whose name I didn't catch, and to a young violinist whose schmaltzy Borodin I had heard a week previously. All the conversations began with Chankin and ended with Telgrin. It was as if Tchaikovsky himself had come back from the grave: Yuri was having a complete triumph.

He caught up with me toward the end of the party and drew me slightly aside.

"You were right. After you left I bucked myself up and acted on your advice. I went directly to the house of Olga Sergeeva. She was preparing to go to bed but she came to me in a minute. I was impulsive, I was rash, I was daring — oh, I *was* an Onegin. I was, don't you see, simply wonderful. That very night everything was arranged between us. She does everything. She sends out to the commissary for little delicacies, she has agents in London, she buys I-don't-know-what, we ride out to her dacha, we stroll around the grounds — all alone, no one else in sight. She doesn't oppress me with gifts or money. I have simply to *want* — and it appears, as if I have a golden chicken. I do, in any event, have coupons and I shop in the foreign stores — just like an American, what! She wants me to play — and I *do* play, better than ever, everyone says so. At least they tell me it's wonderful, for few of them are old enough to have heard me when I played last in public. *She* remembers, and she tells me I'm supreme."

I looked at him as hard as I could, since this was such a complete change from the misery I had last seen him wrapped in. But he seemed to have accepted everything. He was sliding along like an arpeggio on the smooth surface of life, while I was looking for the hidden disappointments that must have come with his decision. So, I thought bitterly, even now he has tricked me: we've changed places, and he has left me with all his doubts.

Before we parted, his wife rejoined us. They were full of plans and the idea that I had played a part in their happiness had settled upon them, so they wanted me to share in their plans. I was made to look at my appointment book (which, in truth, was always practically empty) and to put down dates when I would visit their house, accompany them to their dacha for a weekend and — above all and most immediate of all — attend the recital. Not a ticket was available in all of Moscow, they assured me; but of course they would supply me with one, on the left center, so that I could observe the master's fingers flying over the keyboard. They were swimming in a golden sea of satisfaction and expectation, so much so that by the time we parted, saying our goodbyes to Ambassador Stoessel together in the entrance, I was beginning to feel self-congratulatory. I thought jokingly to myself that instead of struggling with literary criticism I should have taken up the profession of matchmaking.

The next day a man delivered a concert ticket to the *dezhurnaya,* the old woman who sat inside the entrance to my apartment building to keep account of my goings and comings. I took the ticket and pinned it on my bulletin board and recircled the date on my calendar. No reason existed to call Yuri or his wife, especially since I imagined him to be sequestered, practicing for the great event.

On the appointed Saturday night I took the Metro down to Biblioteka Lenina and strolled up Gerzen Street. I was rather early but I wanted to watch the audience going in to try to gauge the social character of Telgrin's triumph. Besides, this would be a rare opportunity to see the sort of Russians one seldom sees en masse, the old upper classes, the artists, and the top politicians.

As usual, when I turned into the little court of the Con-

servatory with its statue of Tchaikovsky in front, a few au-
tomobiles were slowly pulling around the circular drive,
dropping people off in front of the Large Hall.

But the Small Hall was completely dark. I went over to
the entrance and peered through the glass doors into the
empty lobby. Along with a few others who showed up
from time to time, I looked at the locked doors and
searched in vain for a poster announcing the evening's
program. Even that had disappeared. No one hung
around very long, as if fearful of being photographed
there.

I was lucky enough to get a taxi that was dropping off
some Pakistani diplomats for the symphony performance;
and, by promising the driver two roubles for a sixty-kopeck
trip, I got taken to the Hotel Peking.

Some premonition had told me that Telgrin would be
waiting for me in the cafeteria. But I was entirely wrong. I
scanned the room carefully and he was not in it.

I stepped out of the doorway to let a young man pass by,
but he was heading toward me. "You do not remember
me," he stated in flat hurried Russian. "I am the son of
Marta Ivanova, neighbor to Yuri Ivanovich Telgrin. He
instructed me to wait here and, if you arrived, to bring you
to his quarters."

I probably could have found the way there myself, but I
would not have gone without this prod. The young man
led me through the streets silently. By now, the end of
April, the last of the winter's accumulated snows were
rotten and melting. The pavements glistened in the blue
lights.

Marta Ivanova's son and I went up those old stairs together. When we got to the top landing, the fellow disappeared into the door of his own flat. I was left blankly
facing the door of Telgrin's room.

Even now I wasn't sure if, on my own, I wanted to

knock. I could still turn on my heel and hurry off. But suddenly the door opened and Yuri stood there with a wild look in his eyes.

"My God," he whispered, "I was afraid it was she standing there, unsheathing a dagger to drive into my heart."

He couldn't stop talking. "Come in, it's all over, you know. Oh, not just the performance — everything. We're getting divorced. Probably I am denounced as an enemy of the people. I have come back — as you see —to my old room. I am here."

In this place nothing had changed. Telgrin wore the same painfully neat layers of garments as on the first day I had met him. No new furniture or whatnots gave reminders of his more recent opulence.

He simply stepped back from the door, not even asking me to come in. We had the strangest — and I suppose the most common — of relationships, after all: on one point only did we share some knowledge that made us intimate. On all others he was perfectly indifferent to me. My interest in him, when I really looked at it closely, was hardly higher than curiosity on the level of gossip. I thought of him as a denizen of the Hotel Peking, and I had written a sketch about him in my notebook.

"I came to the door of the Small Hall this evening," I said.

He only said, in Russian, "I'll make tea, at least."

There was no point in my asking any questions. In and around our irrelevant chatter he himself introduced the subject in fragments: "Everyone in Moscow knew two days ago. Not many of the 'audience' showed up, I suppose — eh?" And again: "I practiced, yes, but there was no need: I was superb." Later: "Olga Sergeeva is heartbroken. She would be happy if you paid her a visit — she particularly liked you, don't you know?"

At last he said, "It came over the question of the piano. *This* very piano." With his forefinger he touched the black monster that filled his room. "As the time for my performance arrived I realized that a way must be found to get my piano to the hall.

"Sergei Vasilyevich, the director at the Conservatory, was aghast. 'Yuri, dear,' he says, 'we have our own Steinway already in the hall.'

"Everyone derided my idea. Perhaps it was a mania, an artist's obsession. But, why not? Even Olga Sergeeva asked if it wouldn't be just as well if I used the piano provided, as others did. You see, the problem was that there were only two ways to get my instrument out of this closet: to take it down in pieces or to tear down the walls on this floor.

"I was for the second. Obviously, there was no one in all of Moscow who could have put an instrument back together once it had been disassembled — they are all mechanics here. And besides — I will admit it to you, sir — in my pride I remembered the days when this was a grand, spacious house, when my family occupied it in my boyhood. After my father's disappearance, my mother and I were crowded into the top floor, and then, after she died, this little cell was partitioned off for me, and I, with my piano, was sealed into it. Somehow, now that I was emerging I wanted — as your Whitman puts it, eh? — to tear the doors from their jambs, to free the old house again. To liberate my old companion.

"But I simply explained to Olga Sergeeva: 'Listen, this very piano was given to me at my fifth birthday party by our beloved Nikolai Rimsky-Korsakov, in the very last year of his life. On the day he presented it to me he himself sat down at it and played little pieces from *Le Coq d'Or* to amuse me. 'Listen to how it sounds, your new piano, Yuri,' he cried. He held out his arms and I ran to him.

'Now Yuri shall play,' he laughed as he lifted me up on his lap. He smelled of Polish cologne. But I did play — I made noise. And he clapped his hands and cried in a big booming voice, 'Wonderful, Yuri, it plays itself. I shall make a ballet from your melodies. Bang away!' And as I did, he put his big arms around me and played melodies at each end of the keyboard all around and through my thumping, until my beat and his melodies seemed to go together and I was enchanted by my skill.

" 'Olga Sergeeva, it *does* play itself,' I insisted. 'I cannot do without it. I must have the pleasure of making my return to the stage with this very instrument.'

"At this she clapped her hands gleefully and promised to have everything done. She was good. She was everything.

"But it was not that easy. The Ministry of Housing and the Bureau of City Improvements and the Office of Demolition and a dozen other bureaus all became embroiled in a dispute over the proper licensing procedure. Apparently there was no dispute over tearing down the walls, only over who should be responsible for it. Department chiefs could not be gotten on the phone; office managers fell ill; deputies went on vacation. The Ministry of Culture and Sergei Vasilyevich entered the controversy and only made things worse.

"At last I was informed that the walls would indeed be removed and that the floor would be restored to the approximate character it had possessed when I and my mother lived here — only this would take three months.

"I fell into a rage and I wouldn't budge. Everyone begged me, but I said no. I did it all. I held out against them, I was proud, yes, absurdly proud, but I won. Everyone is made to budge in Moscow. The whole country is combined to condemn you for holding out. But I didn't budge.

"On the day that they announced the cancellation of

my concert and took down the posters I came to Olga Sergeeva's sitting room and said, 'I am going back to my own little room. Dear woman, it is not your fault. We come from different worlds.'

"She didn't understand and she cried. But I was gentle and at last she accepted it all. The only difficulty I had was in getting my old clothes back from the gardener. He had already sold them. But I was determined not to have any profit. 'Come and visit me sometime, then,' my wife sighed when I left.

"By now, I am sure, General Matveyev is by her side trying to hold her hand and tell her, in his hissing way, why she should hate me. He hopes to become a marshal — before he is shot."

He made our tea from a samovar stamped all over with seals. "Someday you will see this in a commission store," he said. "Such samovars fetch a good price with foreign diplomats. But I and this piano will stay in this room together until we both dry up and turn to sawdust."

Finally, as I was bidding him goodbye and turning away to go out the door, I felt his lips come up quickly toward my ear. "Krupskaya and St. Cecilia!" he whispered. And then he shut the door.

For a long time I stood at the head of the stairs thinking about that—"Krupskaya and St. Cecilia . . . "

I must have stayed there longer than he thought I would or until he had forgotten about me. For suddenly, for the first time, I heard him start to play the piano. At first he struck the notes slowly, with very long intervals between them, as if he were playing an ancient piece from memory. Then it all came back to the performer and the music swelled. He really was magnificent. It was the choral melody from the last act of *The Invisible City of Kitezh* — the mystical song of the triumph of faith. The music followed me all the way down the stairs.

IV

The Sick Rose

One of the last things I did in the United States before packing my bags was to compile a list of Soviet artists and scholars whom I hoped to meet there. This was certainly a grab bag, for people got on the list for all sorts of reasons.

Arkady Pavlovich Malevsky was on my list because I regarded him as a complete crank.

During the nineteen-sixties he became famous for his uncompromising stand against "decadent modernism." Everywhere he looked in American culture he found disease: in literature, films, art, architecture, cartoons, dance — everywhere. One of his articles stuck in my mind as typifying the slashing — completely wrongheaded — character of his approach. Titled "Dial M for Masochism: Miller, Motherwell and Manson," this piece was a wholesale attack, a slaughter. With a brilliant disregard for detail, Malevsky dove into his subject like a dog digging for a buried bone: the dirt flew in all directions.

He started with Henry Miller, whose works, he claimed, typified the disease of the American mind and American society during the nineteen-thirties when capitalism had to face up to its shortcomings for the first time, when the pretense of the capitalist success was stripped away. Miller's women were lascivious bitches, while his men

were egotistical and brutal. Not as obviously obscene as
Miller's work, Motherwell's modernism conveyed fundamentally the same obscene values, through evasion. Ab-
stract Expressionism, according to Malevsky, was intended by the American rulers to destroy the proletariat's
consciousness of social reality, reason, scientific analysis,
Marxist truths. Charles Manson, he concluded, really exposed the essence of the others, scorning human dignity,
order, regulation, and reason, while celebrating the impulsive, disorderly, outrightly sexual aspects of existence.
In him, Miller's or Motherwell's fantasies became real,
murderous, the tag end of capitalist decay.

This attack was made with the same finesse that ax-
wielding Russian butchers use on sides of beef in the
stalls in the Central Market. Malevsky didn't need a very
sharp blade because he had a heavy hand and he was willing to chop and chop. But it was just the kind of writing
that was likely to be successful with the Soviet establish-
ment. Malevsky was referred to frequently in Soviet jour-
nals. And he was often brought forward as a reviewer to
put down a new book by Mailer or Roth. He was a useful
fellow to have around.

I didn't want to debate with him but I did want to meet
him. I guess I thought of him as a type, the kind of person
I didn't want to miss seeing, a sort of rare Russian bird
that I must see here or never.

By the time I had been in Moscow for six weeks most of
the people I had anticipated meeting, those on my list, had
appeared at one of my lectures or come to a party where I
had been present. Malevsky stood out not only by his absence, but also by the fact that no one seemed to know a
thing about his current activities. I was always asking my
colleagues about everything. And so, naturally, among a
thousand other matters, I inquired about Malevsky. Perhaps he was dead? "No," they said evasively, "had he

died it would be known." He had simply dropped out of sight.

Often I exceeded the bounds of Soviet courtesy. I was accustomed to American universities, where talking usually half consists of asking questions. Here, asking direct questions immediately takes on the ring of an interrogation. More than one colleague probably took me for a spy — for the Americans, for the Soviets. I didn't get many answers.

But it's also true that Russians simply don't know much about each other outside of a small circle of intimate friends and family. Colleagues, students, acquaintances all come and go, rise in power or fall from position, in mysterious ways. Who knows why? Better not to know why. Better not to chance implication. Better to clothe safety in ignorance.

Yet by the way that a few people responded to my query, I began to infer that something was known, something had indeed happened to Malevsky.

"I really don't know the details of his sad case," one person told me, then shut his mouth tight.

The "sad" gave me a clue that I tried to follow up.

"Is he still a researcher at the U.S.A. Institute and the Gorky Institue, then?"

"His positions are still there, certainly."

"But he doesn't occupy them?"

"I'm not acquainted with the details . . ."

2

One day, late in the afternoon, I met my friend Marya Fyodorovna in the cafeteria of the Hotel Peking. It wouldn't have been appropriate for me to have picked her up in the lobby of the Ministry of Defense when we had a date. On this particular evening we were going to dinner at the Baku Restaurant, only a short walk away from the Peking.

Marya always gave the impression of speaking freely because she knew exactly, to the comma, what she could safely say. She spoke her lines, I came to think, with the impromptu infallibility of a practiced actress. She tossed out her observations as if they were perfectly natural and spontaneous, but over the years she had certainly rehearsed her lines. To have survived the curious life *en marge* that she lived she needed this talent to perfection. That's why I liked to be with her. It was safe. She protected herself so perfectly that I could never make her make a mistake. And so she protected me from the fear of compromising her.

That evening while we sat in the Peking waiting for our reservation time at the Baku, Marya again entertained me with stories about Nikita Khrushchev's intrigues. Her talk was always full of sudden disappearances and mysterious changes in the lives of the great. Occasionally she'd say in an offhand manner, "Then, in October, Colonel Gruchkoy simply vanished." Or, "One day Lev Kamenev was wealthy, the head of the food program. The next day he was 'pushing up potatoes in Siberia.' " The last remark she regarded as a fine joke and she giggled with nice abandon.

"I have a mystery of my own," I said. "There's a critic named Malevsky. I supposed I'd meet him in Moscow sometime. But I never have. And now he's become a fixation with me. He's probably ordinary and dull, but for me he's a figure of mystery."

It hadn't occurred to me that Marya would even know the name, but she smiled mischievously at my first words.

"Arkady Pavlovich, you mean. Of course. He *is* a mysterious person. Yes, very much so."

"So, *you* know his story then?" I said, showing my surprise.

I didn't have to worry about exposing my foolishness to her. Male denseness was one of her axioms. Marya always accounted in advance, I think, for the stupidity of all her male friends.

"Know it? Well, perhaps I do," she remarked in a secretive tone. She tried to make it sound like a dark secret. She looked around quickly as if to assure herself there were no secret agents about. But I could see (and so I suppose she wanted me to see) the glint of merriment in her eyes.

"Yes, the story of Arkady Pavlovich is a deep secret. Perhaps you would find it a dangerous thing to know."

"Perhaps if I knew," I said, joining in her play, "I would report it to to the CIA and the whole Soviet state would come tumbling down!"

"Ah, you are clever, you American spies. Does your CIA pay you, then, to squeeze these secrets out of helpless Russian women?"

"I have my means," I said, making a poor imitation of Erich von Stroheim as a Gestapo officer. "After all, I could refuse to take you to dinner until you give up your secrets."

At that she looked serious.

"Reservations at the Baku are not easy to get. We must go to dinner. I trust that Herr Goebbels will allow me a last meal of *zakuski* and chicken *zatsivi* at least."

She gave me a splendid languid look.

"As to the question of Arkady Pavlovich Malevsky," she added, "I am prepared to satisfy your curiosity instantly. It happens that there is a person in this very cafeteria who can tell you all there is to be known concerning Malevsky."

She rose from the table and touched my cheek playfully.

"As a matter of fact," she said, "I have plans for us tonight. First dinner. Then from the waiter we'll buy a nice bottle of Yerevan cognac and take it back to your apartment. And then" — she winked — "you may try to extract any other secrets from me that you wish. But concerning Malevsky, wait just a second, you'll have your wish."

I watched her go across the room and the way she moved made me forget all about critics or commentators, Azerbaijani dinners, and the Soviet state.

But I also learned something about her as she walked. She knew everybody, just everybody. She tossed little gestures of salutation to several people. Then, two thirds of the way across the room she stopped at a table occupied by two men. She greeted both and then directed her attention to one. Without long delay he arose and she brought him in tow over to my table.

He was a large, bearlike fellow. Though probably he was in his late forties, the hair in his great mustache and on his skull was still dense and black; only here and there a few wiry gray stands appeared. He wore a gray gabardine suit with a black turtleneck sweater. All and all, though he was obviously Russian, he had a slightly Turkish look. I guessed that he came from the area of the Black Sea — Sochi, perhaps even Batumi.

"Allow me," Marya said in her most courtly fashion, "to introduce you to Professor Jay Martin." She pointed toward her companion. "This gentleman can tell you all you may wish to know about Arkady Malevsky."

He nodded monumentally toward me. He waited for her to sit down and then seated himself. Apparently she was not going to give me any further aid, at least for the moment, and I felt reluctant to ask questions of a stranger. "What is it you wish to know?" he asked in an interested but distant fashion.

"Marya exaggerates. It's nothing really, I was just mentioning my interest in this Malevsky whose total absence from the scene has been a mystery to me."

"Malevsky is dead," he said blankly, as if he were reading stock quotations.

"Dead?"

"Washed up."

"I don't follow you. He's dead — or washed up?"

"What's the difference? Here, in Moscow, when one falls out of his position, he's dead. Without an important job how can he get money? Privileges? Where can he go? Who will talk to him? Washed up. Dead. Suicide. What more do you need to know?" All of this he uttered in the same lugubrious tone that one would use at a funeral.

"You make him more a mystery than before."

"Perhaps he is an enigma even to himself."

After a minute more of spasmodic conversation he pushed his chair back and said, "I must return to my friend." He nodded curtly, in the Germanic fashion, and said, "Professor Martin."

As he turned away, I said to Marya, "We should be going too. The reservation."

She gathered up her purse and the plastic bag she always filled with novels and other purchases fate sent her way. As we walked toward the door, the large dark man inclined his head toward us. She wriggled her fingers in a little gesture of farewell to him, and then tapped my shoulder.

"Wave goodbye to Mr. Malevsky," she said, laughing.

3

The sour-milk soup and the *zatsivi* and the rice with pomegranates were all excellent. The white wine was of the ordinary Moldavian variety, barely worthy to be called *vino*. Marya obviously was proud at having played such a splendid trick on me, and this improved her mood even beyond her usual gaiety. We talked and laughed and played with each other. By the time the coffee and ice cream came around she began to tap my knee under the table.

We did buy a bottle of Azerbaijani cognac. It cost fifteen roubles, but it was fine and fiery. We had hardly gotten home when she poured herself a tumbler of cognac, downed it, almost purred — and, putting aside all preliminaries, stripped and hopped into bed. We had a marvelous time.

But with regard to Malevsky her lips were sealed. She was nothing if not clever and she knew very well how to keep up interest in a relationship. Like any intelligent woman she stored up little remembered, shared bits of conversation, private jokes, and special allusions to personal intrigues, which she could bring out unerringly if ever our talk paled. Like a musician who has only a few notes assigned to her part, she played these for all they were worth.

And it was obvious that she saw in this particular bit about Malevsky a glittering secret that she could bring up again and again. If something funny happened when we were together, she might say, "Do you remember that joke I played on you that time with Malevsky?" ... Or, perhaps I would tell her that something perplexed me. Then she'd say, "Yes, as enigmatic as Malevsky." . . . Often she disagreed with me over things, and she might say in a pleasant, unaggressive way, "Oh, Jay dear, you don't know any more about this subject than you do about poor Arkady Pavlovich!" She was, in short, always teasing me about this idiotic journalist.

But though I saw exactly what she was doing, actually I liked her for it. Her manner implied a certain attentiveness to my presence, an acknowledgment that we had shared something, and an assumption that we would see each other again. Considering all the men she must have been intimate with, for her to keep the special details associated with each one clear was a miracle of memory and a tribute to the enthusiasm she still put into relations.

At the end I didn't care whether I ever solved the enigma of Malevsky. I preferred her manipulation of the mystery to the mystery itself.

4

A strange collection of diplomats, workers, and military personnel worked at the Embassy. Though I saw them less often, the American businessmen who were living in Moscow were an even stranger lot. I was not long in discovering that most of them actively hated living in Russia. Purely and simply, the Americans regarded Moscow as a hardship post.

They had obvious justifications for thinking this. They were forced to live in the Embassy or in apartment structures specially designated for foreigners, diplomatic ghettos watched continuously by Soviet guards. Even in the apartments of the Embassy itself a husband and wife had to assume that the room was bugged and that they couldn't hold a conversation concerning any matter of importance. Like two grumpy old folks on the farm, they hardly could talk at all; they just passed telegraphic notes back and forth. No one could travel freely; to go a few kilometers outside the city required a visa.

But they also plainly disliked the Russians: despite détente the Soviets were simply *the enemy*. They disliked the lines in the stores, the delays over everything, and the poverty of the television offerings. Secretly they blamed the Russians for not knowing English. They were nice, conservative, patriotic Midwesterners and they regarded the Soviets in the same way that their ancestors had regarded the Indians.

But they found ways of living as if they were still in America. They jetted off to Helsinki or Stockholm on Government R&R. They shopped for samovars and other trinkets in the commission stores, they went to the bear circus, they ate in the Hotel Rossiya. They made believe they were tourists in Moscow.

American movies, more than anything else, tied them to home. Most Embassy parties were organized around a screening. A large number of films circulated in Europe and were made available through military or international business channels. And as these streamed through the Moscow post they were picked like plums off a tree, brought home, and shown on apartment walls.

Though Embassy personnel and members of the tightly knit business community seemed to regard American visitors with indifference or annoyance, I had given a couple of talks to the wives' club and apparently made a success at this because I soon received several invitations to movie buffets.

Truthfully, I enjoyed these entertainments. The screenings occupied most of the evening. But during drinks and breaks for changing reels the conversation had a lot of lively, simple charm. I liked to hear Americans talk. I liked their way of looking at things, mixing the mores of Sioux Falls with experiences in all parts of the world. They were attached to America, but they had chosen to live their lives outside it. They were dispossessed, thrown off base, and they were interesting for that reason, and almost as much of a mystery to me as the Russians were.

Besides, films had always played a large part in my life. I soon became bored with the standard fare of Russian films — lines of tanks heading toward Germany, banners waving, clenched fists of military heroes, noble sacrifice, the rapport of a worker with his tractor. Of the best Soviet film makers, Tarkovsky was silent; and Shukshin, at the age of forty, was already dead. So I was soon glad of any chance to see an American picture.

The choice of films that people made told everything about them, of course. One man, high up in the cultural affairs section, showed nothing but Walt Disney films. Colonel Paul Nikula, the Air Force attaché, and his wife Loretta gave wonderful movie parties, the nicest ones I attended really; all the air attachés of the major embassies came and swapped "unofficial" information explicitly intended to be passed on in the Nikulas' elegant apartment just off Leninsky Prospect.

The businessmen's parties were not usually so international, though occasionally I'd meet someone from Mitsubishi Shoji or Banque de Paris at a Finnish or American party. But the most international and certainly the most singular parties that I went to were given by Art Stevenson III of South Carolina. So far as I could tell, he was even more successful in his negotiations than the Japanese — not because he was so patient but because he gave the cleverest parties. He was a fat little man in his early forties, but he was a genius at sensing anyone's point of vulnerability, and he knew exactly how to put together a successful evening. He even got Russians to come to his soirées. His secret was simple. He showed porno films at his gatherings — a sensation in Moscow.

Art represented an array of American scientific companies, computer and optical and electronic — I never knew exactly which ones. Obviously, he moved freely amidst the mysteries of the Soviet Ministry of Foreign Trade; he was acquainted with executives in many Soviet technical companies; he knew several chiefs in the Academy of Science; and he even helped some scientists at MGU to get equipment they needed — gratis.

All these people came to his parties, along with those in charge of the science desks at the various embassies, an assortment of business contacts and a few stray curiosities like me.

All men, of course. There was always a lot of hard drinking at Art's and he kept a few mattresses in one of his bedrooms for those who didn't want to risk being picked up by the Moscow drunk patrol. But the main feature, as I say, was the films. Most came from Europe, but he was a true chauvinist and he declared his favorites to be American films. The first time I went to one of his parties Art announced triumphantly that this was the sixteenth time he had screened *Deep Throat* — and it was to be the last.

"Finally," he gloated, "every scientific technologist worthy of the name in Moscow has seen this film. What a bore for me! Think of it! I have made a computerized calculation. For the sake of my colleagues, I have been obliged to watch our fair Linda perform her sword-swallowing act one hundred and twenty-eight times. Thirty-eight thousand, four hundred seconds of my life have been consumed in this activity. All in the name of Fair Science!"

He made an esoteric, formal little speech about the importance of the biological concept of man. He praised Darwin — then Pavlov. He referred wittily to historical materialism. He offered to prove that *Deep Throat* constituted America's chief contribution to the science of man. He was really amusing with this sort of mock-pedantic approach to things. He took nothing seriously. Probably he always prefaced his film showings with such a speech. The only other time I went to one of his parties he gave a similar burlesque talk.

"You will observe," he began, "that contrary to my usual custom, I have invited none of our Russian *confrères* here tonight. We have a Swedish engineer, a Spanish chemist, a French businessman, and an American intellectual . . ." He meant me by the last phrase. He glanced about the room, nodding formally at each of us in turn. "But we have no Russians.

"I do not need to tell you this, of course: you have already noticed it for yourselves. You are thinking that I have become disenchanted with the citizens of our host country. You suppose that I am prejudiced against them merely because they squeal like wild boar every time our dear Linda Lovelace swallows someone's tool.

"But you are wrong. I deal with men of science, and scientists have no prejudices. I am happy to see the eyes of our Russian friends glow when they observe the horny antics of some Tijuana tamale or Scandinavian slut. They go home and talk seriously to their wives about western corruption. This makes them smug and happy.

"No, I have left them off the guest list tonight because science declares it illogical for them to see this evening's film. Every Soviet citizen, including its scientists, knows that in the pure heart of socialism no concupiscence exists. It is capitalism — *our* dear capitalism — that causes the decay in morals. A Soviet woman would rather throw herself under a farm tractor — or die in a Samar-

kand dentist chair — than submit to the indelible nonso-
cialist stain of — shall we name it baldly? — group fuck-
ing. Should I try to convince our Soviet friends that the
Muscovites themselves make porno films, veritable skin-
flicks, they would believe me to be thoroughly unscien-
tific. They would trust me no longer. After all, there is
not a word in Lenin about the historical laws governing
Russian raunch. Q.E.D.: it must not exist.

"But, among ourselves, we of the decadent, doubting,
cynical west, I can make my announcement. Tonight we
have a special, one-time-only showing of a Russian fuck-
film. It has neither a list of credits nor even a title, which
gives me the chance to tell you that after extensive research — and a little invention — I have discovered that
the stars are the Marx Sisters and the proper title is: 'Kum
at the Komsomol; or, The Soviets Suck.'

"*Roll it!*" he cried in a supreme gesture of closing,
spreading his arms in the air.

Poor as it was, Art's speech was far superior to the film.
He was well aware that the main interest of the evening
would not be in the film itself, but in the fact that such a
film could be made in Russia at all. In a country where
sex is so taboo that even Freud cannot be mentioned in
public without causing pained embarrassment, the mere
idea of this film's subterranean production gave the evening a special spice. The film itself was done in the style
of private porno films of the late thirties. The hero was
dressed only in a Stalin jacket. He plucked his mustaches,
rolled his eyebrows, and fucked a troupe of big, awkward,
bored women in all the usual positions.

Afterward, several of us drank too much. Art's overnight accommodations would have been strained except
that a science officer from one of the embassies called his
motor pool and had a driver pick up a carload of men and

deliver them to their apartments. I stayed at Art's because I preferred not to wobble past the woman who sat at the entry to my dormitory. At 2 A.M. she would probably be asleep and I didn't want to have to wake her. So I picked out one of Art's mattresses and slept beautifully.

He woke me around ten the next morning to say that he was going to drive into the office to sign some papers. Did I want to go?

On the way in I tried to tempt him to take off from work.

"Come with me, for starters, to the Chekhov museum, Chekhov's house," I proposed. "It's not far from the Embassy, just a few blocks up the Sadovoye-Kudrinskaya." He had an office on Ulitsa Tchaikovskogo, close to the U.S. Embassy.

"To tell the truth," he said a little wearily, "it doesn't interest me. But I'll make you a proposition. Instead, I'll deliver you right to the door of the Gorky Museum. I have to stop there. Why don't you take a look at that place first? It's only a block or so from the Chekhov house. I'll drop you off there."

"Sure. I don't mind walking over. What's at the Gorky Museum for you?"

"Nothing at the museum. I'm making a rendezvous outside it to return this film to the owner. I had a hard time getting it at all last night. The guy says it's in use every night — it's more popular than *Izvestia*. He has to have it back this morning because it's booked at lunchtime — by the North Korean delegation. It's top-secret, cloak-and-dagger stuff, to get it at all. I have to deliver it to him where I picked it up, to a car parked outside the Gorky Museum — of all places!"

Art pulled up across the street from a light green Volga that was parked directly in front of number 25a Vorovskoy Ulitsa. We both got out. As we approached the car, Art slid the big reel out of his briefcase and in one arc swept it inside the opened window of the car, as if he were exchanging state secrets.

The big middle-aged man sitting alone at the wheel didn't look at him or at the film, even as he took it with his large hand. He kept his eyes fixed on me. Then he nodded.

I nodded back.

"Mr. Malevsky," I said stiffly.

5

Some weeks later, I was waiting in the Hotel Peking for Marya to join me so that we could go together to the Uzbekistan restaurant. Malevsky appeared at my elbow.

"Marya says that you are a person of great charm. Forgive me for answering your question so curtly on our first encounter."

"Sit down, won't you!"

"With pleasure."

"I've read your articles, you know," he said. "It isn't that I was prying into your personal affairs. I did want to meet you — I'm writing a biography of Henry Miller, whom you've attacked. Now it looks as if I'm spying on you and I just wanted to say — well, I suppose I don't want you to think that I've been tracking you down."

"My articles are non-articles now. No newspaper editor knows me."

His tone changed. "Listen, let me explain to you a little. We don't know each other at all, so let me say a few words."

He spoke with deliberation. "Perhaps you won't think that I am telling you the truth when I claim that I believed in my attacks on your western decadence. I still believe in them. "Did you ever see my article on the Southern writer William Faulkner? Despite all I said about Faulkner's degeneracy of mind and morals, he had one true observation. You remember in *Absalom, Absalom!* he says about the shady deal Coldfield made with Sutpen, that the raw state of Mississippi society gave Coldfield the chance to make deals which exceeded the bounds of the criminally culpable, but Southern frontier puritanism also gave him a conscience and made him feel guilty about the deals. "That's the way it is in the Soviet Union. Everyone is a criminal. To do more than merely survive a person requires use of the black market and access to foreign currency. He must gain and use influence and bribe in small but illegal ways. To drive a car, to go to the opera on a good night, to get edible food, to place one's son in a good school — all that makes you commit crimes. You know that by needing these things and doing what you must to get them, you must give your soul, your life, away. Once you do one thing, take one privilege, you're lost. Someone always knows how you've gone out of bounds. You can be brought up on charges any time. Sooner or later you forget, and become a real criminal. You can't worry about crimes anymore: your whole life becomes a crime. But you always feel shame and fear. The system that makes you a criminal makes you ashamed and fearful of it. It places you in the deepest of all prisons."

Marya came up breathlessly.

"So you've met — really met — Arkady Pavlovich, then?"

She gave one of her hands to each of us.

"Listen, we must forget about our restaurant dinner, Jay dear. My chief has given me two tickets to Pliset-skaya's *Carmen* suite — I'm dying to see it. Wouldn't the Marshal be disturbed to learn that a ticket purchased on the budget of the Soviet Department of Defense is being used by an American? Dear Malevsky, I wish you could come too. Oh, Jay dearest, hurry and get me a little dish of meat — yes, roasted meat, any sort. I'm famished! Then we can have a nice bottle of champagne and the Bolshoi's wonderful cherry torte during the first intermission. But do hurry — before I expire!"

When I came back Malevsky was gone.

"He had everything once," she sighed, "really everything that a man could want: power, position, money. Editors depended upon him. He had the approval of politicians, he was known high, very high up — at the very top. And so a journal was sure of him: an editor was a genius when he got Malevsky to write an article for him. He didn't write books, he never sold in the millions the way a children's-book author might do, someone like that mechanic Mikhalkov — but he was right at the head of all the writers in this nation. He could sit all day in the U.S.A. Institute, reading American magazines if he chose, and no one dared complain. Eventually he'd quietly, confidently, put an issue of some big Russian journal on the desk of the head of his institute, opened to one of the articles — 'The Corruption of *Cosmopolitan*: The Selling of the American Female' — or suchlike. Graduate students waited on him. Women adored him.

"That was his downfall, the women. That and the reading of Henry Miller. You once mentioned his article on Miller. It was a sensation here. Certainly he attacked Miller, but afterward Arkady Pavlovich's thinking began to shift. He took a trip to East Germany and came back with a wonderful motion-picture camera that ran automatically, and he began to take pictures of himself and his women, porno pictures. He showed them to his friends. He invited them to participate in little parties that always ended up on mattresses. He began to have this other life, a very strange one. The highest people came to his parties.

"But pretty soon they began to wonder about those pictures, to worry about him, to fear him. What would happen to a Party member if a film got out that exhibited him in such an embarrassing postion? They hated him for the threat his camera posed to their weaknesses . . .

"You see where it led. Because he had so much, his crime was great. He lost everything. No job, no salary, no royalties, no pension from the Writers Union, and no hospital services, no apartment. Nothing. He lives poorly — anyone can see that.

"But it's the shame that's killing him. They took away everything but that. They left his shame. He was right when he said to you the first time I brought him over, 'Malevsky is dead.'

"My darling, if you ever write about Malevsky, describe him as a man in hell. He feels the flames, but he doesn't even believe in hell, that's the worst of it. He's burning alive — and he's cold as ice."

We took a bus down to Gorky Street to the ballet. Plisetskaya's *Carmen* was noisy and stagy — a too flashy vehicle for an aging prima.

But after it she performed a very short piece based on William Blake's "The Sick Rose," with music by Mahler:

> *O Rose, thou art sick!*
> *The invisible worm*
> *That flies in the night,*
> *In the howling storm,*

Has found out thy bed
Of crimson joy,
And his dark secret love
Does thy life destroy.

She danced it severely, beautifully, with an absolute purity of movement. That made nothing right, except my heart.

V

The Invisible House

My sister Elena wants me to ask you how you enjoyed the thousand-year-old eggs, Professor. She's a student at the dietary institute, you know, and concerned with such matters," my student Tatjana Efimovna asked me over the phone one day.

I hadn't heard from her for a couple of weeks, and I understood that by reminding me of our early conversation concerning the Hotel Peking, she was just re-establishing communication.

"Tell her that I haven't had them yet. I want you and Elena to come with me to the hotel, and we'll all try them together."

I knew that if Tatjana came along, she'd find some way to get us seated in that sumptuous restaurant, no matter what the regulations might be.

Without Tatjana Efimovna I would have been a prisoner in Moscow. She was the person who arranged for all my trips. On my own I would never have been able to work through all the complicated forms to be completed and rituals to be observed simply to get a visa to visit the sights farther than twenty kilometers outside the city.

But Tatjana knew everything. She was a graduate student in literature, but she had worked for the Foreign Office, she had been a guide for Intourist, she spoke English well. And above all she had endless tenacity and a genius for making her way through any bureaucracy.

She herself had performed the most difficult task in the Soviet Union. She had managed to escape her rural, proletarian origins, move from the country, and establish herself in Moscow. If she could do this, she could do anything.

Born in the Urals, where her father had been sent during the war to work in the mines, she grew up in a village on the Ural River, which divides Asia from Europe. She lived on the European side, but to play in the town park she had to cross the river. Perhaps that absurdity — going from Europe to Asia just to play a game of rope or ball — had an effect on her: it made her want to travel, especially to get away from the Urals.

"Any time I walked over that bridge," she told me, "I would stop in the middle of it and fall into reveries. There on my right hand was Europe and over there was Asia. And I — I liked to pretend that I was nowhere, there in the middle between them, nowhere — or else in some other, completely unimaginable country. I played that like the yellow-colored river, I too was going somewhere — anywhere beyond — oh, not just beyond the town, but beyond beyond, to some beautiful spot."

She was usually decisive and full of business, but when she mentioned those melancholy, youthful times, her one romantic streak appeared and the terrible drama of hopeless yearning was real to her again and her eyes grew wide and sightless.

"My mother understood how I felt. Coming to the Urals had been like death to her. Before she had been there for five years she was saddled with the two of us, Elena and me. My father was wrecked, his lungs were shot from the dampness underground. Later, his legs were taken off in an accident in the mine cars. He had his pension there, he had to stay. Besides, Mother had a job checking gears in a tool factory. She had no chance for escape.

"But we did — one chance. Our aunt lived in Krasnodar in Caucasia, and we could be permitted to go there for high school and live with Aunt Ilona.

"What a wonder Krasnodar was. All my life in the Urals I never knew it was possible for anyone to have meat more than once a week. Back home we had never seen rice — but the province of Kuban was full of it, growing in great flooded fields. And there were fresh vegetables, taken right from the ground, the dirt still on them. That was joy.

"Krasnodar had plenty of parks, too, fine places with trees planted thickly in them. On a Sunday, it was possible to stroll across the grass arm-in-arm with a girlfriend and wear a nice red lipstick, the way Krasnodar girls did. And stand near the brass band and listen to them play 'The Red Army March.' And talk to boys — and maybe even have a special boy of your own to meet in the park. This was indeed 'beyond' — more wonderful than anything I'd known.

"To deserve Krasnodar — that was the trick. My classmates sat in high school during long hours, doodling, writing their names over and over. I daydreamed only about one thing — not slipping back. Maybe going beyond Krasnodar — to Moscow or Leningrad. In my nightmares I saw a black line being drawn across my permit to live in Krasnodar. Someone was placing me on a train to Magnitogorsk.

"Then one day the head of my school called me into his office. I was terrified.

" 'Your records show,' he said very deliberately while

my heart beat fast, 'that your father is part Czechoslovakian and that you speak Czech.'

" 'Yes,' I said, since to deny it was useless.

" 'Then speak Czech to me,' he demanded.

"I was so scared I could remember only the first sentences I had ever learned. I said, 'My name is Tatjana. Here is the bridge. How are you today?'

" 'What does that mean?'

"I felt ridiculous, but I told him.

" 'Wonderful,' he said, breaking into a smile. 'So you have a job by which you may serve your school. It will count toward your duties in the Komsomol.'

" 'A job?'

" 'Yes, I am asked by Intourist to give them aid in guiding a group of thirty farmers from the Czechoslovakian Socialist Republic who have come here to learn from the experts in our Krasnodar Institute of Agriculture. You are chosen to aid in this important enterprise.'

"So I learned the secret of rising in the world: to know foreign languages was to be an important person. I studied hard.

"When I learned enough English to work with Americans the whole world opened up. Once, thirty-four farmers arrived from your state in Iowa. The Americans disturbed me. They were cheery and called me Little Miss, but I had been trained in British English and these men, I thought, spoke English so poorly I concluded they were spies — I have since adjusted myself to your flat American accent, however. Besides, they didn't seem serious about farming. They did go to see our collective farms, but I could tell they were more interested in eating at the Cossack Village, going to our tearoom, and buying souvenirs at the Intourist Hotel. They had no interest in agricultural statistics. They listended politely when I told them about the rate of kilograms of Kavkaz wheat pro-

duced per hectare, but I sensed that they were more interested in hearing the Kuban Cossack Choir sing or
watching the Adyghei dancers.

"I learned languages as fast as possible. Bulgarian, Polish, German. I was allowed to enter the university. Finally, a dream came true: my chief at the Kuban State
University informed me I would be sent with a good fellowship to Moscow State as a graduate student in order to
study modern languages. A teaching job would await my
return, it would be in my plan.

"Moscow! It is as far ahead of Krasnodar as that city is
beyond the Urals. I wish to remain in Moscow always.
Despite my plan, I dream of getting a job here. Where?
Well, in the Institute for Foreign Languages. You've met
Professor Lydia Suronova who is director there, haven't
you? Wouldn't you consider mentioning my name to her
favorably? Dear Professor, thank you! You've made me a
happy person."

By nature as well as necessity, Tatjana was a thorough-
going Darwinist. She told the tale of her rise from the dep-
rivation of the Urals to the splendor of Moscow with a
certain amount of wonder, but also with an unmistakable
undertone of determined calculation. She sounded a little
like John D. Rockefeller or a business tycoon in a Dreiser
novel. She had her own program for existence, and it dif-
fered from her official plan, registered in the employment
director's office of the state of Kuban. She herself was the
center of her world.

Tatjana had seen from the first that marriage was the
trap for Soviet women. Because her girlfriends had
wanted to get married and raise kids, they were now stuck
in Novorossiisk, married to merchant marines; or maybe
they lived in Maikop or Eisk, looking out of kitchen windows at streets full of mud and oil derricks. Tatjana took
her boyfriends as they came, and fundamentally each one

came speaking a new language. She even took up with a Rumanian for six months — and she regarded Rumanians as the lowest order in the male romantic species. But she got the verb endings down pat.

If she had any weakness at all, it was for her sister. They had a kind of affectionate symbiotic relation based on the principle of specialization in the evolutionary process. Tatjana concentrated on languages while her sister took up the study of diet in the Institute of Home Economics. She couldn't speak a word of any language except Russian — but she managed to bring home little bags of food every night. Fuel and mobility — it was all the organism needed. And so together they thrived.

I'm just trying to say that Tatjana Efimovna had developed one skill to perfection: she knew how to get what she wanted. She worked like a weasel and she had a personal appeal that made her determination appear not merely acceptable but actually attractive. So, whenever I needed a travel visa I always appealed to Tatjana, handed her my passport and left the rest to her. Within a few days, she'd have all the documents properly authorized, and we'd be on our way. "We," I say, because she invariably accepted my invitations to accompany me. Probably I was part of some complicated plan of hers which would eventually land her in Paris or New York as part of a Russian diplomatic mission. Still, how could I complain?

2

In the beginning of April she got me a visa to visit Abramtsevo, the country estate where Gogol and Turgenev had often spent long holidays during the days of the czars.

In the eighteen-seventies, Tatjana informed me, the estate was purchased and restored by the wealthy railroad entrepreneur Savva Mamontov. He invited painters like Repin and Serov there to help make Abramtsevo a center for the revival of traditional Russian arts. Now the Artists Union kept the place in its original state.

We started out early on a Friday morning. Tatjana was dressed in boots and her best jeans suit and a turtleneck sweater beneath her duffel jacket. She kept the hood tossed back and wrapped a Scotch plaid scarf around her blond hair. All in all, we might have been going on a New York subway to visit Central Park, instead of on the Metro to Komsomolskaya to board the suburban train.

The first thing we discovered when we arrived at the Kazan Station was that the army was repairing the railbeds along the line between Moscow and Zagorsk. Instead of a train running through to Abramtsevo every twenty minutes, we would be required to wait two hours.

For Tatjana this delay presented no problem — rather, a welcome opportunity to investigate the little stands that various sellers had set up in this yard between the Leningrad and Kazan stations. She was mad about shopping. Whenever we went anywhere, she shopped at every opportunity. It was one of her ways of keeping up combat with the world.

"Who knows what might turn up?" she said, just as a grizzly bear might wonder what luscious mouthfuls might be nestling under a stump he was about to flip over.

"You know," she explained, "this is the best spot in Moscow to discover bargains. Those with food and little treats and specialties set up stands here. And from the outlying districts, as far away as a hundred and seventy-five kilometers, the country folk come to buy. Sometimes a group of a dozen families will send in two burly guys to

do their shopping. Moscow, as we say, is the stomach —
this is where the food is. Moscow is downhill — everything slides down into Moscow. Sometimes the peasants
trade their handicrafts for food — like carved nests of
Easter eggs: Byelorussians still make them. Today, not
long before Easter, might be a good time to find them.
They go for big prices on the tourist market. Or, there
might be the kind of fancy lacework the Ukrainians still
know how to do. Sometimes they bring in samovars and
desk sets to trade for food. In the backwoods this sort of
stuff is just a drag on the market. But the right person
would know how to dispose of it at a good price."

We agreed to meet after an hour, meanwhile she'd shop
and I'd wander around. I handed her ten roubles. "Bring
me back something interesting, then." I didn't think she
had much money and I figured that buying something for
me — just for the pleasure of buying — would satisfy her
almost as much as acquiring something for herself. Perhaps, too, I was a little infected by her own passion for
purchases — not enough to shop with her ferocity, but
enough to wonder what her luck would uncover with my
ten roubles.

I went inside the station and stood at a table and tried to
read a volume of verses by Bella Akhmadulina. By the
time I reached a poem devoted to a celebration of a motor
scooter, I decided to make Tatjana a gift of the book. More
than cute blond bangs and a marriage to Yevtushenko
would be required to make this woman into a poet.

I wandered about outside. Spring was coming and for
the first time I spotted a *kvass* wagon. A little line of men
and women stood waiting behind the yellow steel barrel on
wheels. A husky woman with a red face sat on a folding
chair and opened the spigot to allow the brown frothy
liquid, fermented from black bread, to shoot out. Of
glasses she had three, each a different size, designed to

satisfy various levels of thirst and pocketbook. After each was used she turned it over and rinsed it out on a little jet of water. Out of curiosity I waited my turn, gave the lady four kopecks for a small size, but got a medium since the smallest glass was being used.

Later, when Tatjana met me, I mentioned this drink of *kvass*. She was shocked.

"Pooh! That's for peasants to drink, that filthy stuff. It's full of germs, besides. The Ministry of Health should close those wagons down! I've bought some oranges for you, seven roubles a kilo. Not a bargain — but did you ever expect to find oranges? Just to get them is a miracle."

For herself, she had assembled a collection of articles in her string bag. I could see a few choice objects: a can of pineapple from Hanoi, a small, paper-thin gray record, and a bar of Warsaw soap, scented and colorfully wrapped. By stuffing sheets from *Izvestia* around the outside of the bag she managed to conceal the rest of her purchases.

The train was now required to handle a two hours' assemblage of passengers and naturally everyone made a rush for seats when the cars were backed into the station. I would have been left behind except that I followed in the tracks of Tatjana, who set out like a ferret for the cars at the head of the train, while most of the first wave of riders crowded sheepishly into the nearest cars. As it was, we barely got places on the hard wooden benches. In a moment the aisles were also completely packed.

Almost every passenger had been shopping and most were carting back enormous loads. One gigantic man who pressed his hip hard against my shoulder held a cardboard box of fresh-cut meat in his arms. He tried to rest its weight on his stomach but it kept slipping down. Within a few minutes a dark moist spot began to show at the bottom of the box, between his hands. It began to bulge wetly, and finally blood started to drip through his fingers, splashing on his gray lumberman's jacket until it looked as if he had been shot in the stomach. A woman standing directly in front of me had her string bag crammed with an assortment of purchases, two dry fish, a big bologna, a few dirt-encrusted beets, a cabbage.

Soon all the odors in the train bloomed, like juices mixing in a stew, from the odor of soaked boots, armpits, and bad teeth, to the musky fragrance of rabbitskin hats. I felt completely worn out, my eyes stung. I closed my eyes tight and felt tears rolling under my eyelids.

Suddenly, Tatjana called, "Professor, dear. Now we must hurry to get through the crowd. Here is our stop." I opened my eyes and watched her push and wriggle her way down the aisle. She used her shopping bag as a wedge, held in front of her to thrust her way through the crowd, and as usual I followed in the path she broke.

"You slept for a half hour, I think," she said. "And it is still morning."

On both sides of the platform, pine trees towered. A fresh breeze cut through my overcoat like an ax, and I shivered.

"Which way do we go?"

"I've never been here myself," she remarked. At the same moment she caught the sleeve of an old man who was hurrying by. He wore a Cossack's hat made of gray Persian lamb. There was much pointing and gesturing before she was satisfied.

"Well, let's go," she announced in her typical cheery, brusque manner. We walked to the end of the platform, crossed the tracks and took a dirt path which immediately disappeared into the woods. Though the Moscow streets were filled with puddles, here the thaw had not advanced so far: ice and mud mixed together. The path had the consistency of frozen oatmeal.

Birch trees soon intermingled with the firs, until they drove the firs out and dominated altogether. The bare boughs made a spidery filigree against the pale blue sky over our heads. We seemed completely encircled by the forest: our rural path seemed to be going nowhere. There was nothing to do but slog along and hope to avoid the waffles of snow that occasionally slid from the branches and glided down about our heads.

But after about fifteen minutes we came out to a cleared asphalt road and faced a fruit and produce and general store that was closed. Tatjana was sure that we should turn left here. The road was elegantly named Boulevard of Artists and Authors. The Soviets had put up dachas along this road for the use of prominent members of the writers and artists unions.

After a few hundred yards the road turned down toward a bright, rapidly flowing river. A bridge crossed the river, then led to a road which twisted and turned until it disappeared up a hill.

"Up there is Abramtsevo. It must be," Tatjana said.

Two men and a boy were fishing from the bridge and another man was casting from the bank below it, getting upstream from the others. They were in good spirits and waved to us before we reached the turn. We waved back and when we came up next to them we asked if they had had any luck. "Show them, Vanya," a jolly, shrewd-looking little man in his mid-twenties said to the boy. Vanya opened the lid of a wooden box. Someone had filled the bottom with sedge and on it were three bream and two kinds of perch. Their heads all pointed in the same direction. The gills of one perch twitched slightly.

"Good," the other man said with satisfaction.

The approach to the house was arranged with a characteristic nineteenth-century emphasis upon scenic views. The path twisted around the meandering river so that we had to cross another little wooden bridge. The overflow of water created by the thaw covered the rickety foundations. Woody bushes and a few bare birch trees bent over the stream. Reflected in it, they looked like the circle strokes of a Japanese brush painter.

Just before we reached the crown of the hill we looked back and the jolly man, who was looking our way, waved again. "I believe he has his eye on you, Tatjana," I said, and I laughed at the sly, pleased look that came into her face.

At the summit we came upon a parking lot, beside which stood a café that was closed. As we turned right, into the little Abramtsevo compound, the buildings also seemed closed. The scene looked like a poor, deserted New England settlement of the eighteen-fifties that had failed even before beginning to develop. A few buildings were arranged around a cleared oval of ground. Farther to the left other buildings were tucked in among huge trees. The main house, which lay directly across from our path, turned out to be an ungainly two-story affair. Mamontov hadn't quite restored it — he had just added to it, piling a large central addition onto a low roof. The house looked low and mean.

While I wandered around, Tatjana went to a gatekeeper's lodge to see if she could locate the museum guide. On either side of the main house cottages were built in the old Russian carved-gingerbread style, looking just like big Bavarian clocks.

All this was ordinary. But I was suddenly plunged into the strangeness of Abramtsevo. Down toward the other end of the oval was the most astonishing building. It looked like a square, rough one-room log cabin, a child's playhouse. But it also had a fanciful entrance with a slanted snow roof held up by two carved pillars. Nailed across its gables was the outline figure of a great bat, his wings spread wide, holes drilled for eyes. The snow had frosted the carved bat ears like white fur. Somehow this sad Hansel and Gretel cottage with its absurd bat and the dark recesses of the surrounding birch tree woods whispered of the dense ambiguities of Russia. Here, the darkness all too clearly peered out of the sunlight.

This was not all. The spongy ground was strewn with gigantic petroliths, stone phallic figures that looked like monkeys' heads. A printed sign explained that during the construction of Mamontov's railroad these monsters had been dug up near the Black Sea. The bulging stone eyes looked at the world with dumb hatred, as if the creatures might struggle out of the earth in the dark of the moon and gather in a silent circle around the toy cottage with their unblinking brother of the air.

Tatjana strode resolutely toward me across the gravel path and put an end to these fancies. Due to the construction on the tracks the guides had assumed that no one would visit, and so they had all gone home. The caretaker had set off to fetch a guide, but as he had no car and the closest one lived five miles away, he would not be back for at least two hours.

We walked around the oval, past a little chapel imitating the Novogorod style, beside which we found Madame Mamontov's grave. The exhibition hall of the Artists Union was closed.

"There's no point in waiting," I said. "Why don't we go over to the house and just look in the windows?"

Tatjana was angry with these country people for their patent inefficiency.

"This place has no dignity anyway," she said. "Can you imagine, the guides do not speak any language except Russian. They have tape recordings in several languages explaining each of the rooms. They try to guess what language you are speaking and then they put that tape on the machine as you go from room to room. How stupid! Probably they make a bad guess most of the time and give Italians Bulgarian and Swedes Spanish. Certainly they are just peasants.''

All the rooms in the house were visible from outside. The sun flooded through the curtained windows, making V-shaped patterns on the herringbone parquet floor. In the corners of the main rooms were glazed porcelain tile fireplaces. Abramtsevo was famous for its vivid porcelains, and it really was a remarkable technique that had produced these incredible yellows, greens, and blues.

Seen from the windows, in fact, the whole place was quite splendid. I changed my mind about it entirely. It was filled with art. Many of the artists who had stayed here in the summertime had painted from the landscapes of the vicinity. Paintings of the outside hung inside, on every wall, as if, like the dazzling fireplaces, they could continue to radiate summer's warmth. Many portraits also hung on the walls, probably in the very rooms where the subjects had posed for them. The furniture those now-dead persons once sat on could still be seen. A fine painting of little Vera Mamontov in a pink dress rested on an easel in the dining room; she was painted sitting at the very table which still stood in the room, with her back to the sunlit windows — had Serov been painting her at this moment, he would have seen my face behind Vera, gazing through the parted drapes. So the house was like an infinite regression. It had ghosts — delicate ghosts, artistic ones.

Above all, the rooms gave the feeling that they were still lived in. At any moment Gogol might stroll up the path, unlatch the door and, with the greatest simplicity, take his place at the cherrywood desk, light the candles and oil lamp, and start composing a story. The whole house conveyed a sense of an ageless, uncomplicated passage through a time; it possessed an atmosphere slightly charged by a sacred sense that the house appreciated itself as a treasure and a repository and reliquary for the people of sensibility who once occupied it. For some curious reason, it reminded me of Conrad Aiken's house on Cape Cod where I had lived during the summers when I was a student. The same rich, simple consciousness of art hovered over it.

A guide showing up with several taped-recorded reels in hand could only have shattered this consecrated aroma, and after a half hour I declared myself satisfied and proposed to Tatjana that she lead us back to the Kazan Station.

"I hope that you do not attribute the failure of these guides to perform their job to our socialism," Tatjana said, still irritated.

"No, not at all," I assured her. I was afraid that just for the sake of making the caretakers do their duty she might insist that we stay until Abramtsevo had been inspected down to the last stitch in the tablecloth on which the Mamontov daughters had embroidered the signatures of famous guests.

"Very well, then," she said. "Let us see if the café is open before we go back."

Ever since our arrival, she had pulled a succession of chocolates, hard candies, dried fruits, and cookies from her purse, rapidly but delicately popping each sweet morsel between her red lips.

A twinge of disappointment came into her pursed mouth when we came in sight of the still-closed building. But her face brightened immediately when she noticed that the man cleaning the windows on a little van in the parking lot was the very same jolly young fellow with whom we had exchanged a few words on the bridge earlier. Her mind, I think, was full of fine gears that continually spun around, seeking to mesh with any new opportunity. In the end, she liked to accompany me, surely, because the presence of an American professor gave her one more lever to work and multiplied the opportunities for manipulation at least to the second power.

In a businesslike way she hurried over to the fellow and asked him to give her and her "distinguished guest of the Soviet Socialist Republic, Doctor-Professor," et cetera, et cetera, a ride back to the station in his van. At first he refused pointblack — at least I guessed he did, because though I had followed at a distance, I saw her roll her eyes to heaven in her characteristic gesture of exasperation. By the time I actually came up to the van, though, he had changed his mind. He told me in English that he would be honored to drive a professor from the United States to the station. He introduced himself as Alexander Petrovich Yushkevich.

"Once I gave some assistance to a traveler from Edinburgh," he confided, "and this man told me that in Scotland I would probably be nicknamed Sandy. In honor of our conversation, do call me Sandy, won't you? And we'll all speak in English, just as if we were in Chicago. I get so little chance to practice."

"But first, honored sir," he said, holding his arms out, palms upturned, in a warm, embracing gesture, "I must ask you if I may know how you enjoyed our fine Abramtsevo? I myself have studied in our English school and I know that removed as we are from Moscow many visitors from English-speaking countries visit our museum each year."

I tried to keep the waters smooth by saying simply that the house was fine. But Tatjana took this opportunity to scold him, as a representative of this country place, for the unforgivable defection of the house guides. Her city-acquired haughtiness concerning country things came out all too plainly. She really lit into him, and for a moment he took it like a slap in the face. But even before she finished her tirade against this primitive outlying district, he stopped listening. He didn't need to listen because he had decided upon his defense.

"Ah, it is no matter," he said, ostensibily answering her, but looking at me. "For I myself, when I studied English, I practiced by visiting the house and listening to the English tapes in each of its excellent rooms. For practice I memorized the tape for each room. And therefore I may now, if you are willing — yes? — make suitable recompense for the most unfortunate absence of our official guides, who after all are but dear ladies of our town whose chief care is for the dust on the furniture and the airing of the rooms. Now, since you have looked at the rooms through the windows — yes? — I will speak the tour and you will hear of the special wonders of which you may not be aware fully."

He spoke all this with such a perfect sincerity that even Tatjana swallowed her Muscovite ridicule. She had to go along with his plan. There wasn't the slightest possibility of silencing him. First he walked us around the parking lot, tracing out the dimensions of the house. He brought us to an imaginary front door and issued us in. Then he started talking at once in the exact words of the recorded tour. And so we followed him around the imaginary rooms of the imaginary house built on the parking lot, while this plump young fellow gestured at invisible pictures and objets d'art or called our attention to an exceptionally fine carved cabinet, all the while mouthing the recording he had memorized right down to a tone of voice that was not his at all.

It was a perfectly ghostly performance, and therefore perfect in every way. Old ladies with dust rags seemed to hover about. I almost felt that all the ancient aristocratic fellowship of the house had gathered in spirit shape to see what new revolution had despoiled them from their house into the new apparitional dwelling around which we were guided. Perhaps even the ghosts, with their diminished sense of materiality, became confused over whether the house they had once inhabited was the palpable, closed-up museum or the invisible mansion that was being so vividly described.

Those were the sort of thoughts I had while he droned on and I followed him about, nodding as he described each invisible object. At first Tatjana seemed absorbed, but in a few moments she reassumed her attitude of scorn and applied it to his performance. Undeterred, he continued his feat of memory to its conclusion. In the voice of the record he wished us a pleasant stay in the U.S.S.R. and a safe trip home.

When he had finished, Tatjana remarked in a cold neutral tone, "That's all very well, but who can put the house and the tour together? It doesn't make any sense at all."

However, he was so perfectly pleased with himself that he heard only my praise for his feat, not her criticism.

For me, it had been a perfect day, a real Russian day, and I was content to have it end right here. In advance I imagined how it would be on the train. The car would be warm, filled with sun and human odors. Tatjana would pull out a big novel by Frank Norris, on whom she was writing her dissertation, and fall to reading. I'd press against her and doze and dream about the wooden bat and toy cottage and the stone giants, and I'd look again in all the rooms of that incredible invisible house. Maybe this was romanticism of the most sentimental sort, but I let myself sink into its rich oozy bottom. Sandy tucked us into his van and started toward the station, but I dreamed my way there ahead of him.

None of these contented visions was to be realized, as

things turned out. We never did ride back in the train, and by the time Tatjana and I got back to Moscow my whole mood had changed.

What happened was so opposite from what I expected and planned that it became a completely different story for me, and I have to give it its own special place in these legends.

VI

The Lady with the
Blue Moskvich

Alexander Petrovich took us to the station along a
paved route. When we passed the general store he said,
"It's already afternoon and I should be opening up the
store. I am its manager."

He showed an obvious pride in this fact. Like Tatjana at
least in one way, he thought himself a successful person,
competent against any accidents of fate.

But he had no control over Soviet trains. When we arrived at the station we found a surprising number of people there. The wooden benches on the platform were all
filled and many people were leaning listlessly against
poles, pacing up and down, or loitering back and forth
across the tracks to a little *tabac* shop and newsstand.

Sandy made the inquiries that were called for. Shaking
his head he came back to report that there would be a very
long delay. An enthusiastic group of Komsomol students
had arrived twenty kilometers up the track to aid the soldiers in repairing the roadbeds. These young Communists would not be content with the slipshod work of the
soldiers: they'd want to remove ties and replace supports,
and in general they would take great pains to prove their
socialist seriousness. The result, the stationmaster had
said, was that it would still be at least two hours before the

line would be open. Sandy made the obvious deduction and declared that this really meant at least four hours.

"How lucky that we happened to meet. Come to my store. It's no Macy's, but it does have a good trade. We can sit there in comfort, have a bite to eat if you've a mind, and talk English. Why, this is a real stroke of good fortune for me!"

His store resembled little country stores anywhere. It was meant as a food store, but it had a varied assortment of goods on the shelves. We pulled a few chairs up to a board fastened to the end of the counter for use as a table. Sandy hustled to the back room to make some tea.

While he was gone Tatjana made a hurried but undoubtedly thorough inspection of the wares lying on the shelves and counters. For the most part she maintained her attitude of scorn for everything associated with Sandy. But apparently a few of the items surprised her, since like a seismograph she gave off slight clickings with her lips and teeth whenever she came across something of interest.

Soon he brought out a little stoneware pot and cups decorated with gay orange designs, meant to represent Chinese willows. He poured out our tea and began to chat pleasantly. Tatjana busied herself in silence with dumping cubes of sugar into her cup.

He hadn't raised the window shades on the front door, and so I assumed that while technically he fulfilled his official duties by being present in the store, he also wanted to give the appearance of its being closed so that he could devote his time to us. But somehow word got around that the store was open and we had hardly lifted our teacups before two women came in the door. Each was already so loaded down with goods packed in heavy duck shopping bags and cardboard boxes that it was impossible to imagine how even these powerful women could have carried more. Sandy ignored them, but if they came to buy they seemed in no hurry either. They simply stood around and scanned the shelves, all the while whispering in low tones to each other. After a few moments one of them drew a copy of *The Leninist Banner* from her purse and they both stood in a corner poring over the news and poking each other over juicy items.

Within a few moments a middle-aged man opened the door and walked in, without salutation. He was not silent from gloom, it seemed, so much as from expectation. He looked like a heron who barely rested his thin body on solid ground.

From outside came the sound of an automobile squeaking to a halt and a thin young woman walked noisily up the two steps and quickly came in. She approached our improvised tea table, instinctively seeming to know that Tatjana and I were strangers and Sandy was the boss. She leaned her head over to him and whispered. He went to a glass case and fetched a package of cigarettes for her and handed them over without taking any payment. As she slit the silver wrapper with her fingernail she scrutinized the room's occupants again and continued to throw little glances our way. She drew out and lit a long Russian tube cigarette.

I was following her darting glances, trying to learn what she was searching for, when her eyes fixed suddenly on the activities of the thin man. On the counter, unnoticed, he had placed several pairs of ladies' beach slippers and three pairs of stylish boots, in black "wet-look" vinyl, which he had removed from a paper bag. From another parcel he took out a pile of brightly colored scarfs.

Before the woman with the car could move, one of the two burly ladies stepped over to his side and proposed, "Let me see those boots. Hm, last year's style. These are available through Poland now: one needn't go all the way to Turkey for them anymore. They'll be in the state stores soon."

"My dear woman," he said, "they *are* in the state stores. But, as usual, the employees buy them up first: these boots were sold, and sold again, before the store even opened. The same with my other things. I make no false claims. I do not deal in the black market. All my goods are available at state prices — plus a tip, shall we say? — for my services."

"We two have come all the way from Kharkov by rail to trade in Moscow, and here we are stuck in Abramtsevo," the other woman said. "Do you take us for country bumpkins? What's your price for these articles, inferior though they are?"

"Certainly, I can see that you understand how to buy. These were made in Leningrad. Fine, aren't they? For the boots, fifty-nine roubles — just a little increase above state price, eh? And for the scarfs, forty-seven roubles twenty kopecks — wonderful colors, wonderful feel to the cloth, almost handmade. But don't you have anything to trade?"

"Yes, but only the best goods made right in our factory — not on company time, but on an 'extra shift,' don't you know?" They both winked loudly. "Here, see, lipsticks in gold cases: two gross. Sparkplugs — the longest lasting: four dozen."

"And what do you have in those boxes over there?" the man asked, gesturing at two boxes tied together with twine, an ungainly package that one of the ladies had dragged in.

"That's for trading in Moscow. It's of no use here, that's for sure. Eight hundred and thirty-five dozen prophylactics. 'Cossack Condoms. Strong, Most Sensitive Made. Machine Tested.' We're going to try to sell them

to a hospital. We overproduced on our quota last year —
you know how it is."

The Russian reticence about sex went out the window
when it came to a trade.

I calculated quickly to myself: "ten thousand condoms." Something about the number was stunning.

I saw Tatjana's eyes light when the bright fingers of lipstick flashed in the air like bloody claws. But at the mention of the prophylactics her eyelids fell, like the hoods on
a serpent.

"Let me buy two lipsticks from you," she said, getting
up. "How much?"

"Four roubles," the taller, slightly younger woman
answered.

"All right," Tatjana said, and handed over the money
readily. She rolled the lipsticks in and out in complete ab-
sorption, like an idiot, while the woman with the car
crushed her cigarette out in a glass ashtray and said, "I
want to trade with both of you, for a few lipsticks and
maybe beach slippers. I just have to go out to my car."

As she reached out to grasp the knob, the door opened
and two men walked in. They were dressed in suede
jackets and hats with goggles that closely resembled the
soft helmets worn by pilots during World War I. The
woman went out as they entered. These two men were
motorcyclists. They had ridden here together on a bike
with a sidecar. Seeing that a trade was already in
progress, they quickly came to the point. One man unwrapped a dozen mohair sweaters, in four or five different
colors, but all the same cardigan style.

"Anyone interested?" he said in a tough voice. By now
I understood — as doubtless Tatjana had instantly understood — that by accident we were in the Russian equiva-
lent of a Southern California drive-in on Swap Meet Day.

Officially it was a food store, but Sandy had developed a thriving business on the side, acting as a kind of middleman and broker between the country and Moscow.

At the same time the other motorcyclist opened his briefcase and took out a half-dozen long-playing records. The one on top was by Blood, Sweat and Tears. "These are the big ones," he urged, "Wings, with McCartney, Credence Clearwater Revival, David Bowie."

While this was going on Sandy went over to the Kharkov ladies and apparently arranged a big complicated deal. They lifted their four dozen sparkplugs onto the counter and he whisked them under the other side and produced a certain amount of money, two Scotch plaid blankets, and some small clear plastic packets containing foldup raincoats. He took two pairs of boots and four scarfs from the thin man and handed them over to the ladies. Then he turned back to the fellow and gave him a record turntable, three bottles of Rose's Lime Juice — taken from the back room and clearly marked "By Appointment to Her Majesty" — and a few bars of Moscow chocolate.

The nervous lady came back from her car.

"If you'll give me four lipsticks," she proposed, "I'll give you the name of a butcher in Moscow who sells out of the rear of his store. You follow my meaning?"

"How do we know this is true?" the older Kharkov woman muttered suspiciously. But they were pleased with having gotten rid of the sparkplugs and they took a chance. And, in turn, so that something tangible would change hands — "for luck," she said — the woman with the car gave them a package of record needles she had found in her car.

She turned to the thin man. "For a pair of these boots I'll give you this fur hat — hardly worn," she said, hitting it against her arm to show that it was not dusty and that no hairs fell out.

"It's an old thing," he grumbled, "practically ratty, too."

"Well, add two pairs of beach slippers — they're the plastic and not the good rubber ones, aren't they? — and I'll throw in these windshield wipers, hardly used. And this cigar lighter from my car."

"No, these don't interest me."

"Wait a moment." She went outside again. From the sounds she made, she must have opened her trunk and then reached into a hiding place — perhaps under the spare tire — for it was over a minute before she slammed the lid and came in the door with a short-wave radio. Everyone gaped.

She sized up the two men. "This for a record and the sweaters. Take it or leave it?"

Instantly they became joint owners of the radio.

"Now, I'll give you four sweaters for a pair of boots, two scarfs, and a couple of pairs of beach slippers, perhaps," she told the thin man.

The man asked for a record also but when he understood that she would hold stubbornly to her proposal he gave in and took the sweaters.

"Say, let's have a peek at that radio," Sandy called cheerily to the motorcyclist. Actually this was merely a manner of speaking; he hardly glanced at it. His method of trading was exactly the opposite of the others. One could see that instead of downgrading an article he wanted in hopes of lowering the asking figure, he'd be more likely to praise it to the skies. Then, when he'd made the owner take a sunny, positive view of things, Sandy would offer him an article of his own in trade and praise it with equal enthusiasm. How could the other fellow say, "You are right about the value of my offering, but yours is beneath contempt"? More often than not, Sandy would be likely to come out on top in this puffery contest. "Yes, it's a fine radio — what does it matter if it's illegal to possess? — a fine radio, if only one had a converter for it, since, you know, it wouldn't work on *our* current. Where would anyone ever find a converter?"

The two men looked at each other and at the lady with the car, afraid they had been fooled, when Sandy said brightly, as if to aid them, "Who cares? I'll take a chance. Maybe with my connections I can get a converter. Say, look, here's a stereo speaker, a Sony, from Japan — the finest — hooks up to anything. And this" — he brought out a little cardboard box of pint bottles — "this is, you know, eh, 'cough medicine' from Turkey. I can't read Turkish, but, well, I wouldn't be surprised if the bottles weren't filled with opium — wonderful for chills and arthritis, eh?"

The two men hesitated, uncertain, but Sandy adroitly added, "Ah, and a bottle of lime juice from the tropics! Oh, and here, two pairs of fur-lined gloves. Sure, they'll fit. Take that from me as a friend." The radio changed hands. Who could tell if it would bring in anything but static?

While this deal was still in progress, to my amazement I heard Tatjana coolly say to the nervous woman, "Why don't you let me buy your car? I'm sure you want to sell it. What kind is it?"

"A nice Moskvich. Blue in color. Runs good," the woman recited. "I don't think you have enough money."

"Name your figure, anyway."

The lady proposed an outrageous price: "Well, cars are going up so fast in price, and I've spent a lot of money putting this one in shape, I would just break even if I let you have this for twenty thousand roubles."

By the way he unintentionally flinched at this figure, Sandy, I noticed, was listening. Tatjana would not have failed to notice it too. "Not bad," she said quickly. "I've got a taxi driver friend looking for a car. Give me a chance at it."

Sandy tried to interrupt, but she waved him off and silenced him for a second. "I mean, look, let me make you a gift of this can of pineapple — from Hanoi — and these bars of scented soap — imported — and this ten-rouble note. It's all yours to keep just in return for an option on buying your car. You take these. Just don't let anyone else buy your car for the next two hours, eh?"

Tatjana slipped the articles out of her bag and pushed them at her. What did the woman have to lose? This was a sheer bonus she was getting. Tatjana took her off for a little whispered conference, woman-to-woman, in one corner of the room.

Outside, a man pulled up to the door on a racing bicycle. He leaned it against the front step railing, locked a chain around it, and removed some packages from his wire carryall.

Everyone gave him sidelong glances to see what goods he might produce, but at this point in the trading everything was going along so smoothly that no one cared to stop and wait for the new arrival. His coming, in fact, seemed only to accelerate the rapidity of their dealings.

At this point Tatjana showed a depth of calculation that even I had not anticipated. Putting her head close to mine, she whispered, "If I can get them, I always keep one or two of these with me — for trading with men." She opened her large purse and brought out two magazines sealed inside plastic wrappers.

"Take a look at these," she said offhandedly to the motorcycle guys. The bicyclist and even Sandy let this development distract them. The men held the two magazines gingerly, almost with reverence, and looked at the front and then, reluctantly, turned each over to look at the back. "*Playboy*, the famous *Playboy*. And also a Danish magazine. Interested? What will you give me?"

"Two records?"

"All of them."

"But there are six records and only two magazines," one wailed.

"Well, I can get plenty of records," Tatjana remarked indifferently, and reached for the magazines.

While her hand hovered, she added, "O.K., forget the records, just give me that useless speaker." Then, as soon as her fingertips touched one magazine, crackling the cellophane, the man said,

"All right, that's all right. We'll keep them. Take the speaker."

"I hope you don't think you can buy my car with dirty pictures," the woman said to Tatjana as she lit another cigarette.

Sandy had already gotten into a discussion with the two women, who had occupied themselves trying on their new sweaters.

He was saying, "See here, those boxes of yours must weigh a ton, don't they? Why don't we make a trade for one of the two — how many did you say?"

"Almost eight hundred and fifty dozen," one answered. But the other corrected her, "Eight hundred and thirty-five exactly. It's every one that we had left in the warehouse."

"Well, I can take half of them," he said. "It'll take me a century to get rid of them. But why not? Let's trade."

From his back room and various drawers Sandy extracted a changing collection of articles, placing them on the counter and rapidly removing them as he proposed various combinations of goods in exchange for the prophylactics. Four calendar watches, two dozen French-style lace bras, in assorted colors and sizes. Ten jars of Maxwell House Instant Coffee. Three dozen pantyhose. Three pennants reading "Moscow Dynamo." A case of water-packed peaches from Bulgaria. Six tins of snuff. Lip balm. One bottle of cognac. A bolt of colorful material, Uzbek pattern. Chewing gum. He made such articles pass across the counter in the same fashion that a pitchman passes a pea under walnut shells. At a certain point, the women just gave in and turned the heavy cardboard box over to Sandy.

Now the dealings really started in earnest.

"No, certainly," the jolly fellow explained then, he had not promised them "*all* these things." Hadn't he used words like "these . . . or," "either . . . or?" Didn't words mean anything? Finally they agreed on the appropriate combination and the women were pleased that, after all, they had gotten so much and lightened their load into the bargain.

"If you don't like this book of poetry," Tatjana asked me, "can I have it? I can make good use of it now."

With a big smile Tatjana congratulated them on their good fortune. "Just for my own luck," she suggested, "won't you trade that little box of record needles to me for this volume by our greatest female poet, Bella Akhmadulina. I'm sure that as a woman you know her work. Supreme, isn't she? — fit to stand with the revered poets of your mother's generation, Anna Akhmatova and Margarita Aliger. Please let me make you a gift of this." She handed the volume over and swept up the package of needles in the same motion.

Sandy attempted, without success, to work the magic of his apparently endless supply of Rose's Lime Juice upon the bicyclist. They finally made a deal by which Sandy gave up the short-wave radio in exchange for four rolls of

Greek toilet paper, an old copy of *The Watchtower*, a bottle of German Köln-Wasser — and the bicycle.

The two motorcyclists had drawn into the shadows of the farthest corner of the little room and were staring hard at the magazines. One of them had opened a pint of medicine and they took turns drinking from it.

"I want a box of that medicine, Mr. Yushkevich, if more is available," Tatjana said to Sandy. In this forlorn, frigid place, where Sandy traded frequently with peasants living in even greater isolation, this elixir of Turkish opium must have been one of his fastest moving items. Probably in the back he had a dozen cases.

"Yes, I have another," he told her. "But perhaps you would prefer a single bottle. It makes such wonderful cures, who could put a price on it? — but naturally it is frightfully expensive."

They proceeded into complicated negotiations and I turned my attention to a development of a minor agreement between the lady with the blue Moskvich and the Kharkov women. Clearly, I now understood, Tatjana must have been right: the nervous lady *had* come to sell her car, and she really had little else to trade. I made up a story about her. I imagined her to be from some provincial city — Minsk, perhaps. She may have gotten the car from an uncle who died. Now it was her capital in life, her one chance. She had to sell it, but she couldn't let it go cheaply. Any price she was offered seemed just a little less than she needed to have.

Here she had been both encouraged and stymied by Tatjana's sudden proposal to give her some desirable goods gratis, just for an option to buy her car at the price the woman dreamed of. Yet, that immobilized her. With little else to trade, she was obliged to stand around uselessly and watch articles passing from hand to hand. She looked as miserable as a lioness unable to touch the tender lambs that frisked about her flanks.

"I'm interested in a trade," she said to the women, who were already packing away their acquisitions, satisfied with the trading they had already done. They perked up their ears at once, for they heard what anyone who listened would detect: the voice of desire, a voice like a child's.

"What interests you, then?"

She spoke in low tones to them.

"Pantyhose and bras, you say?" the older woman asked.

"Yes."

"We've packed them away already. It's hardly worth our while to get them out. We think that when the railbeds are fixed we'll just go on to Moscow and do some trading in the market outside the Leningrad station. We've been there before, you know. And have no fear, we do a good business there." On the other side of me I heard Sandy say to Tatjana, "Your duffel coat *and* your boots. This medicine is expensive."

The woman who was talking to the Kharkov ladies obviously wanted to make a trade. They knew it and they just waited her out. Finally, she drew a package from her purse about the size of a compact tape recorder. That's what I thought it would turn out to be until she took the tissue paper off it and brought up a portrait painted on ivory. I myself sauntered over to get a closer look. The ivory, which was over an inch thick, had been reduced in thickness except for a strip of about three quarters of an inch around the edge, so that the painting was framed by the very ivory on which it was painted, all in a single piece. The subject was charming. A young lady with masses of curled brown hair falling on her shoulders, wearing a white organdy dress with blue ribbons at the neck and waist and puffed sleeves, was holding a loose bunch of purple irises in one dropped hand. She had a deep, meditative look in her eyes. The technique was exquisite.

"I'll trade this for three pantyhose — say — two bras —and a can of peaches, for my little girl." There was too much of an edge on her voice.

"Not interested," the old woman said without even looking up from working over her bag. "We've got this stuff just about packed away."

"Forget the can of peaches, then," she whined as she finished lighting another *papirosy*.

"Such pictures are in every commission store in Moscow. Can anyone eat them? Who wears one? What good are they?" the Kharkov lady scornfully said.

"It's a thing of value. Look at the beauty."

"Forget the beauty. Where can I trade it? *Two* pantyhose and *one* bra," she grumbled and laid her hand on the picture.

The nervous woman made a motion as if to pull it back, but then she let it slip out of her hand indifferently, the way a drowning man lets go of a log. She took her undergarments, folded them neatly and put them in her bag, and then she turned back toward the corner where Sandy and Tatjana were swapping.

"Wait a moment," the older woman commanded. "Take these peaches as a gift for the little one. A gift, remember. Don't trade them away before you get home, understand?"

Dumbly she nodded and accepted the can.

"It is a very tender portrait, isn't it?" I mentioned to the younger one.

"Are you British?" she asked with wonder.

"American. You have a good eye. My overcoat is English — Scottish, actually."

"Your Russian is not bad," she said. "Most Americans can't speak Russian, we think. Is that right?"

"Yes."

"I have a school friend who went to live in Kiev and married a Greek and after two years she was allowed to leave the country to go to Athens with her husband. Now they live in Chicago in your country."

"And does she like it, Chicago?"

"I have only heard from her once. She is afraid to walk around the city. She does not work. She says it is no fun shopping. Shopping is too easy: one just goes into the store and buys whatever she needs, anytime. Is that possible?"

"Yes, in the supermarkets."

"As our Universals — yes? But what good does it do to be a clever wife when anyone can find and buy the same thing as you? She was a most clever girl. She had good training. I'm afraid she'll be wasted in your Chicago."

"I have no cleverness for bargaining either. It's not the kind of talent we learn, I guess. But I'd like to buy that portrait from you. Will you take money?"

"Perhaps, since you are a visitor in our country. Is eighty roubles fair, do you think?" the older woman asked. "I believe it would bring a hundred and twenty in the commission stores."

"It's fine, yes." I took my wallet from my inside pocket and removed my bills and started to count them out, hoping that I still had eighty remaining from the 240 that I was paid each month. There were ninety-six.

"But, please, sir, if you will forgive me," the older said before I recounted eighty. "I see you have some American money."

"Yes, but not much."

"Let us be honest with each other. It is the only way. We both know that it is illegal for a Russian to buy for-

eign currency; likewise for you to sell it. But if, in counting your money for your own satisfaction, you were to
leave twenty American dollars on the counter by accident
and we were to make you a gift of an ivory miniature on
behalf of Soviet–United States friendship, who could
object?''

First we shook hands and then we accomplished the
few gestures in this little playlet. Officially, a rouble was
supposed to be worth $1.33, but I knew how magically
useful hard currency was and I figured that a dollar would
be worth at least six roubles.

By this time Tatjana had secured a case of elixir and was
engaged in a trade with the thin man. Ever since his first
few swaps he had apparently had little luck and he was
anxious to make some kind of deal. I saw her take up the
record player which the thin man had gotten from Sandy.
She spun the turntable around: it wobbled noticeably.
But apparently she wanted it, for she nodded her head.

Sandy approached the woman with the Moskvich. "I'd
consider buying your car. Part trade. Part cash. Of
course, not at that ridiculous price you named.''

"I've already sold that young lady the right to buy my
automobile.'' She appeared dazed and immobile. Obviously Sandy was frustrated.

"Well, let's talk about it,'' he said, and drew her to one
side.

Tatjana had disposed of the thin fellow and busied herself with the bicyclist — now without a bicycle. Apparently she had developed an interest in the short-wave
radio he had acquired. After a few moments, he walked
away from her in my direction. Over his shoulder she
flashed me a big smile.

"Your friend is a demon in a trade,'' he sighed. After a
pause, he added, "So you're an American? I had a cousin
in Leningrad who was a guard outside the American Em-

bassy. Look at these poor clothes" — he rubbed his hands over his sleeves — "real thin synthetic material, cold as hell in the winter, the wind goes right through them. Not like yours. Did I mention I am a tailor? It's a pleasure to look at your clothes. English, aren't they? Everyone has heard of Burberry's. Austin Reed. Have you ever been to Bond Street? Savile Row? I dream of going there. Was this jacket handmade, possibly? I have been to Finland. Very cold. You know, with clothes like these one could get a part in a Russian movie, I'm sure of it. I see I'm boring you. Please excuse me." He bowed slightly and left me in confusion.

Tatjana said a word to him and came over to me. "I've traded him your clothes for the short-wave radio."

"You've what!"

"Your clothes. Every stitch. Don't worry. Wait and see. It'll be all right. I can't talk now." She rushed away.

Sandy and the woman with the blue Moskvich had been outside looking the car over. Now they huddled with Tatjana.

"I've never heard of such a thing," he sternly stated — "trading for an option to buy. Are you a filthy capitalist? Look, take back your stuff. She's ready to trade with me."

"Of course," the woman said anxiously, "I'd rather sell it to you for twenty thousand . . ." Her voice trailed off like her hopes.

"Naturally," Tatjana said confidently. "I am prepared to pay you."

Sandy reacted quickly to this. "Where are you going to get the money? How? You have only a little over an hour left on your so-called 'option.' The train couldn't reach Moscow in that time, even if it started running now. Do you have the money here? When your useless *option* runs out, I'm trading, right away.

"If you don't trade with me now, the price goes lower

every minute," Sandy said sternly to the nervous woman. I was sorry to see that he was losing his cheery disposition.

"Don't let him bully you, my dear," Tatjana cooed in a motherly fashion. "Please do relax for a moment.

"I have a friend in Zagorsk," she continued, "the administrator of the Beriozka, in fact, who will buy the car. The town is hardly ten kilometers away. I have but to drive there and bring her back," Tatjana told Sandy and the woman in a confident tone.

He was hard-faced. "How do you propose to get there? Let me inform you, in case you are thinking of it, my telephone is out of order."

"Really," she said abstractly. "But this woman and I will just drive over in her car, Mr. Yushkevich."

Sandy almost leaped between them and the door. He glared and pointed his finger at the woman. "Think of the deal I mentioned. It's down the drain, you can count on that, if that car leaves this spot. All right, listen, I'll add a case of canned stuffed cabbage from Hungary and a hundred rolls of toilet paper to my offer. I stick to that. My word's good. But suppose you drive off with her, you might wreck the auto on an icy spot. These roads have big ruts: you might knock the suspension off. Some dumb palooka of a truck driver might run into you. And suppose she doesn't have any friend in Zagorsk? She looks like an outlaw to me with her foreign clothes. That guy over there" — meaning me — "may be from Chicago — a real gangster. They'll murder you in the woods. Who can take a chance? Believe me when I say the deal's off if that car leaves this spot. It's for your own good."

Tatjana hadn't shown the slightest interest in this tirade, but remained busy arranging her goods on the counter.

When he finished she stepped back, ignored Sandy, and addressed the two motorcyclists. "Look here, count these up. See what I've assembled. Here is a box of phonograph needles. Here a stereo speaker. Here a turntable. Here a short-wave radio, which can be hooked up to the speaker — a child could do it. And here, a record" — it was the paper-thin gray disc she had acquired before we left Moscow — "in short, a complete stereo set. This kind of thing is worth a fortune. Look at it. Who ever saw such a thing before? And this could be yours, perhaps, in exchange for the use of your motorcycle for merely two hours! What do you say?"

"You mean we keep it?"

Tatjana nodded. "Yes, of course, you keep it. Understand, it is a rental price. I'm just asking you now, *if* I want to rent your motorcycle and sidecar for two hours, will you take this? I'm just asking."

They said yes. Though befuddled by the opium and agitated by the magazines, they still could not have failed to see that the balance clearly fell in their favor.

"So," Tatjana said to Sandy, "you can stick to your deal. You see, I don't need your phone. The car doesn't have to be moved a meter. This poor woman and I will just hop in the motorcycle and ride over to Zagorsk while the car remains here. Are you satisfied?"

She turned to the nervous woman. "Even were the deal to fall through," she said, "I'll have you back in an hour. He's given you a promise to keep to his deal for that time. You have nothing to lose."

"What are you trying to pull?" Sandy shouted.

"You've gotten me angry," she said. "Why don't you behave? Maybe I didn't want the car at first. Let's say I didn't. But you've been so unfair I'm determined to have it, just to spite you."

Sandy changed his tune immediately. "Come on, be reasonable," he said softly. "Let's take a little break. Everyone should be happy. Say, I have a bit of homemade vodka right here, made from grapes on my aunt's plot of land in Dushanbe, and carried here by the little dear herself."

He matched his conciliatory speech with actions and set a row of glasses on the counter while he spoke. "Yes, everyone join in," he hummed, as he poured the pewter-colored vodka.

Tatjana downed hers in one gulp.

"Let's finish the bottle," he urged. "Better a broken back than a half-filled bottle."

"An Armenian proverb," Tatjana hissed. "Not for me, thanks. Time is precious, you know. We must start for Zagorsk."

Then she smiled sweetly and seemed to change her mind also.

"Of course, if you want the car so much, I hate to break your heart. Perhaps you're not so bad a fellow after all."

In an instant he was suspicious. "What will you take?"

"I don't know. There's not much here of interest. Maybe you have something in the back? I could go for a few cases of the 'cough medicine.' Some canned fruit. A case of cognac. I guess you probably have lots of bras and pantyhose. I don't know. Well, I'll start with that half case of prophylactics. You know what we use them for in Moscow? Balloons and bottle caps. It'll prove an amusement."

He looked relieved. "What else? You don't expect me to toss in anything else?"

"One can of peaches. Just to be friendly."

"All right. But that's it."

"Of course, there's one other thing," she added. "I'm not going home in the nude, not in this weather. And I swapped all my clothes to this fellow" — meaning the thin man — "in exchange for the turntable. And I've traded *his* clothes to this bicyclist for the radio. An American would freeze to death in a Moscow April without his reversible."

"So, why don't you just drop the trade. Give them back the radio and turntable. No deal if you expect *me* to buy them for you and make you a gift of them!"

Tatjana drew herself erect. "This is our deal — and it's a good one for you, believe me. I give up my option. You give me that case of rubbers and a can of peaches. Trade these guys something for our clothes. I'm sure you can satisfy them. Buy the car, drive us back to Moscow, and just wait a minute at the apartment door and we'll hand you out the clothes."

The wheels going around inside his head were almost visible. There were perhaps a thousand roubles in the deal for him from resales of the clothes and the car.

"Done!" he suddenly announced, and hit the counter.

"I *will* have that other drink," Tatjana said, and slid her glass to the bottle. Before he could refuse, the others did the same. It had a bitter fiery taste, like sucked cherry pits. The two motorcyclists almost immediately felt the effect of combining the opium and the vodka. They became playful and started cuffing each other just as bear cubs do.

When she put her glass down, Tatjana turned to the ladies of Kharkov. Their tired eyes were moist from the drinks, but they were alert.

"What would I need with a stereo set? Now I don't need it to trade for a motorcycle ride. And I *have* a stereo set, at home. Take it all — take these pieces and I'll take the rest of the condoms from you. So they were produced in your own factory?"

"Yes, that was last year. I guess no one wanted them.

This year we were retooled and now we make rubber nipples for baby bottles. You can have them for all those phonograph pieces — gladly."

I gave Tatjana a murderous look. She led me into a corner while Sandy traded hard to complete the deals for our clothes and the car.

"Don't kill me," she said, playfully cringing. "I was in a pinch. I just had to have one more item to trade and make everything fall into place. I confess, I wasn't prepared to come across a chance like this, or I would have had some valuable things with me and everything would have gone easier.

"But now I'm a wealthy woman, a genuine robber baron. And of course, you won't be sorry. I'll make your sacrifice good. In fact, why wait? — I'm prepared to do so now. I have something for you that you'd be glad to trade your clothes for."

From her purse she withdrew a package identical to the one in which the ivory portrait had been wrapped. "Take a look."

It was the companion to the painting that I had purchased from the ladies, a portrait of a fair young military officer with a clipped blond mustache and a painfully erect carriage. Together the paintings were obviously a pair of love pictures, probably commissioned on the anniversary of some romantic occasion, a year of marriage most likely. Each of the lovers would have exchanged his portrait for the other's. How charming the Russian customs of the eighteen-nineties were! When the portraits were thus placed together, a sweet old aroma of betrothals, plighted vows, bittersweet departures and passionate returns hung about them. They worked their magic on each other, like dry patchouli cast upon warm water. The odorless fragrance of romance generated by the portraits made the fourth rich distillation of mystery dropped upon the simple surface of the day: the bat and stone monsters at Mamontov's, the invisible mansion, the complicated swap, and now these.

"You've noticed," Tatjana whispered, "that the portrait of the man is signed."

"Yes, but could it really be V. M. Vasnetsov?"

"The pair is worth two or three thousand, if the signature is genuine. Only outside the country, of course."

"Better say, a fine souvenir. But how did you get this other? It's the pair that's really valuable — in every sense."

"I had it almost from the beginning. You remember after I made that big deal about securing an option to buy the blue Moskvich, I took the lady aside for a quiet talk.

" 'Let me see what else you have to trade,' I told her. She had only a few poor things, as you know. But I spotted the portrait of the young prince at once. I'm afraid she had the girl's portrait hidden. I slipped up there: it was my only mistake in the whole negotiation — but you made it right, with your good instincts.

" 'Dear woman, why else would you come here if you did not wish to sell the car? Come out with it,' I told her.

" 'I must sell it,' she said in agony. 'It's all the extra money I'll have for me and my little girl to make our way ahead. My husband's killed. The car's all we ever had.'

"I told her," Tatjana related: 'Trust me, will you? Alexander Yushkevich knows well you want to sell the car. He's the kind of person who knows how to turn it over for a profit, too. Next week a taxi driver in Yerevan will be behind the wheel. I don't really want to buy your car, but I'll help you to sell it to Yushkevich. We'll make believe we're trading. In exchange for my aid I want that portrait for myself, and I'll get a good deal for you. I'll help you get the price up.'

"She had the pictures from her husband, who got them

from his grandmother. She didn't know their value. She would have exchanged them for trinkets. She lost nothing.

"Myself, I had to think fast and provide for all the roadblocks Yushkevich would put up. The key was the motorcycle, mobility. Otherwise we were stuck here, we couldn't move. Here he was in full command. That's why I had to put together that phony stereo set. The turntable must be held together by rubber bands — it won't last five hours. The rest is junk. The short-wave radio is 'short' all right: I'd bet it won't pick up Helsinki. But put altogether it looked dazzling enough. If I had anticipated how stoned those motorcycle pilots would get I wouldn't have had to work so hard. They would have taken anything that looked shiny from me — I wouldn't have had to trade your clothes for the radio to complete the outfit. Sorry.

"However, that doesn't matter. The important thing was for Yushkevich to think I was ready to spirit away the woman with the blue Moskvich. He himself knows five or six people in Zagorsk who would buy it.

"Of course the car is junk too — perfect for the Armenians. It's a 'sixty-four. That year all the transmissions that came out of the Tallinn plant were defective. It'll never go a hundred thousand kilometers, and this car's already got eighty-odd thousand. The brakes are nothing to brag about either in those models. Bad drums.

"I wasn't doing all this for my entertainment. For me the deal with the car was a smokescreen. Any person from Moscow could see that the only thing of any value in the whole place was that crate of condoms. Why, do you know, there isn't a factory in the whole of the Soviet Union that produced a single condom this whole year! And these are not things that sit around on shelves in Moscow, believe me. Nowadays the girls buy them and make their boyfriends and husbands use them. I don't know anyone who wants to have a baby. It's impossible these days to get along when you've got kids. A mother's just a slave. Forget it! We have our own quiet women's movement here. Let the Asian population grow. Don't ask us to have babies.

"I don't know why they stopped production. The story is that the previous year there was a shortage of rubber nipples and the chief of the latex products branch got censured for that. So naturally this year he went into high gear on nipples: all the condom factories were converted.

"Next year, of course, there'll be a new chief and then production of prophylactics will resume. In the meantime, unless people are really careful, we're going to need those nipples.

"I figure I have three months before the changeover. Even if I sold them by the piece — as I plan to do — these will be gone long before then.

"Sex is a wonderful thing, isn't it? Even in Russia, isn't it? Even in MGU. What else do we have? Who wouldn't pay five roubles for one of the last condoms in the nation? Cunning as he is, Yushkevich didn't know their value. He doesn't understand the city. He's only a man.

"But he wasn't so stupid that he'd let them go for nothing. He had to calculate my threat that I'd whisk his deal for the car from under his nose. He figured up his margin on the Moskvich. He saw that I was tossing him four or five hundred roubles with the clothes. He took what he could get. He doesn't know what he lost.

"I have my fortune. And of course, this portrait is for you. So you have a pair of remembrance portraits. I nearly jumped out of my skin when I saw that woman pull the other one out of her purse. You were very quick!

"And what have we given up? Soon your English

clothes would be too warm, even for Russia. You have a trunk full of clothes anyway, and only two months from now you'll be going back to California.''

"It's all right. I wouldn't have missed this day — any of it.''

The former owner of the blue Moskvich had been hovering in the distance, balancing on one foot then another and looking our way for the last minute. Tatjana signaled her to come over.

"I made a fine deal, thanks to you,'' the woman said. "How wonderful, too, to have gotten — well, some nice women's things. Tatjana Efimovna, I also want to return those articles you handed over to me merely for our little game. I understood the rules of our make-believe trade.''

"Be quiet. Yes, pass the ten-rouble note over here — but keep the pineapple and the rose petal soap for your little girl.''

The woman squeezed her hand. It was comforting for me to see that no one was a complete Darwinist.

"Well, we're on our way,'' the two Kharkov women also announced. Their load was much lightened.

"But what about the stereo set? Where is that?''

"To tell the truth, dear, we didn't think it was worth much. With great pleasure we traded it to those two gentlemen with the flyers' caps.''

"For —?'' Tatjana opened her eyes.

"Yes, of course, for the motorcycle. We leave for Kharkov at once!''

The former motorcylists sat sullenly at the hinged table board mixing cough medicine with cognac.

"Ah, then, *do svidaniya,* watch out for the ruts. Go with God,'' I said to them.

They bowed in the old-fashioned Russian way.

Sandy walked over, looking completely drained.

"That bastard won't give up your clothes for anything,

Mister Professor. It turns out he has a friend in the Moscow Film Studios, and he feels sure that with those natty clothes he can get parts as sinister American spies or corrupt businessmen in our Soviet films. No one in Moscow has a costume as good as this. His clothes will make him a fortune. However, sir, he knows that you weren't part of the deal, he sees that he's on shaky ground, and so he's agreed to give me a ten percent commission of his earnings if I bring your clothes back. I've settled for that. It's not bad."

We got ready to leave. I carried out Tatjana's fortune, putting the two boxes on the front seat of the Moskvich. Sandy drove and the two of us squeezed into the back seat. Tatjana purred with satisfaction and excitement all the way back to Moscow. The transmission also made little grinding moises.

When we arrived at the door to my apartment, I carried the case in and dropped it in my bedroom. Sandy agreed to wait inside the little vestibule alcove leading to my two rooms. We'd hand our clothes out to him. "I'll say goodbye to you now," he said. "I've enjoyed our meeting."

Tatjana went into the room where I had my couch and table and TV set, while I went into the bedroom and closed the door. As I took off each article I made a neat pile on the bed. Last, I put my socks on top, opened the door and handed them out to Sandy. When he took them I could just see that he was already holding Tatjana's clothes.

"Good night, then," he called to the two closed doors and went out of the apartment. I could hear the latch snap.

On my night stand I propped up the two ivory miniatures against a lamp base.

For the first time, this day struck me as the most absurd day of my life. And the most ludicrous moment had been saved until last.

Here I was, completely nude. My feet were freezing. Tatjana stood in the other room. I pictured her, naked, unconcerned, trying out her new lipsticks in my mirror. The two of us in that condition, Friday night, and no lectures to give for two days. *And* 10,000 Cossack Condoms in my bedroom.

I started to laugh quietly and I couldn't stop laughing even when I heard a little light shivery knock on my door.

VII

Death on the Pale Horse

More than a month passed after I started going to the Hotel Peking before I saw the student Andrei Nikolaivich Kavelin again.

There was nothing unusual about this. One day he simply showed up at my class again and occupied his seat. He looked paler and thinner and even more nervous than when I had seen him last.

After the class was over I found him lingering in the hall near the door, waiting for me — yet, in his usual indecisive, diffident way, not wanting to speak right out. I approached him. I wanted to start a conversation and make things as easy as possible for him.

First he made a few distant observations about my healthful appearance and the good qualities of the day's lecture. Then, with little transition, he launched into his favorite interest. He was the only Soviet art historian to have taken up the study of eighteenth-century American painting. In particular, he was concentrating on Benjamin West, the first great American painter, who succeeded Sir Joshua Reynolds as official painter in the court of George III.

The title of Andrei's proposed thesis was "Benjamin West: Historical Painter in the Age of the American Revolution." When he had first told me this title and described the outline to me I had concluded that he was performing beautifully in the intellectually opportunist tradition of the post-Khrushchev period. He had managed to get in the sacred Soviet words, like "Revolution" and "History," and his subject could really raise very few political problems for him. West hadn't been involved in politics of any sort, much less the kind that could get a Soviet researcher in trouble. How else could an American artist have retained his post as the king's painter when the king was warring with America? West was important but strictly noncontroversial. So it appeared to me that Andrei had chosen wisely.

But this day I realized that he hadn't chosen to work on West merely as a safe accommodation to the Soviet system.

"I do not always understand West's paintings," he remarked, "especially his religious works. Oh, but those are his masterworks for me, *Christ on Calvary* and *Christ on the Mount of Olives*, and all the others. The great holy pictures."

"*Death on the Pale Horse?*" I asked. It was West's great painting of the Apocalypse. A terrible figure on a sickly white stallion harrowed the world with fire and sword.

"That most of all. He was supreme. I dare say he was the last religious painter in England, the last genius of religious subjects anywhere."

"You've seen many of his religious paintings?" I was thinking of the complete suppression in Russia of the great religious painters, except for those like Rublev, whose works carry important elements of the Russian tradition.

"Certainly not all, but some — reproductions in books, of course. As you know, I am not allowed to travel to the museums in England and America. I dream of doing so someday. And it is a problem to find books with illustrations of West's work, even in our Lenin Library. But I read descriptions of them in studies of West, in auction catalogues, or in exhibit announcements. I seek them out. I work hard.

"Unfortunately, there are many additional difficulties. For instance, as you know, I do not have an edition of the Bible that West used. Or the *Book of Common Prayer*. And this makes my work of interpretation very difficult. You haven't, by chance, brought any such books to our Soviet Union with you?"

I hadn't, but I assured him that I would stop in to see the Episcopalian chaplain and some of my friends in the British Embassy. I would see what I could do.

I didn't do as much as I should have to keep my promise. Maybe I felt some suspicion about his request for a Bible, and I let it drift along. Whenever Andrei came to class, afterward we talked about the Christian symbolism in West's paintings. We met in the Hotel Peking a few times, too. We spent a long session there going over every iconographic detail in *Death on the Pale Horse*. Once I asked him about Lev Dahl, but he answered ambiguously, so that I let that matter drop.

One evening in March, Andrei called me up and invited me to accompany him to the Sunday matinee performance of opera at the Bolshoi theater.

"It's a good cast," he observed. This point was fundamental since below its first-line singers the Bolshoi could be quite awful. "It's *Katerina Ismailova* — I think you will enjoy it. Do come with me."

Actually, though I didn't recognize the opera, I gladly said yes. I felt that he was indirectly attempting to show his gratitude for my possible help. I told myself that covertly, in his own cautious way, he was reminding me about the religious books I had promised to get for him.

Even the best Russians fall into thinking that bribery is justified if it is accompanied by the proper courtesy. But I had really intended to do everything I could for him in any case.

Soon I learned that I had been mistaken. His motives turned out to be quite different from what I supposed.

The opera surprised me too. The music was fine, but for me the whole production was marred by its attacks on religion and by its obvious anti-Semitism, yet these were the aspects of the opera most applauded by the audience. After Katerina has evaded her father-in-law's watchfulness and taken a lover from among the workmen, she gives the old man poisoned cabbage soup. Later, with her lover's help, she strangles her husband. Then, in a scene of marriage celebration, Shostakovich brings a drunken, lascivious priest on stage to mock the church, its representatives, and its ceremonies. What is worse, this character is made to sing with a Jewish accent and to ape Jewish gestures. All the while that this hefty priest pulls at his beard and sidelocks, he is draining numerous bottles of wine and goosing every female in sight.

"Let's ride up to the Peking and talk it over," Andrei suggested when the curtain came down. "How did you like it?"

"I appreciate your taking me, but I'm a little surprised that you picked out this particular opera."

While we were waiting for the bus he drew me aside. "Let me give you a tip. Next Thursday there will be singing of chants and canticles at the Novo-Devichy Convent. Go there at five o'clock. You will find it very worthwhile, most interesting."

As always, the bus was crowded, which made nothing but casual conversation possible, even though we spoke in English just as if we were two tourists. Before we had ridden three blocks, just beyond the Central Telegraph Office, he pointed down a street to the left. "There — do you see it? — that's St. Nicholas' Church." I did catch a glimpse of it as the bus slowed. When we got off the bus at the Sadovoye Ring, I asked, "Wasn't there some trouble at that church a few years ago? Or was it another St. Nicholas?" But for an answer I got only apparent inattention and the whistling sound of snowflakes sweeping across Mayakovsky Square.

2

We stepped into the cafeteria upstairs and Andrei immediately led me to a table in the rear. Two men sat there who rose as we approached them.

"Professor Martin, allow me please to introduce to you two of my dear friends. This is Nikolai Nikolaivich Leschenko, who works at the Institute of Astrophysics," he said, indicating a short heavily built man whose eyes were sunken deeply into dark furrows, but who smiled at me pleasantly enough. "And this is Alexander Samoilovich Rosanov, one of our scientists of the French language in the Institute for Foreign Languages."

These two gentlemen greeted me affably and begged to know my opinion of the opera. They seemed a little on edge to me but I told them my reservations.

When I finished Leschenko remarked, "Ah, but *we* consider it a religious opera. Unconsciously religious, I mean. Or, if one would not wish to go that far — for assuredly Dmitri Shostakovich was not a religious man — then an exposure of the dirty lives of the proletariat when they lack religion."

"That's a curious interpretation, isn't it?" I inquired.

"Well, you see, what Brother Nikolai means," the other gentleman said excitedly, "is this. Look at the priest in the play — he's the center. Certainly, he's a dirty fellow, a real pig. He's a priest who's gotten so far away from his priesthood that as you observed a moment ago, he talks like a Jew. All right, when the church has forgotten itself, what kind of society do you get?"

"A murderous one," Leschenko interrupted. "Exactly what we have here in this opera, in the Soviet Union. Gross, brutal workmen speaking filth, whores and sluts, overstuffed animal-like fathers, sensuality, license, complacent husbands. All fuckers. It's real murder, I tell you."

"Yes, Katerina is just following out the logic of her time, her class, her politics," Rosanov said vehemently. "Spread your legs for the first guy who winks at you. Fill your enemies up with rat poison, strangle them in the dark. Maybe Lady Macbeth was just a murderess too, but Shakespeare made her noble. Not Katerina, not in Mtsensk, not in the province of Orel. Not after nineteen seventeen."

"So maybe he didn't know it, Shostakovich, but he did have counterrevolutionary tendencies," Leschenko added. "He was an artist, after all, and that came through: he hated the society around him, the materialism, the technology, the loss of our Russian spiritual heritage — a society of only Katerinas, gross and sensual and utterly without vision. He tried his best to write our wonderful Socialist Realism, to be like any dolt. But he couldn't do it all the way, only on the surface. Still, it took the censors, the guardians of the Party, those idiots, two years to understand what he was saying. And then Shostakovich was finished. He would have ended up in a labor camp, probably, or whiling away his time in the country like Pasternak. It took a war to resurrect him, it took the destruction of Leningrad and his Leningrad Symphony, it took our dear leader Stalin's decision to allow religion to revive in order to rally the people. Sir, you see what it cost for you to witness this opera today? If it hadn't been for all this, Dmitri Shostakovich would have been an exile in New York, or Paris, having his coffees with Marc Chagall or Igor Stravinsky."

Andrei had been up at the food counter buying bouillon and meat pies for us all. He approached the table, balancing his tray with utmost care.

"How is your wife, then?" Rosanov asked Andrei.

"Better today, yes, better, I am told," he muttered in a hesitant, broken way as he set the tray down and placed the plates before each of us.

"I remember meeting your wife," I said. "I didn't know she had been ill."

"Oh, she was sick the day you met her. She was suffering terribly. But what is one to do? She had to wait her turn to get into the hospital, since the director of the Medical Institute placed her in the classification of nonemergency patients. She had a kidney infection, and it was serious all right. But she was already waiting for six weeks to be called in when, just a few days after you met her, she came down with a bronchial disease due to her general weakness."

"And still they wouldn't admit her," Rosanov said to me. "Maybe they didn't like her politics, eh? Anyway it was fortunate that you had such suitable housing arrangements, with plenty of people always about to help take care of her."

"Better for her if she had stayed at the apartment after all, with or without pneumonia. The hospitals are sure death!" the other man moaned.

"She developed pneumonia and we got her reclassified as an emergency patient, but no sooner had she been admitted than a staph epidemic broke out in the hospital and the whole building was quarantined. I was lucky — I was already inside the place. They had agreed to let me sleep on a pallet next to Flora's bed, and so now I had to be kept inside in order not to spread the infection. The only ones they let out for three weeks were the corpses — in sealed boxes — to be buried without a funeral."

He looked seriously at the solemn faces of the other two men.

"Fortunately, Flora had not yet had her operation. Those who did developed running sores all along their sutures and had to be sliced open again. I myself got only two boils on my arm and a sore under the nail." He raised his forefinger; the nail had been completely cut away.

"But Flora wasn't so lucky. Probably someone had forgotten to wash the sheets they put on her bed, because the poor girl developed sores in lines all along her back, just as if she had been lashed with barbed wire. Now, at least, the epidemic is over and they've let me out. Well, God's will be done."

"Amen," echoed both men.

I needed no special acuity to see that, as we turned to begin our soup, Andrei and his two companions, as by secret accord, paused in silence for a moment. Instantly I sensed that some compact existed between them. And prayer before meals was part of it.

"Perhaps you've been to one of our religious museums already," Rosanov said slyly.

I decided to play along. "Certainly, everyone goes to St. Basil's as soon as he arrives in Moscow. Next week, I believe, I am to be taken by an art historian to the monastery where Andrei Rublev painted his icons."

"Didn't you find St. Basil's — ah, cold?"

"It was freezing. My window thermometer registered negative twenty-five degrees on the day I went."

"But perhaps there was something else? Something lacking?"

"The shadow of the Kremlin falls on it. That makes it colder!" Leschenko growled.

Those were unexpectedly strong words and could not rest there. Either they had to be withdrawn or expanded.

"Andrei tells us that you go to the Mass in the Embassy, and also the Lady of Hope Chapel," Rosanov began.

I couldn't remember whether I had ever mentioned this to Andrei.

"It is my own dream," Rosanov continued, "to go there myself someday, to hear Mass celebrated in French! To be sure, I have the wonderful benefit of possessing a missal in French, and I say the service every day to myself. But to kneel before Father Robert and hear him whisper, 'Le corps du Christ,' would be an ecstasy almost too grand to imagine."

I was surprised at finding a Russian who was a Roman Catholic, and I said so.

"I beg your pardon," he said, "I am a Catholic. In Russia, I must be orthodox — but I recognize no difference of geography in the faith. We are all Catholics."

"However, you *do* make too much of the French; Professor Martin is right in noting that, Alexander Samoilovich," Leschenko said. "In Rosanov's case," he added for my benefit, "it was the Lenin Library that was at fault, and that must bear the responsibility for his awakening."

One could see that here was a story Rosanov liked to tell, and his friend had charmingly given him a cue for it.

"Yes, when I was writing my thesis on French literature in our national prisonhouse of books, the clerk delivered to my place one incorrect book in among those I requested. I think I had asked to have Taine's work on the Dutch republic brought to me, but instead of Taine, I was brought a volume by Jacques Maritain. Imagine, in the

Lenin Library the clerk brought me *Man and the State*!
I'm surprised they hadn't burned it. Well, to this day I
have yet to read Taine on the Netherlands. But I have
read everything written by Jacques Maritain.

"I was just a rough student from the Ukraine and I had
never heard anyone talk about God and the Saints and the
Blessed Mother except to say how Darwin had exploded
them. I was just going mechanically through the books
that had been brought to my place, taking each as it came
to hand, making notes on my topic, my ridiculous topic —
'Henri Barbusse and Leninism.' When I opened this
Maritain book and started reading I couldn't understand
why I had ordered it. Naturally, I didn't know what to
make out of Maritain at first. You understand, I was just
doing what I had been told to do. My adviser had given me
a bibliography of books to read for my topic and had demanded, 'Don't come back until you've read this list.' So I
just made out cards for books on the list — I hardly looked
at the titles, I certainly didn't try to guess what would be
in the books. I was just doing a job. Almost at once I realized some mistake had been made. I checked my bibliography. No entry for Maritain was on it. I was ready, in my
arrogance, to have the page who fetched the book brought
up by the scruff of his neck before his chief: 'What does he
mean putting this book before me? Is he a papist spy?'
But something impelled me to read on.

"I know now, of course, that God was guiding the hand
of the page, using his stupidity to open my eyes. And my
eyes *were* opened. But neither now nor then did I ever
think that the authorities of the library were stupid. One
slip, yes, but no more. It was up to me to be careful, and
believe me I had to be. By the time I had come to the end
of that book the whole world had changed for me. I vowed
to read, not just Maritain, that sainted man, but all those

he mentioned, the great ones, Aquinas and Scotus and Pascal.

"I made no mistakes, I proceeded with the greatest of care, for I was completely convinced of the future direction of my life. I went to my adviser. It was not enough to read Barbusse alone, I argued; but to appreciate the power of his thought, and that of his followers, I should read the bourgeois, monarchist, papist works of their opponents. I proposed a chapter called 'The Triumph of Barbusse and His Followers Over Right Reaction.' My adviser gave me a quick, curious look, and then said offhandedly, 'Well, go ahead. But you understand it is not necessary to read any of those royalist works. You can know just what they are like from what our progressive critics have said about them.' This was simply to let me know that if I wanted to proceed on this dangerous ground it was my own lookout; he washed his hands of me. He was just one more Pilate.

"From Maritain I went, of course, to Léon Bloy. And then, later, to Ernest Psichari and Julian Green, Claudel, Péguy; and naturally, in time, across the channel to Hopkins, Eliot, Charles Williams, C. S. Lewis, and all those other remarkable men. Even your own American Thomas Merton.

"But somehow for me it all comes back to the French. Finally, nothing means more to me than the vision I have of Cocteau returning to the church in old age."

"You see, he really isn't an authentic Russian," Leschenko said, smiling in an admiring way, however. "His soul's over in France. He'd give anything to go hear Vespers at St. Chapelle or Notre Dame or to wander about the grounds of St. Germain des Prés — I've heard him say such things. Be assured, however, Alexander Samoilovich, they'll never let you go to France. Perhaps they may allow you to visit Warsaw. Would that do? And so he misses, don't you see, the glorious — I must say — the unequaled traditions of our Holy Mother Church in Russia."

"It's not true, and you should not joke of such things," Andrei said with boyish seriousness. "Alexander Samoilovich has a true faith. It begins in Paris but ends in Zagorsk and Rostov."

"Probably our own Russian church is not of the slightest interest to you," Leschenko remarked to me. "You, with your American refinements — with, if we hear truly, your guitars at Mass, or even rock bands — you probably think of us as practicing some antiquated superstitions."

"Of course I've been to St. Basil's and to the Church of the Smolensk Mother of God — to the museums, that is. But," I added, "I've also attended service at the working church near MGU."

I felt I should be completely honest. "I think I should also say, though, that I don't believe I have the same kind of fierce religious devotion that you seem to have. I simply rather enjoy the service, including the guitars if they're present, and a cup of coffee afterward. I admire you, but it's much simpler for me."

"For the best of us, at our best times, it should be simple. But where are the best times? Nothing is simple in the Soviet Union except dying. Do you think it is easy to talk to you? But Andrei spoke often about you," Leschenko said, "and we wanted to meet you — well, to talk to you, just to speak to someone who is not afraid, someone — precisely — who finds it a simple, unthinking matter to go to church. Oh, we are far from that. Just to go to church — it's the old Russian way. You can't know what it means to hear you put it in just that simple fashion. A saint, a Russian saint, might have put it that way."

I was embarrassed at this turn of the conversation, but Andrei changed its course.

"So in the west, then, you've heard about the controversy that occurred in St. Nicholas' Church?"

He turned to his friends to explain: "Professor referred to it when I pointed the building out from the bus."

"We went to hear Father Dmitri's lessons — until he was silenced, sent away," Rosanov said. "The three of us and many of our friends."

"But," Leschenko added quickly, "we never revealed ourselves to him. We didn't know him — I mean we weren't sure of him. It's easier to be sure of an American than a Russian. Father Dmitri spoke so openly we were certain that he must have been an agent. Otherwise, it seemed, he would never have been permitted to talk so. Then he was, we are told, sent to an obscure rural church to silence him."

"If it is true that he is there," Andrei said, "then we made a mistake in not seeking him out; for then, assuredly, he was a very brave man. But where is he? Who hears anything of him now? Is there such a person? We are told many things."

"Well, you must come to services with us and learn our Russian ways," Leschenko urged me.

"Andrei has already mentioned singing at Novo-Devichy this Thursday."

"Yes, in the Assumption Cathedral — not in our cathedral-museum, of course," he said sardonically. "Good. We will see you there."

They asked me a number of questions about the controversies among traditional and progressive theologians in Europe and America and especially about the situation of the Charismatics, a movement they viewed as very Russian. Was it really true, they wanted to know, that the

Pope had washed the feet of the Orthodox Patriarch? I'm afraid I gave them very little information — these were matters I didn't follow closely — but they were elated just to chatter with an outsider. Rosanov became so excited that he began to speak French and for a time, at his urging, I even limped along in my bad French through a conversation concerning the relative merits of the cathedrals at Beauvais and Rouen, French mysticism, and Port Royal logic.

"When I speak French," he said with a sigh, "for those moments I am not Soviet. I am a Russian still — but not *Soviet*. Think, think, how things would have been had Napoleon only settled the problem of his supply lines before stretching them to Moscow. Then he would have won. The churches would have joined hands again, and a new Christian age would have come to Europe. The refinement of the French spirit and the power of Russian holiness! What a powerful force that would have been! I am sure, just as Dante was sure of his enemies, that General Kutuzov rots in Hell for his triumph at Borodino."

Andrei mentioned that the hour was approaching when he would be allowed to pay his wife a visit. His friends urged me earnestly to accompany them to the apartment that they all shared, while he went to see Flora. He promised to join us later.

3

We took the Metro to Kropotkinskaya. They led me across the embankment to an apartment building in an old section in back of the open-air swimming pool. Clouds of steam hovered above its heated water.

When they opened the front door I was caught by surprise. Several people were apparently already inside the apartment. Andrei's reference to the communal apartment hadn't sunk in, and now it hit me with real force.

"Even by Moscow standards of nine square meters allotted to a person, this is an overcrowded dump," Rosanov said. "But we don't dare to apply for a change of residence for fear we'd all find ourselves at the end of the Metro line, an hour from the city center, in one of those sardine-can apartments that start to fall down even before they're built. Here we only have three floors to climb — no need to worry about broken elevators. And this building lasted through German bombing, so we don't have to be fearful about a strong Moscow wind blowing it over.

"More important though, we've formed a religious community here in these six rooms. We all want to stay together, even if we're crowded. What does it matter if we have twenty-one people here, counting the little ones, so long as we can trust each other? Certainly, most of the people here are workers, old ladies, people of simple faith.

"It took us a year to achieve this community of the faithful. Naturally we had to bribe the original occupants officially assigned here in order to get them to move to another apartment. We had to find other housing for them. We had to spend our money freely, I can tell you. And finally we had to bribe the clerks at the Bureau of Permits to authorize all the changes in and out that this required. But at last we are all Christians here."

The rooms led from one to another, just as they had in the Brooklyn tenement I lived in as a boy. As we walked through them the two men were cordially greeted by those sitting about. A few quick words were exchanged to indicate that I was "safe," but no introductions were offered. The apartment was apparently well-organized for its communal purposes. Several rooms held chairs and lumpy couches, while one room next to the kitchen had a miscellany of bumped and scratched tables and wooden chairs arranged as if to make one long refectory table. To call this a monastic room would give too favorable an impression, for the tables were of several different heights and all of poor modern construction. Nevertheless it was easy to recognize the monastic intent. Another room was filled with mattresses laid on the floor, a few beds, and some pillows stuffed into boxes to serve as bedding for the children. Probably ten or twelve persons might sleep there at any time. Another room was closed. Nikolai said, as he gestured toward the door, "There's no window in there. It's our dark room. Those who work at night sleep there during the day."

In another room we found a seat on a fairly good couch with a folding back for conversion into a bed. Leschenko went to a glass cabinet and brought a book from it to show me.

"Can you make the title out?" he inquired, still holding the book himself, as if unwilling to place it in my hands.

I shook my head. *Vehki* meant nothing to me.

"*Landmarks*," he translated. "Don't you know Lenin's article about it in *Novy Dyen*? ... It's just as well, it's a calumnious piece.

"Look though" — he pointed to the title page — "here is an article by Nikolai Alexandrovich Berdayev. My father was christened in his honor and I was likewise. What a man! Russia's finest philosopher. But look, here is Bulgakov too — and, see! Kistyakovsky, Alexander Izgoyev, and Struve and Frank. What a wonderful collection! Rosanov talks about Napoleon. But Russia didn't need the French to save it. We Russians were certainly able to save ourselves. These men, had we listened to them, could have set it on the right course. Look at the publication date. Think about what this means. Here it is nineteen-nine, years before the October revolution. Still a chance, still a chance remained. Why didn't the people hear Berdayev and the others when they spoke of the need for 'repentance,' 'humility,' oppositon to the 'pride of the intellectual,' and the importance of 'the plain, coarse food of our Moses' Ten Commandments'? The Bolsheviks frothed at the mouth over these recommendations and babbled like devils so the masses wouldn't hear these truths.''

"Pardon me, I have heard of your lectures and your help to Andrei Nikolaivich, Professor," a neatly dressed elderly man said from across the room. He astonished me by speaking in stiff old-fashioned English. "May I present myself? Stefan Timofeyevich Samokhvalov, at your service. May I call your attention, Professor, to a not unimportant and interesting fact that has been neglected? We call this our 'Heritage Room,' " he said, waving his hand toward the bookcase. "Here, in this case, where Nikolai Nikolaevich keeps his *Vehki*, the others who live in these rooms have also placed the books they value, so we can all share, at whatever level, in each other's spiritual ideals. I myself have placed here a volume by Pyotr Chaadayev whom, I'm afraid, no one understands but myself. They say they understand, the others, but it is a book to be comprehended, I think, only by a Cossack!

"However, in this same cabinet you will also find the four Gospels, hand-copied by a fellow who can't even read. It's a wonderful book!

"Let me draw your attention to the wall, Professor. You've noticed already, I'm sure, that this is a veritable secular iconostasis. Covered — isn't it? — by pictures of the greatest interest. Here again, each of us has placed the pictures of those persons who best match his ideals. Here, as you have observed, are three pictures that must be the contributions of Alexander Samoilovich: these are,

namely, Renan, Maritain, and Cocteau. Look here: post-
cards of Dostoevsky and Tolstoy — of course. Here also,
however, are some faces unfamiliar to you, perhaps.
Clipped from an old newspaper — Khrapovitsky, Arch-
bishop of Kharkov. Also Pavel Florinsky. Could this steel
engraving represent Alexander II? Patriarch Pimen —
torn from a western journal. Pope John the Twenty-third.
Probably you recognize Berdayev's features. Here is Pasternak. This is Pavel's mother, I think, whom Pavel re-
gards as a saint. Perhaps she was. Well, it's a remarkable
gallery."

Almost pointedly, he had neglected to single out any of
the several cabinet photographs, neatly arranged together
at one end of the wall. "And those photos there?" I
asked. "Those are precisely mine," the Cossack said
proudly. "These too, no one but me understands."

These wouldn't have meant a thing to me and I probably would have ignored them altogether, except that I had
seen a collection of similar photos many, many years before. One Saturday afternoon, while I was a student at
Columbia College, Conrad Aiken brought me along to
lunch with Edmund Wilson, and when Conrad went back
to his flat to nap, I walked with Wilson up Third Avenue as
far as the mid Fifties.

"I have to pay a call on old friends," he had explained.
"I won't be long. Stay with me, won't you? I want to talk
to you about U. S. Grant. Amazing to find someone so
young who's read his *Memoirs*. Come in and sit. They're
wonderful friends, old friends, revolutionaries long ago —
when there *were* revolutions. Elegant people. White
Russians."

I never found out whether Wilson's call was anything
other than social. A beautiful old couple greeted him at
the door. They welcomed me; then they took Wilson off to
another room and left me alone in the corner of a room

filled with art treasures, and also with a lady whose age and ivorylike skin made her look like one of the treasures herself.

I must have seemed very young to her. She looked at me for many minutes. She was considering, I think, whether it would be proper to entertain me by reading me a fairy tale or perhaps by getting out a picture book and saying things like, "Look at the horsies!"

Instead she pointed to a little collection of photographs on the wall. "See," she said, using a child's picture-book tone after all, "these are very interesting, don't you think?"

At that moment I had been staring at a large, unusual Malevich on the opposite wall. But I turned my attention to the photographic history lesson she wished to give me.

"Here am I as a young woman," she said abstractly — uncertain, it seemed, what possible connection she could claim with that thin, heavily bundled-up young woman standing on a platform among many men. All were looking fiercely into the camera. She pointed to another photo. Some of the same people were in both pictures. "Here is a photo of the Constitutional Democrats who participated in the first Duma. Here, see in this photo, the third from the left, that is Kerensky. Here is Viktor Chernov, a good man."

She pointed a long finger at another photo. This one was of a group sitting around a table stacked high with papers. She made no mention of the fact that she was in this photo again, but I recognized the same burning eyes in one of the two women in the group. "Here is a working group of the Constituent Assembly, just before it was disbanded."

Her eyes lit up a little again and she said, "How fast civilization slipped though our fingers . . . I am sure none of these old faces interest you."

And now, in a communal apartment less than a mile from the walls of the Kremlin, I was looking at those same faces all over again: Kerensky, Chernov, Social Democrats and Mensheviks, Whites. Many men and a few women whom history had blown about Europe and America. Blown to smithereens. Probably all of them were dead now. Outside these rooms, I thought, few people even remembered any of them.

The photographs which the old Cossack had pinned on the wall brought back that afternoon nearly twenty years ago. I didn't have to look closely at the photos. I knew that the faded woman who had sat in the quaintly fashionable room in the East Fifties was in them. The eyes gleamed from a faded sepia print.

"I myself was an officer in the Crimea on the staff of General Wrangel!" the Cossack said, interrupting my thoughts.

I hadn't noticed that the late afternoon sun had broken through the clouds, but all at once, when I looked up at him, the wall behind him seemed ablaze with the separate flames of the sun striking the glass covering many of the pictures, as if each one were a tongue that could speak. This antiquated Cossack had very prettily called the wall a "secular iconostasis" — but now I saw that it was really a wailing wall, the blank void of history against which we throw ourselves over and over again, a wall that remains unchangeable — merely a wall, nothing more, just the dead surface of broken images.

"Come on," Leschenko said, "there's another room to be seen in our humble apartment." He motioned for me to follow him and Rosanov.

I thought I heard Andrei's voice in the entrance and just at this moment he stepped into the room where we were rising.

To our unspoken inquiries he said woefully, "She's not

good. She's in awful pain. They still haven't operated. Perhaps tomorrow, they say."

"Come with us, then; we were just going to go in and pray," Leschenko said in a tone of real sympathy.

We walked down the central hall to the very rear of the apartment and quietly opened a door.

It was like stepping through a looking glass — out of space, out of time — to go from the lumpy poverty of the other rooms into this incredibly rich one. The first thing that I took in was the forest of candles, like a miniature birch wood, each tree aflame at its tip. These candles, in their gilded stands, threw a shivery light on all the other objects in the room. At one end of the room, a priest dressed in golden vestments over a silver-white tunic swung a gilded censer, which threw off platinum-blue puffs. Four persons stood before him, chanting with him, murmuring like summer bees. Another was bowing to kiss the margin of a book opened on a stand. Their faces were all lighted a deep, antique yellow, the tint of parchment paper. The censer and the chain from which it swung and a massive gold ring on the priest's left hand gleamed.

We stepped farther into the room, entering the hum of voices. The yellow light bathed us too. The clouds of incense drifted above us. A heavy scent from them fell upon our heads like welcome rain.

The priest was a large, heavy-faced man with a big black beard and thick black hair curling down over his ears. With his rimless glasses tilted down his nose and his great barrel chest and stomach he looked almost comic.

Behind the priest I could see that the whole wall was decorated. In the very center of the wall was a golden tabernacle with a candle burning above it. The rest of the wall seemed to radiate from the sacred cabinet. On it were many holy pictures, painted directly on the wall.

Each was about twelve by ten inches in size, and they were arranged symmetrically. Individual saints, saints in pairs, groups of saints, or holy angels, and Christ and Mary and God the Father filled every inch of the wall. On second glance I saw that in three or four of the rectangular spaces actual icons were nailed. Here, the Virgin and Child were sheathed in silver. Elsewhere, a figure of Christ, painted on wood and richly gilded, hung on the wall.

By this time I had reached the center of the room. My eyes were better accustomed to the darkness. A movement by Andrei at my side made me look up. Just a few feet above our heads a large face of Christ was painted on the ceiling. Two great luminous eyes burned through the blue incense fumes. Andrei, who always seemed agitated, but who was even more on edge after coming back from the hospital, stood transfixed, looking at those eyes, and then he let out a little cry and dropped to his knees and began mumbling and whispering, and moving on his knees toward the priest.

The priest couldn't fail to notice him, despite the rapt attention he gave to his canticle. He hung the censer on a hook and turned to Andrei and lifted the young man up, showing him the cross which he held in the other hand. Andrei leaned over and kissed it fervently. The priest inclined his head to hear Andrei's word of sorrow. Then, putting his arm around his shoulder, he led him to where the other believers stood. He linked their arms into Andrei's, holding them together. Then, he resumed his chant.

After a few minutes the chant ended and the believers filed out of the room. But the priest motioned to us in particular to follow him into the opposite corner. There, behind a screen, was a bureau and a chest and a thin, rolled-up pallet. He removed his chasuble and other vestments, carefully folding and placing them in a drawer. He gave the impression that until he had divested himself of his ceremonial robes he should not participate in conversation.

Then, wearing his black cassock, he turned to us and shook the hand of each of us in the most friendly manner. He came to me last with a warm greeting.

"This is a great pleasure," I said, "a double pleasure, in fact, because, after all, this is the second time I've seen you perform today. And both times as a priest. First in *Katerina Ismailova*, now here."

"But not the same kind of priest, eh?" he said with a big sensual grin. Or do you like it better when I seize a wench and say, 'Come here my yittle vun. Giff me a smoozle on der cheek'? It's a wonderful role Shostakovich wrote, isn't it?

"But it is true, I am a real priest. I was trained in the seminary at Zagorsk and I served for a very little time in the parish at Peredelkino as a very young man. Later, I managed to get alternate papers — not so unusual a thing after all — and I joined the Bolshoi as a singer. There aren't that many good singers around. Who asks questions? And as a boy I had studied in the Academy in Odessa. Now, the priest in *Katerina* is one of my regular roles. So everything worked fine. As a man in holy orders I have no existence: the part I play is my real life. It's a perfect, a characteristic, Soviet disguise.

"But you. Andrei has told us fine things about your lectures. We're grateful for the help you've given to him. We are glad that you are here with us so that we can thank you. We all talked about you, we asked the priest at the American Embasssy, Father Robert, about you, we read your works — they are very difficult. We voted on having you here. We think you won't betray us."

"Shall we have tea, Father?" Rosanov asked.

"Yes, I just have time before I must go to an appointment," the priest said. "That is, if Professor Martin has a few moments to spare."

Before we opened the door, the priest asked warmly; "Wouldn't you light a candle for our community, dear sir?"

I did. And I quickly prayed for them, too. For the priest, with his double life. And Rosanov, dreaming back to the last chance at Borodino. And Leschenko, with his idealization of Berdayev, for the old Cossack, with his memories. And Andrei, frightened by visions of his wife's pained face. For Flora, tormented by infections. And for the whole nameless community, who in order to devote their weekends to prayer must have pretended to outsiders that, like members of many other communal apartments, they got drunk and stayed drunk all weekend. And last for myself. I don't know if any of this did any more good than a candle melting away. But since no one but myself knew of my prayers, what did it matter?

Andrei looked completely worn out. Leschenko offered to walk to the Metro with me, insisting that Andrei rest.

On our way he said, for conversation; "Do you know how he became a priest, Father Vasily? It's most amusing. When he was a voice student in the Academy of Music in Odessa he had a friend who was captain of one of the vessels that run along the Black Sea coast, trading with Bulgaria and as far away as Turkey. Together they made an agreement: the captain smuggled back Bibles and other religious articles from Istanbul, and Vasily peddled them. Any sort of Bible is a hundred roubles on the black market, you know.

"It was inevitable, of course, that one day he should want to look at one of these books that people were so keen to get. You can guess the rest. And it happened just that way. God works even through the Soviets, behind their backs. We see that all the time."

After he gave me instructions about how to get home he said; "We'd be very happy if you would come to Novo-Devichy on Thursday. Andrei told you. Five o'clock. Do come. Someone will wait for you outside the door of the Assumption Church, opposite the cell of Irina Godunova. Do you know where I mean?"

We shook hands.

4

Thursday glittered. On Wednesday the weather had turned warm and all the snow and ice began to melt. But overnight the temperature dropped suddenly. When the cold morning fogs cleared away around noontime, everything was covered with a layer of brilliantly glistening ice. The ice-coated snow gleamed as if it had been varnished. The bare trees and the dark green branches of the firs clustered around the university were all plated and jeweled with silver. Eventually, this would be a bad thing for the ash trees, losing the warm snow cover and being imprisoned in ropes of ice; but for the moment it made an incredibly dazzling display in the sun. Across the gleaming white snow or the green surfaces of the fir trees flew the large blue-black Moscow crows, shaking down splinters of ice from the crackling trees as they settled briefly on the branches.

I decided to leave my dormitory early and walk to the convent. From the square at the end of the university mall, one could look over the river and see the Novo-Devichy buildings, with their golden onion domes flashing like metal in the sun. But to actually get there I had to follow a circuitous route. First I had to walk along the rim of the Lenin Hills to the tiers of glass boxes which housed a gigantic escalator taking me down to the river level. At the bottom I strolled through the riverside park, making crunching noises on paths that I was the first to break. I found the footpath under the Metro bridge and walked across the river on it. The water was frozen blue-black. Underneath the hard top layer of ice, the rotten melted and refrozen ice was visible.

Once on the other side, I cut across a soccer field, already broken up by morning players. Little glaciers, moving rivers of ice, had formed in the gashes they had made in the field. The ridges were hard against my boot soles. Frozen blades of grass stood up stiffly like little swords. I passed between the Lenin Stadium on the left and the automobile storage areas on the right. Icicles hung suspended from everything in sight. Finally, over an hour after leaving my room, I turned right toward Bolshaya Pirogovsky Ulitsa and the eastern gate to the convent, just past the entrance to the adjoining cemetery.

I was deliberately early because I wanted to make a stop at the Beriozka store directly across the street. This emporium was strictly for foreigners and accepted only foreign currency, which the Soviets were not permitted to have. For a few dollars I made a little collection of treats, a few packages of Gauloises Bleus for Rosanov, a can of Smokehouse almonds for Leschenko, a slide viewer with slides of Vladimir and Sudzal as well as a chocolate bar for Flora, and some little presents of tea and Dutch cookies for the occupants of the apartment. I had all of these wrapped separately and marked and packaged in a plastic shopping bag decorated with a picture of a smiling matryoshka doll.

And in my pocket I had the Anglican prayer book that Andrei had desired.

What with the long walk and the sudden warmth inside the store, I was overheated by the time I walked into the convent grounds a quarter of an hour before five. And soon, as I strolled about the area around the bell tower near the southern gate, I felt completely chilled. The tower bells gave off a cold, hollow sound. So I finally stood still beside the side entrance to the refectory, stamping my feet and trying to push my neck into my collar, and looking in vain for one of my friends among the surprisingly large number of people who were passing inside. When at last the bells stopped and an old fellow came out of the church, unlatched the open door, and started to close and lock it, I slipped inside.

As always, the entryway was packed closely with ancient women, but I also saw some younger people, Andrei's age and even younger; and even, for the first time, a few men in uniform. Their long gray coats with red epaulets stood out against the black and brown garments of the others.

It seemed impossible to move in such a crowd. But everyone was moving, following intricate paths cut carefully through the flowing mass. The crowd moved as each individual slid off of others, each person gently grinding along on his own circuitous course. And I too, without direction of my own, was moved by the drifting floe.

Aimlessly I picked out one woman who slid by me and followed her, pushing along in the vacuum of her movement. She seemed to know exactly what she was doing. First, she made her way to a counter at the far rear of the church and from the ladies there she bought two large candles and a handful of small ones. I watched her pass the crumpled roubles across the counter. Then she cut diagonally across the crowd into an anteroom where the walls were lined with large icons. Against one wall was a kind of iron cage, inside of which was a representation of the infant Christ. She placed a large candle in a stand before it and lit it. Through the bars she dropped a few coins.

Quickly she passed to another room, placed her candle, and went out. I followed her into the center of the church. Before certain icons whose location she obviously knew exactly, she stopped — only for an instant — and kissed a corner of the frame or the glass protecting the painting. From some of these holy pictures towels were suspended, and before kissing the glass over the foot of a Mary or a St. Vladimir, she would wipe them perfunctorily. Finally, she came close to the iconostasis, where she left her last candle before a painting of St. Jude.

Now, for a moment, she seemed lost, purposeless; she raised her hands to the heavens and then let her arms fall loosely in despair at her sides. For some moments she stood there, desperate. Then, with a look of resolution, she pulled her little money purse out of her coat pocket and with it in hand again she made resolutely for the counter where the candles were sold. I let her go her way.

Others were crowding forward toward one or another of three priests. Each priest seemed to be engaged in his own ritual. Most of the worshipers gathered around the prelate on the left side and responded vigorously to his chant. Three hundred thin voices answered his deep bass voice. The group was enlarged steadily, too, by the worshipers in the center of the church. They stood on line at the end of a service waiting to kiss the icons held by the priest and deacon. After doing so, most of them joined the singers.

As the central part of the church emptied, I saw that on the right side a group of about a hundred and fifty worshipers crowded together in silence, listening intently to the discourse of a thin, boyish-looking, unbearded priest. The members of this crowd looked younger than those in the others. The faces of several men and women who were still in their twenties could be seen above the bent figures of the old women.

As I drifted toward this assemblage, I suddenly saw a face staring at me, the old Cossack's, Stefan Samokhvalov. He looked as serious as if he were posing for a photograph. The whole dark scene suddenly looked like one of his framed cabinet photos. Though he didn't move, I knew he recognized me. Then I felt a tap on my shoulder. Rosanov.

"Yes, it's here," he whispered in a strained voice. "Follow me."

We went around the group to the other side, where I found many of the apartment community, including Leschenko and Father Vasily. Vasily was dressed in an ordinary overcoat and suit. They listened to the sermon. No greetings were exchanged.

The priest began to swing a censer handed to him. His talk, which I hadn't understood, changed to a high-pitched singsong. The center of the crowd opened and pushed back to where I stood and suddenly, in the opening, I saw a high-domed painted wooden coffin lying on a rug on the stone floor. It looked too small to contain anyone but a child. Andrei was standing in back of the casket, terribly pale. His long thin wrists stuck out of his coat sleeves as he wrung his hands. But otherwise he was composed.

Four men picked up the casket and, with Andrei following in his still tottering fashion, carried it through the parted crowd. From the worshipers in the group at the other side of the church came a heightened sound, a fervent chant of supplication for divine favor, divine mercy.

After the coffin passed and the crowd closed behind it, Father Vasily laid his hand on my arm and said softly, "Never did we expect to have a funeral today. Andrei Nikolaevich will be glad to know you came. I don't think he saw anyone. But I shall tell him."

"She wasted away like a candle," Leschenko moaned.

I walked outside with them, following Flora's coffin as if I were part of the community. The old Cossack Samokhvalov told me that after she died on Monday night he placed a photograph of her on the wall with his other mementos. "Flora Tursunovna was made of the right stuff," he announced sternly, as if she had been a comrade-in-arms who had been dropped in her tracks by a Mauser bullet.

Increasingly I felt out of place in that mourning community. We had gone less than halfway to the grave site where, in the distance, a knot of people had already formed, when I drew Rosanov aside and begged him to pocket the cigarettes himself and distribute the other gifts. I asked him to give the slide viewer to Stefan Timofeyevich, the old Cossack.

The others went on, but I wandered apart in the cemetery. Somewhere within the walls of these burial grounds lay Gogol and Khrushchev, Kropotkin and Chekhov, Nadezhda Stalin and the generals purged after her husband's death. Their stones and busts were all covered by the snow and the coming night. Only one grave opened a black throat to the sky.

I touched my side pocket. Unfortunately, I had forgotten to ask Rosanov to pass on the *Book of Common Prayer* to Andrei. I promised myself to mail it to him on the following day. But I wondered about Andrei. Would he continue to work on Benjamin West, on *Death on the Pale Horse*? I looked about. The distant mourners assembled in the gathering night. The scene bore no resemblance to

West's great painting, with its deathly pale horse and its mysterious rider, the rider named Death, with all Hell following at his heels as he devastates the earth with sword, famine, plague, and wild beasts. No, it was just an ordinary death, a common burial.

The promised end was still far away. The wall of history had yet to be filled with photos of all the fallen. For a long time yet, I supposed, we would still beat against that unyielding barrier of time, like the ice-burdened trees in the unchanging wind.

VIII
The Ski Jump
at Leninsky Gory

On the Lenin Hills, at the north perimeter of the
university grounds, stands a gigantic ski jump, which I
never saw anyone attempt. Many afternoons at sunset I
leaned against the marble balustrade at the crest of the
hills and in my mind traced out the jump's arc. No doubt
existed that the skier would fall from it in one magnificent
curve and end up in the Moskva River.

The ramp was impossibly monumental. Many things in
Russia seemed to me to be like that — opportunities were
always being offered that would be suicidal to seize.

In a lesser way, this was also true for any temporary resident in the Soviet Union. Various sights existed to be
seen — but when were they open? How did one gain
entry? Whose permission was needed?

Whenever I mentioned to a Muscovite that I hoped to
visit some special monument or museum, I'd almost always get the same answer: "Wait until the weather is
nice." As if they had never experienced a taste of an endless Russian winter, they always counseled delay — until
the weather was nice.

I began to see that this response was a form of white
magic. When enough hopeful travel plans were deposited
in some mythical meteorological account book, some mag-

ical good weather–bad weather set of scales, the balance would be thrown over on the side of fair temperatures.

But through February and March the same bad weather continued unabated. For myself I decided that the weather would never be "nice" — certainly not before June, when I had to leave. And so I began to shuffle and slide through the snow and ice of Moscow streets to the various museums, sometimes with Tatjana, more often alone.

More than any other place, I wanted to see Andrei Rublev's museum. Who could leave Moscow not having seen the very spot at which the greatest painter of icons had worked, more than two centuries ago?

Unfortunately, I found, one could not simply stumble into the Andronikov Monastery and ask to be shown about. All my attempts to make arrangements to be admitted were in vain. I spoke to my department chief, hinted about it to Tatjana Efimovna, and applied for a guide to the University Foreign Office and the Ministry of Culture. But, as if I had shouted into a vacuum, no echo returned.

I believed that this neglect was not at all premeditated. I was sure that no official prohibition against my visit existed, so I decided to imitate the Russians and wait patiently until some chance occurrence brought me to Rublev's museum. "*Nichey-vo,*" the Russians often say, meaning, "It'll get arranged eventually." I said *Nichey-vo* to myself.

One evening the phone rang. The man on the other end started out talking in very rapid Russian and at first I thought he must have gotten the wrong number — a frequent occurrence in a city of eight million inhabitants without a phone book. But when I caught the name of Rublev, I asked him to go a little more slowly.

If I were free, he explained, he would take me to the monastery three days hence, in the morning. He himself was a researcher in Russian iconology. He promised an expert tour. How had he learned that I wished to go there? Had we met at some university function? No, he answered, he hadn't had the good fortune to make my acquaintance. Miss Gorbunov in the university's Foreign Office had mentioned my interest in Rublev, however, and he wished to put himself at my service. Should I meet him at the monastery? I asked. The usual polite Russian answer came back: he would bring a car to my apartment and telephone from the lobby when he arrived downstairs. I said my few words for "Fine" and "Thank you" and put the date in my notebook.

Three days later a fine continuous snow fell all morning. The phone rang.

"Shall we wait until the weather is nicer?" my guide asked.

"I'd prefer to go today, if it's possible."

"Very well, then. In fact I am waiting downstairs," he said.

I had expected him to be a student, say in his mid-twenties, but he was almost my own age. At once, I noticed that instead of a right hand he had a stiff black leather glove fastened to the end of his arm: probably an accident had deformed or crippled or removed his hand. He was old enough for it to have happened when he was a child in the Great Patriotic War. Instead of shaking hands, he nodded, almost imperceptibly, to me.

He greeted me in Russian, just as I had expected, since he spoke no English over the phone. But as soon as we walked out of the entrance to my building, past the smiling door lady into the open air, he remarked brightly in English, "You understand that the works of Rublev himself have all but disappeared in this particular place, though he worked in the Andronikov Monastery most of his life."

Like most Russians he didn't want to promise too much.

"But there *are* interesting icons in the monastery?" I mumbled choppily. In my surprise I found myself still using Russian, even after he had switched to English.

"Yes, certainly. And many beautiful ones, too. I am a particular expert on the iconology of the thirteenth to the fifteenth centuries. Some of these jewels of art do exist here, as all over Russia, of course. Nevertheless, here in the Andronikov Monastery, most of the works we shall see are, unfortunately, of eighteenth- and nineteenth-century vintage — the completely decadent period of the Russian icon."

He had a friend waiting outside with a car, a shiny little Fiat-type sedan. I was ushered into the back seat and my guide, who introduced himself as Anton Dmitrovich Dubrovinsky, slid in the front. He let me know that he was "an old Muscovite." Our drive, he remarked, would be along a route that would give me "a splendid view of our city."

So, as we drove on, he pointed out various sights. He seemed to be personally acquainted with every building on our route. About half the places he mentioned were associated with artists. We swung around Tolstoy's house and cut in by Mayakovsky's apartment and the Scriabin Museum. The other half of the buildings he pointed out had been occupied by politicians — Dzerzhinsky, Marshal Zhukhov, Lazar Kaganovich, and so on. I'm afraid I got these so jumbled up that if I tried on my own to go to the house of the composer of the *Poem of Ecstasy,* I might end up in the apartment of a gangster who had arranged for the permanent disappearance of several thousand Ukrainians. We drove through such a tangle of unfamiliar streets, crossing and recrossing the river several times, that I never hoped to take myself back unaided for a closer look at any of these places.

He pointed out a house where Viktor Vasnetsov had once worked. The paintings of Vasnetsov usually had fantastic subjects but were executed with considerable realism. He had worked at Abramtsevo and come under the Slavophile influences there. He looked to me like a Russian Rockwell Kent with his fairy tales, medieval settings, and epic celebrations of burly Russian warriors, or his nostalgic drawings of delicate, wistful peasants. His portraits were different, of course, and I had two of them propped up on the bureau in my room.

"So that was Vasnetsov's house? How do you like his work?" I asked of my guide. I'm afraid I was teasing him. His seriousness made me expect to hear a tirade against this illustrator. I couldn't foresee how passionate Dubrovinsky was or what direction his passion took.

So, rather to my surprise he said, "There's one thing for which he was supreme. That fellow survived among the Soviets. He lived beyond Lenin and died a natural death under Stalin — no easy task for any artist. He knew how to dress up themes in fairy tales.

"Yes, Vasnetsov and Rublev make a fine pair. The older artist, the artist of the fifteenth century, did just what the state wanted. God ruled the peasants. Rublev knew how to represent God so that he looked pretty much like a czar. Rublev held the secret by which the masses could be persuaded to think that the priests and the czars were God. He unlocked the power of the state. He allowed the priests and czars to rule God.

"But he was great. Why? Because he believed. He didn't know he was an artist. He was a believer.

"And the other? Vasnetsov? He too helped to keep the

poor children of Russia childish by showing them tales about people riding on wolves, magic kingdoms, visions. He unlocked the power of the state in a very special way, by tying people to a love of old Russia. This seems paradoxical to you, doesn't it? — when we Soviets are always talking about our newness, our science, our machines. But who ever heard of patriotism being generated by an electron microscope? We Soviets really like to restore the Ostankino Palace, move Peter the Great's cottages from Arkhangelsk, rebuild the Catherine Palace or Pavlorsk. And, of course, we keep up the Vasnetsov House and the Rublev Museum, eh? So long as we can do these things we forget about the other ways we spend our money. Vasnetsov's fairy tales allow the army to exist. They allow us to forget the state, as if it too were a fairy tale. Vasnetsov was great because he believed in nothing — nothing but his art. But he was useful."

He paused and then added, in a matter-of-fact voice, "Of course, you understand me, in the present day, under our present enlightened government, such self-deception or deception by the authorities is unnecessary and unthinkable."

Following a few minutes of ruminative silence he went back, however, to his earlier train of thought.

"Yes, those are the only choices for a Russian. To believe completely — or to believe in nothing. To believe in God or to believe in art."

He mumbled, "That is why there are no artists in Russia."

"Aren't there, really?" I asked Dubrovinsky.

"Oh, thousands, of course. They sit by oil stoves in Palekh and paint boxes or make nests of matryoshka dolls. In Estonia they embroider table runners or weave shawls. In Novosibirsk they make large posters of happy plumbers holding up their wrenches, in order to post them in Red

Square on May Day. They glue balalaikas together. In Novgorod they make papier-mâché cups and call them 'genuine Khokhloma Folk Art' to sell in the Beriozkas. They exhibit in the Central Exhibition Hall in shows with titles like 'Soviet Art Is for the Working Man.' They are technicians, mechanics, joiners. Or are you talking about *artists?*"

By the time this last remark was uttered we had gotten out of the car and were walking through the monastery gate. The car pulled away. The great church of Our Savior loomed up before us. "An artist designed that!" he exclaimed. "Have you taken a look at the Hotel Rossiya?" Then he shut his lips tight until he opened them again to begin his professional tour of the icons and the monastery grounds.

He was indeed an expert. His memory was incredible and his analyses subtle. Any icon he commented on he could connect with other icons done on similar subjects or in a similar style. He seemed able to recall from memory every Rublev icon in the Tretyakov Gallery.

But he was extraordinarily opinionated about all manner of things. He claimed that no painted icon produced after the fifteenth century could pretend to artistry, except for those little jewel-like enameled copper pieces done in Rostov in the nineteenth century. No subjects for icons were possible, he insisted, "except those of Mary and the Babe, the Christ Himself, and St. George." Specifically, he rejected the saints that the Russians had fused onto the Byzantine conventions, Vladimir, Boris, and others.

He had a specialized scholarly interest in art typology and spoke of the St. George cycle with particular reverence. He was fascinated by the representation of the serpent dragon. Dubrovinsky saw dragons everywhere, though, and not just in portrayals of St. George. The

Blessed Mother, he pointed out, often crushed a dragon under her feet. Even the background squiggles and flourishes in many paintings he interpreted as implying the presence of a serpentine devil, whom Christ and the saints were to defeat. The "icon proper" did not exist, he said forcefully, unless there was a serpent in it. It had to have a hidden drama. He was obsessed with the idea of hiding, of deception.

He had many other curious ideas, too. Amidst the dry professional antiquarian patter of the connoisseur he dropped the most absurd remarks. He declared that the bell tower in the Novo-Devichy Convent was far superior to the Ivan the Great tower inside the Kremlin walls. He flatly said that beside the Smolensk Cathedral, St. Isaac's Church in Leningrad was "a big tin balloon." So he went on and on, saying outrageous, sometimes insane-sounding things in the most incontrovertible tone.

I found him boring and interesting at the same time. I suppose I'd have to admit that what was interesting about him was his aspect as a "case" of a mildly pathological sort.

But after a while I began to suspect him. His opinionated observations had a practiced air. He was like a bad little boy who thrusts his finger up his nose, with apparently supreme indifference, whenever he catches an adult looking his way. Under the circumstances I gave him the only possible response. Whenever he issued one of his idiotic pronunciamentos, I simply nodded gravely and looked another way.

Still, I was really grateful to him and so I proposed that since the car had gone we take a bus to the ring road and stop at the Peking for lunch. He readily assented and we hopped a number 10 bus.

We went to a bar first and had two kinds of vodka to drive away the cold. We had the aged brownish vodka first, then turned to the other. "*Starka* for strength," I said rather foolishly as the drinks had their effect, "vodka for energy, and lemon flavoring for vitamin C. All we need. Here's a thimbleful toast to Rublev!"

"And another to Vasnetsov!" he responded, reminding me of our morning's talk. We got some cheese and bread and ordered more vodka. I began to think Dubrovinsky a rather pleasant companion. Just to make the vodka interesting we continued to exchange toasts, until he gave me a look of resolution and cried out, "To the art of children, the only art of Russia!"

At once he added, in a tone that didn't imply the possibility of controvertance, "You will see what I mean. I am going to take you to the Palace of Pioneers. Do not worry. It is near the university, only slightly out of your way." He tossed off the vodka and fairly rushed out of the room, with me in tow, forgetting all about the lunch I had planned in the Peking, with thousand-year-old eggs.

"Yes," he kept saying, "we must go to the Palace of Pioneers. It's wonderful there. The children — the children do whatever they wish. They *can* be artists. Who would say no to them if the little dears wanted to splash the canvas with one big ball of color, to do drip paintings like your Jackson Pollock? Yes, they do Rublevs if they want, or Vasnetsov, or Picasso — or they just make a mess, an excellent mess. They're children, right? In Russia children can do anything. Yes, the place for us to complete our tour is the Palace of Pioneers!"

Tatjana Efimovna had already pointed out the Palace of Pioneers to me and remarked, "Once, when the aristocrats ruled, they had palaces. Now the children run everything and we have turned the palaces over to them."

That was true. Children in Moscow were pampered and petted and allowed every form of indulgence and misbehavior. On the crowded Metro old grandmothers would get up to give children seats. If one had a child with him, it would even be possible to get a taxi. They were kept in a Doctor Spock world, these Russian kids — until adolescence, when the state snatched away their toys.

Actually, I had no real desire to see the inside of the Palace of Pioneers: made of decorated concrete and glass, it was quite ugly enough from the outside. Besides, I concluded that the vodka was causing Dubrovinsky to act rather childishly himself. To put it bluntly, I thought him rude to insist upon my accompanying him wherever the whim took him. I intimated as much while we waited to change lines at the Park Kultury Metro station, but he begged my indulgence in such polite terms and fretted so nervously about it that I went along with his pet project.

The place was pretty much as I expected, with noisy children demanding attention from the huge number of assistants and teachers on the premises. Dubrovinsky led me around in a fashion that showed he was familiar with the place. We peeked into a ballet lesson for a half dozen little boys garbed in tights; we listened for a few moments to another young fellow struggling with a clarinet piece. We took a look at the photography lab and I listlessly inspected the crafts, weavings, batik, and so on. We moved on to the corridor that led to the art studio. He had saved this until last.

"Did I tell you that I work here?" he asked. "Yes, I am an instructor in painting for the children. I teach them everything. They make wonderful things. They are real artists."

But when we arrived at the paintings posted in the long poorly lighted corridor leading to the large art studio, I wasn't at all prepared for what I saw.

My first impression was simply of luminosity. It was like being plunged underwater, into a dim pool, to find oneself inspected by a hundred bulging, liquid fishy eyes, which stared out of the paintings on every side. The display of light was simply dazzling: colors were laid down behind and next to and upon other colors in the most amazingly transparent fashion. Spread thinly on heavily leaded paper, the paints burned in the gloom.

I looked to Dubrovinsky for a clue to this spectacle, but his lips were pressed tightly together and all the color had drained out of his face. I was afraid that the vodka was affecting him badly.

Looking more closely at the pictures I saw that beyond the array of light, there was something in each painting that Mark Tobey calls "white writing" — a language, an emerging shape, a hidden figure that had been pushed out of the foreground but still hovered as a presence behind the surface. The effect was like having a floodlight suddenly shone in your eyes: the light flooded everything, but behind the light one might glimpse shapes and meanings emerging. The more I looked, the more I saw figures, figures writhing in torment or ecstasy, people, saints and sinners, coiled together like a nest of serpents, men and women and children who seemed to be seeing visions, and whose eyes were the lanterns from which the beams of light shot.

In silence I inspected each painting. About twenty were posted on each side of the corridor. And then I glanced back at Anton Dmitrovich, who was leaning against the wall looking quite sick and faint, as if crushed by the fear that I might mock the work of his darlings. On the floor below we'd passed a cafeteria. I led him back there, sat him down, and fetched a glass of tea for him.

I felt I had to say something to put him at his ease.

"Never in my life," I said to him smiling, "have I known a teacher who is so wrapped up in the work of his pupils! The way you led me around this place so familiarly I began to suspect even before you mentioned anything that you taught here. That explained to me why you were so keen to have me come — to see the art your students produced. But I never expected anything like this. How did you manage to convey to ten- and eleven-year-olds your passion for icons? Behind the splashes, that's what they are, aren't they? I see a figure of the Virgin, the Child, St. George — and in all the pictures the swirls of the dragon, like a great river of flesh coiled and congealed around everything else. You're worried that I wouldn't see the really great work you've done with your little ones. But I do see it — and it's astonishing."

"I am a dead man," Dubrovinsky announced in a voice almost as surprising as the paintings. He appeared ready to swoon, but his voice was deep and absolutely unshaken. "You see too much. Even so, you are not right. But you *are* right enough to kill me. Yes, I try to teach my little ones how to keep their blues like fire and their yellows like a southern sun striking quartz. Yes, I show them pictures of icons, I make them look deep into the eyes of the dragon. But what do they see? Only Soyez-Apollo, Sheremetyevo Airport, an ironworker. They see nothing. Do you understand?"

I stared at him hard. He just needed a pause to repossess his voice, not any prod from me to keep going.

"So I destroy their pictures after every lesson, the stupid paintings of rocketships and factories. I tear them into little bits. And every night I sit in the studio making my icons and pasting them on the walls, as if they were done by the blameless children. In all of Russia, only in the Palace of Pioneers would such paintings be tolerated. Here, the mamas walk up and down happily clucking over the bright splashes that they think their little darlings have done.

"Do you see," he whispered, "what I've managed to do?"

With one motion he triumphantly pulled the stiff black leather glove from his right hand. I was horrified at the gesture, but instead of a withered stump he exposed a perfect, white hand. "I paint with my hidden hand," he muttered grimly. "For me this is a sacred act."

I meant it humorously when I interposed, "Why, that's sheer sacrilege," meaning his mockery of the Soviet organization — but he took me seriously.

"No, it keeps the gods alive, the saints and the old dragon. They look at us, they lurk, they wait to come back. I keep faith with them."

"So," I said finally, with no further attempts at relieving his anguish by comedy, "you've taken both ways, of Rublev and Vasnetsov?"

"It's the only possibility remaining, to keep secrets with secrets. Secrets within secrets."

Outside the palace he seized my shoulder, "Remember," he said, "there are no artists in Russia!"

We walked down together to the Lenin Hills and parted at the Leninsky Gory Metro stop. I turned toward the university, along the path that winds on the top of the hill, until I had walked to the head of the long, central MGU mall. It was a perfect Russian evening. I turned my back on the university and stood at the balustrade looking over the river toward the Kremlin.

The darkness gathered so rapidly that the lights of the central city came on almost all at once, like a single salute of fireworks. Above me on the hills was the gigantic ski jump, dark in the moonlight. I tracked its curve downward toward the river.

Anyone who jumped off that, it seemed, would sail into space, over the river and the city, into a burst of light.

IX

The Magicians of Moscow

No sooner had Tatjana Efimovna disposed of my winter coat than the weather turned cold again. One day, near the middle of April, I left the Embassy, where I had been discussing my upcoming lecture trip to Samarkand and Georgia. I set out by foot toward the Rossiya Cinema for an afternoon performance. Tatjana was busy studying for examinations on Marxist theory — Party exams, I gathered. And Marya was out of town for a week's holiday visiting a relative in Smolensk. With no lecture scheduled for the next day I was at loose ends. The sun was shining brightly, I felt good. But hardly had I walked a block, and at a brisk pace, when I felt completely chilled.

On impulse, I turned off Sadovoye-Kudrinskaya toward the entrance of the Planetarium, which looked like a silver egg sitting in an Easter basket. Along with a hundred school children and their teachers, for half an hour I watched the patient movements of the constellations. Then came what everyone was waiting for. The lecturer touched a switch and Soviet sputniks and spaceships shot and reshot across the sky, as if clawing tracks in the heavens. It was a wonderful show. I and the children had been properly awed and thoroughly overheated.

The Rossiya's evening show was still a few hours off and what with the cold I decided to make my way to it by slow stages. Halfway between the Planetarium and the cinema was the Hotel Peking. I conjured up an appealing image of myself bending over a glass of tea, rubbing my hands in the steam, and sitting at a sun-streaked window table, looking down on the bronze shoulders of Maya-kovsky.

Lev Alexandrovich Dahl was already sitting there. He nodded to me in a familiar, half-happy, half-solemn — and wholly practiced — manner.

"Didn't I tell you you would find me here in the after-noons?" Dahl said as I settled down across from him.

I glanced out the window. A fat pigeon perched on Mayakovsky's head.

"You did. But I have looked for you several times since that day I met you here in the company of Andrei Nikolai-vich and his wife . . . She died, you know."

"To my sorrow. It's all very sad. But how did you like our museum at Abramtsevo?"

"How did you know I went there?"

He smiled in a friendly way. And he spoke with perfect sincerity and deliberation . . . But he said the most aston-ishing things in his ordinary tone.

"Didn't I tell you the day that we met here I knew everything about you? *Perhaps* I was giving you a hint, though I had no reason to do so at the time. Now I do have reason, don't you see, and I must tell you straight out that the reason I do know everything about you — from the date of your birth to the size of your shoes — is be-cause I am the person officially assigned to keep you under surveillance. Understand me, please. I'm not a ro-mantic spy or something of that elevated sort. I'm just a reporter, a clerk, a case worker. Yes, I'm, just like a wel-fare worker in New York, don't you know. I'm your wel-fare worker, you're one of my 'cases.'

"I don't by any means keep *you* under surveillance

every moment, or I would never be able to show the least little attention to my other cases. I have many. It's my curse that I speak Italian, and so I get the bulk of the Italians to survey. That's why I'm so often in this dump of a hotel; this is where Intourist puts all the Italians. Besides, at the moment this cafeteria is the best place in Moscow to pick up information.

"Naturally, I use various standard techniques with all my cases, including yours. Whenever the passport of any foreigner comes through the office for a domestic visa, a notice is forwarded to his agent. In your case, naturally the Foreign Office at the university keeps me informed of your activities. By and by I'll get a little report from Tatjana Efimovna concerning your Abramtsevo outing. Jolly, I hope."

I said that it was. But his question was rhetorical and, ignoring me, he continued:

"Oh yes, even before your arrival, while your entrance visa was being processed through the London office, I picked your case out of a hat. I am regarded as a specialist in 'cultural' visitors. You naturally came up on the culture list. I remembered you from long ago and as soon as I saw your name I thought it would be amusing to have you as one of my clients. And I might as well say, I hoped you would make an easy assignment too, since, after all, how dangerous can a professor be? Who could ever suppose you could be a spy or a CIA agent? I wouldn't have to give you a second thought. It looked like an easy job. Why should an internal security welfare worker in Moscow work any harder than one of your welfare spies in New York?

"That's what got me into trouble, my own indifference. That and the ridiculous compartmentalization of our system.

"You wonder why I'm talking to you like this. Why, if I

truly *have* been assigned to spy on you, should I be telling you so? You are thinking that I am a Walter Mitty spy, like Danny Kaye. That I am giving you a line.

"Granted, this is a ridiculous situation. But let me explain. Here's the way it is. Another fellow in the internal security office who specializes in religious dissidents was on the trail of Andrei Kavelin, Rosanov, and those other fellows. Certainly, I myself knew Andrei; naturally I was aware of his activities — highly suspicious ones, too, from a certain point of view. But why should I care? It was not my concern, not my specialty, as one says. Only now that the whole case of the collective apartment and the subterranean, insurgent performance of private religious services there has broken wide open, you are involved. Your name has come up. And so *I* am involved."

"What!" I said quickly, interrupting the perfectly unhurried, unruffled flow of his narrative. "Has Andrei been arrested?"

"Of course. That's all settled. If you'll be calm, I'll tell you how it was. But just let me explain a little, first, as I'm trying to do, why it is I'm speaking to you.

"To tell you the truth," he continued, "I haven't really been paying much attention to your activities. I've just been filing the usual reports, keeping one eye cocked in your direction. My reports say only 'Subject: Martin went to such and such a place . . . Nothing suspicious to report, et cetera, et cetera.' I don't mind telling you that I do have cases that I give close — and I daresay, expert — scrutiny to. Yours — no.

"Now, there comes along this trouble with Andrei and his group, and *your* name turns up in the reports of my colleague. 'Martin, Jay. American Exchange Professor. Meets subjects Kavelin, Rosanov, and Leschenko, in Hotel Peking. Visit to apartment of subjects. Present at funeral of Kavelin, Flora. Telephone calls from Rosanov. Attends

Mass on Sunday, such and such dates, et cetera, et cetera.'

"This makes me look like an idiot. Even though my concern is not with religious dissidents, I should have listed your defections in that area, perhaps have alerted my chief. Unfortunately, I just ignored them — they didn't concern me. Now that group has exploded — and you look, from your visits, like an *agent provocateur* for religious dissidence. Who knows what to think? To my excitable colleague you look like an emissary from the Pope, a Jesuit. I put you down in my files as innocent as a lamb, and you go and get into another agent's books. How do you think this makes me look? It's trouble for me, have no doubt. It's most inconsiderate of you, it's not nice at all."

"But Andrei?" I urged.

I noticed that behind his pretense of anxiety he was really enjoying himself, telling a good story. Above all, he was bemused by the ironies of the complex system in which he was caught, innocently. With great style he was retelling the old, old story of the smart guy who had outsmarted himself.

"Presently, presently. I still have to tell you something about myself. I see that you remember me, remember our meeting in Hollywood, that is. I wasn't sure when we first met that you remembered me at all. Well, why should you? Time makes great changes. But I knew about you, as I've said, and long before you arrived I already had a file growing up on you. I did all the busy work even before you appeared here. I anticipated your every move in advance. I knew all about you, I thought.

"I admit, though, I was shocked to see you walk through the door of the cafeteria in the Hotel Peking. It's the last place in Moscow I expected to find you. Indeed, for a moment I felt a shiver of panic: it occurred to me that you *were* actually a spy — and that you had found me out and tracked me down in order to do some typical American gangsterish thing to me. Shoot me, Mafia-style, maybe. I guess I've seen too many Cagney films, eh?

"It's my profession to remember things," he went on, "and I remember telling you a tale about my life in the labor camps on account of my love affair with Svetlana Stalin. The story was a good one, a true one, and I enjoyed telling it — but as you undoubtedly recognized, it was not *my* story. To the contrary, I have no interest whatsoever in landing in the Urals. I've always kept myself clear of trouble, and I intend to continue to do so. That's why I'm talking to you now.

"To make a long story short, I started out in the theater. I wanted to act, I wanted to direct films. But nothing of that sort worked out. I tried it from another angle and became a photographer, hoping to work my way into films.

"But then the war came and I stayed out of the front lines by being assigned to the photographic corps. I was with the vanguard that entered Warsaw. Many of the members of the Right Resistance that we eventually liquidated were identified by the photos I took during our early days in Warsaw. I survived very well, as you see — and got a nice easy internal security job back here in Moscow after the war. A tranquil job — which you've disrupted by doing the unexpected.

"I was still interested in show business, but I was not Eisenstein. Finally I found my niche. I discovered I was a good organizer and I had a talent for light comedy, for being a master of ceremonies. I couldn't sing, like your Georgie Jessel; I was, shall I say, more the vaudeville type, with a quick patter and a few good lines.

"I know you've been to a few variety shows — I mean like the show you saw in the theater of the Hotel Rossiya, the one organized to welcome the Party delegates to the opening of the Congress. Marya got you tickets, didn't she? I didn't do that one, but it's the kind of show I do well and do often. Who could live on only the salary of sub-sub agent?"

I had lost the track he was following; I couldn't understand the point of his story and must have looked restless, for he said, "Now I'm coming to Andrei. Last Saturday I had a show all organized for the opening of an International Congress of Balneologists. Doctors who run medical baths, spas, hot springs, that sort of thing. I put together several good variety acts for an evening's entertainment in the Hall of Arts at MGU. I had it all ready to go. Then, at the last moment, I get a call from Anna Merchuli, an old actress who is always applauded for her dramatic narrative of those great musical days in the twenties when she knew Chaliapin. It's her standard act. She's done it a thousand times, and I've booked her for this show of mine.

"When I hear her voice so close to the time the performance is to take place, naturally I'm worried immediately. I haven't had much luck recently. As cheerily as I can, I inquire after her health.

" 'Lev Alexandrovich,' she says in her thin old voice, 'I've fallen down in my apartment and broken my hip. It's impossible I should come tonight.'

" 'I could have you carried onto the stage,' I tell her in desperation. It's always happening this way when you organize a show. At the last minute everything falls apart. In Moscow there are too many people who break their hips, it seems. I feel just like a baseball manager who works years to get a good pitcher on his team, and when he does, his homerun slugger goes blind!

"Well, I dove into my little talent notebook for a replacement. But Sukhanov the actor turned out to be booked in Riga; Ulyanova had given up playing the xylophone — she had taken a job in the motor replacement-part industry. And Pitrim Stolypin was under contract to play every night in the bear circus.

"At that moment Andrei, curse him, popped into my mind. You know, perhaps, that his father was one of our great scientists, the founder of a world-famous chemical company before the Revolution, but nonetheless a strong Bolshevik supporter. This Dr. Kavelin had one passion beyond chemical isotopes: hunting. In particular he had a romantic passion for tiger-hunting, and when he was a young man in the eighteen-nineties he hunted tigers in India. He loved India and brought back a group of Indians as servants in his household. That was long before Andrei was born. He was a child of his father's old age, born only a year before Dr. Kavelin died.

"And so he was raised by the Indians, who lavished upon him all their love for his dead father. Among them, the cleverest was a thin fellow who was a conjuror, a magician — the most expert sleight-of-hand man I've ever seen in my life, and believe me I've seen plenty, in and out of the entertainment business. He amused the poor little fatherless child by teaching him tricks. The result was that by the time he was ten Andrei began to appear on stage with a magic act — rope tricks, illusions. Wonderful things. I counted on him as one of my regulars, I often had him in my shows.

"Three years ago, when he became a graduate student and fell under the influence of that phony priest, he abandoned the stage. But I said to myself, 'Good old Andrei will help me out! What a stroke of genius!'

"I called him up. He spoke as if he were knocked on the head. He told me nothing. How was I to know that his wife had recently died? He wasn't one of my clients. Who can follow the troubles of everyone?

"I pressed him, begged him, kidded him until he agreed to appear for my sake. So it was done.

"What a blunder it turned out to be!

"I was patting myself on the back for the first half of the show. Myself and a dumb dora played a sketch about a patient with a bad back who comes to the spa at Pitsunda for the baths and falls in love there with a lady weight-lifter. This was a big hit, given the audience. It had a little sly sex. I wrote the sketch myself. I was feeling good.

"Andrei's bit came halfway through the second act. When I looked at him I was in a panic at once. He tottered out on the stage like a zombie and was greeted by a big laugh. They thought he was acting. I knew better. But he really did look like a comical figure, just as if he had been practicing his hypnotism tricks in the mirror and had hypnotized himself.

"But he hadn't lost a single move of his act. He was sensational because, well, it looked as if he wasn't giving a thought to these intricate tricks, and yet they flowed like silk.

"Why, he'd have me tie him up in knots — I was his stooge and helper — and then he'd just twitch an eyebrow and the ropes would slide off. We had a fellow come up from the audience and put chains all over Andrei. And then the guy wheeled him in back of a screen, and a moment later when the screen was removed Andrei was standing on his head and the volunteer was covered from head to toe in the chains.

"Then he took my hat off my head and pulled a dove out of it. Routine stuff — but that was the start of the trouble. Instead of getting rid of it, he lets it perch on his hand while he stares at it.

" 'May the Holy Spirit descend on us all,' he says.

"The audience figures this is some kind of antireligious

crack, and they're roaring anyway, so they keep on laughing.

"We stuffed him into a coffin, and he lay in the coffin whistling 'Moscow Nights' until we closed the lid. A few seconds later, all of a sudden, he totters in from the wings, stiff as Frankenstein's monster.

"He stares at the audience, big black circles around his red eyes. Who could be sure whether he was a figure out of *The Cabinet of Dr. Caligari* or a clown? 'After three days he shall rise again,' he mutters. Most of the audience doesn't hear what he says: those that do figure they're supposed to laugh at jokes against religion, so they laugh. I whisper, 'Are you crazy? Knock it off!'

"Why didn't I have them bring on the next act then and there? Like that baseball manager, you have hopes. Besides, only one routine was left.

" 'Next, for your amazement, and delight,' I say to the audience, 'The Great Kavelin will read the minds of a few of those who filled out the little slips of paper I distributed before this act. The question you were asked to answer, you recall, was: 'What is your heart's desire?'

"This was always a big finisher. It's a simple trick, but a little complicated to explain and you'll forgive me, I hope, if I don't explain it. Suffice it to say that by calling first on a stooge in the audience, Andrei would have the key to the rest of the answers. Anyway, everyone would write down predictable things like: 'To double my production next year' or 'To witness the triumph of Socialism in the world before I die' — dumb things like that. So it would make a buildup of applause for the last trick, when Andrei would reach into my hat and pull out a red banner with Lenin's face on it. Scenes from Lenin's life would then flash on the movie screen. Cheers! Curtain!

"Only it didn't go that way. Andrei stood on the stage staring into space. He ignored the stooge altogether.

" 'Doctor Ilychev, please stand,' he asks in a voice out of a tomb. This doctor is one of the most important doctors in Moscow, a Party member of course, a fellow who loves to travel to Switzerland or New York to study the latest practices in hospital administration, but seems to visit tailors in those countries even more often. 'Your answer is: My heart's desire is to get out of this god-forsaken country as much as I can. Sit down!'

"It got a laugh. It was daring. These days, there's a lot of satire of corruption — it's a fad, maybe it was started by Voznesensky — and it looked like Andrei had made a good hit.

"But he didn't even smile — and, believe me, I was in no smiling mood. I was frozen where I stood. I felt I was turning into a column of ice. 'Doctor Golubenko, your turn,' he says. 'Your answer is: To sell the medical supplies on the black market.'

"He left poor Golubenko standing. Only one person giggled in the front row. Andrei passed on quickly now. He pointed to one of the *apparatchiki* present, a politician charged with the improvement of health delivery. 'You, Kolchak, your desire is to falsify statistics and to conceal the horrible sanitary conditions. You, Doctor Skrypnik' — he pointed to a well-known physician of the health resorts — 'you wish to get as many female patients, nice young ones, on your examining table — that's *your* heart's desire!'

"Those named stood up from habit, for everyone has seen such acts before and knows what is expected. They just continued to stand there like stumps in a swamp. But in a moment some fellows grasped the situation and stood up shouting at Andrei.

"At that Andrei went through the motions of ending the act. 'Let me see what is on my assistant's mind,' he says, just as always, as he removes the cap from my head. That's when the Lenin scarf is supposed to come out. But this time he shakes out a big silk handkerchief with the face of Christ on it! I didn't know how he got hold of it, but later at headquarters I got a look at it. *Souvenir de Lourdes* was written at the bottom. That damned Rosanov!

" 'Only Christ can save you,' Andrei whispers to the audience. 'Here is the message of the First and the Last. He who was dead and has come to life again. Here is the message of Death on the pale horse, the One who has the sharp sword, double-edged, the Son of God who has eyes like a burning flame and holds the seven stars in his hand . . . I know all about you: I will spit you out of my mouth.'

"Meanwhile the stage manager, who after all can't hear what's going on, gets the cue of the flag waving — he supposes it's Lenin's picture — and he turns on the tape of the national anthem, douses the lights, switches on the projector, and flashes on the screen a shot of the opening of the Nurek Dam in Tadzhikistan. The first burst of electricity lights the sign on a mountaintop: 'Lenin lived. Lenin lives. Lenin will live.' This, you may imagine, draws further protests from the audience — it was a mockery that even Andrei had not intended.

"Within moments we were arrested. Lucky too. The audience was ready to assist Andrei — and me too, probably — toward our maker. I soon wriggled out by identifying myself. But they interrogated him. Files on his activities were hauled out. The apartment was doomed, of course; not one resident there remains in Moscow, except Andrei, who is in a Moscow sanitarium. Doubtless he's being well cared for — lots of injections, electric treatments, and so on.

"But I didn't wriggle out for long. Your name, as I say, came up in Andrei's file and my chief wondered why I hadn't reported your movements in this regard. *His* chief saw something suspicious in the fact that I was working with Andrei, that I had asked him to join the show at the last moment. Believe me, I had to do some fast talking. But, you see me before you, still a free man.

"Your file, of course, has been removed from me. It'll take a little while before your case gets reassigned. By God, Martin, if you *are* a spy, I'm done for!"

"Everyone has been arrested?" I asked.

"There was even a scuffle, when some of the old ones tried to hide photographs and icons. And all the contents of the apartment were placed in storage, for investigation. Including, I should say, a *Book of Common Prayer* with a note in it associating it with you — perhaps a gift."

"And all are sent to — where? — to prison? to camps?"

"Oh, you've read Solzhenitsyn, have you? Perhaps you've chatted with Nadezhda Mandelstam? Nonsense! That's an old story. Let's just say they have been reassigned residences for the purposes of distributing work in our large country. No one is killed, except one old Cossack who died of a heart attack — really, it's true — in the scuffle. Well, should I start running? *Are* you a spy?"

"No!"

"It's a ridiculous question. I'm glad to hear you say no anyway, though. What I really wanted to say was: Be careful, won't you?

"*Save me*, that's what I'm asking you. Don't do anything dangerous in the few weeks you have remaining in Moscow. Play it safe. Don't do anything that will look suspicious. That's why I've told you this whole story. It's just that you Americans can't be trusted to know how to behave. Some dope will ask you to carry out a letter for him or to have lunch with a dissident — and in your simplicity you'd probably say yes. You have no consideration for your agents, what your thoughtlessness might do to them. Please, I'm asking you, *think* before you do anything foolish. I'm putting myself on the line in telling you all this, but I'm appealing to your good sense, the well-known kindness of Americans, to ask you not to do anything to bring further suspicion on yourself — and by the same token, on me. Think of me. Think of my career. At my age, ruin is unthinkable. I'd never work my way back. Think of me!"

"You mean, if I am a spy, if you guessed wrong, then I should be careful not to be caught — for your sake?"

"Precisely."

His monologue had held my attention so completely that until this moment the snow which had begun falling heavily outside hadn't caught my attention. Already everything was covered in whiteness.

I had a good view of the "5" bus stop. A group of people were shoving each other to squeeze into the double doors. I saw an old lady hurry along to catch the bus. In her haste she slipped on the curb just as she lifted one foot toward the platform, and she slid under the bus and disappeared almost as if she were part of a magic trick. A puff of exhaust shot from the rear. I saw her climbing out sideways, clawing at snow and slush for a handhold, right beneath the rear wheel. The bus seemed to start to move. It was a moment of helpless horror. Lev had followed my glance. He gasped. But some people had already leaped in front of the bus waving their arms. The tires just spun in place. Others dragged her out. She was lifted up and left there. The bus went off and abandoned her in the dense snow waiting for the next one, limping around in a pained circle.

"Nothing's to be done to help Andrei, I suppose?"

"His father's name is still famous. He'll be all right. If only he hadn't criticized the doctors in public. Now they have him at their mercy. Nothing, as you say, is to be done."

I dreaded the walk from the Universitet Metro station

back to my apartment. But I decided to skip the show at the Rossiya and, instead, start home before too many inches of snow had accumulated. I soon left Dahl. What promises could I make him?

Many weeks before, Marya had told me that Dahl was a spy. "Everyone knows that he is an informer for the KGB — not actually an agent but one of the *stucikachi,* a collaborator who works for favors, a *seksoty.*

"But most likely he is also a spy for the Americans, a double agent. That is what many people believe, certainly. Every now and then he throws someone inconsequential to the wolves to keep his position. To stay away from him would be best, I think."

Not long after Dahl's confession Marya returned from Smolensk. I had really missed her — more than I thought I would — and the day I expected her to come back on the train I took the bus to her apartment on the outskirts of the city and pushed a note under the door asking her to meet me at the Pechora Café. We had several appetizers and a little vodka and then we got a taxi back to my apartment where we picked up the two Hungarian chickens I had bought for her at the diplomatic *gastronome.* We stayed to have tea.

When I told her about all that happened, including Andrei's sensational breakdown, she shook her head dubiously and said again that Dahl was an informer and not to be trusted on any account. Then she added:

"As for Andrei, it is true that he has disappeared. His friends too. For all I know he *may* be in a sanitarium. But not once have I heard even a whisper about such a catastrophe at a show for a doctors' convention. Does the story ring true to you? Very likely it's been entirely concocted by Dahl to worm his way into your confidence. He's very clever — no one doubts that. Probably, he himself simply informed on Andrei and his friends and made up this story as a coverup. Dahl is a tough guy — no one to fool with, whatever side he's on — or whatever side *you're* on."

"But I — I'm on neither side," I said.

"Then be on *my* side, will you dear, and pour me some tea, and let me look at the photographs in these wonderful American magazines that you bring from the Embassy. That copy of *Vogue* — hand it to me, please. And come and sit by my side as soon as you've brought the tea.

"Oh, there are spies everywhere. Dahl is certainly a spy. Our pornographer friend Malevsky may be a spy. Sometimes when I wake up suddenly in the middle of the night I am not sure just who I am: then I think *I* may be a spy.

"And you. Look at the notes you've collected. You've been very active, haven't you? Are you writing a novel about us — or collecting files for your chief at home? On your desk I have seen notes on Andrei and Dahl and Malevsky, Anton Dubrovinsky, Marshal Grechko, Yuri Telgrin, Comrade Lenin, our dear Nikita, Lara, and the unnamed ones who fill the Peking cafeteria.

"Modern spies, you know, use cameras on those they've got under surveillance. But you're an old-fashioned spy, aren't you? Maybe you're right. We've nothing to fear from the camera anymore. Everyone alive has already been photographed and tape-recorded. But, my dear, from you, with your memories and your old-fashioned vision, perhaps we do, we do have something to fear."

X

A Loyal Citizen

Just a few days before I left the United States, my Russian teacher made a pause in our language lesson. She and her husband had been allowed to emigrate from the Soviet Union only a few months before, but we had never talked about Russian politics or society. Masculine-feminine endings and verb forms had quite adequately occupied our daily hour. But near the end of my last lesson I saw that secretly she was worried about me.

"I am sure you will have no trouble in the Soviet Union," she said. "Tell me, do you have any relatives in Moscow?"

"No, none at all."

"*Then*, do you know any dissidents in Russia? Are you interested in contacting dissidents?"

"Certainly not."

She paused and seemed to hesitate about her next question.

"Well, then. Are you Jewish?"

"No."

"*Then* —" her face lit up happily — "*then, you are a loyal citizen!*"

Many times during my months in the Soviet Union I had reason to recall this little quiz, especially one evening in the middle of May while I waited in the foreign passengers' lounge at the airport in Samarkand.

There, in a quite unforeseen manner, I got into trouble. When the Ministry of Education had approved my lecture tour, I readily agreed to the proposal by Bob Miller, the Embassy's Assistant Officer of Cultural Affairs, that he make a random selection of American books and magazines from the storehouse and package these up for me to carry along and present as gifts to scholars in Central Asia and Georgia. Miller was young and bright, a Stanford graduate. I made endless requests of him for materials in connection with my teaching and he helped me a lot, he even helped arrange for my trip. But on this occasion he let a secretary pick out the magazines, and this got me into the first of a series of embarrassments, difficulties, and, eventually, real dangers.

Everything was fine until I stepped off the plane in Samarkand, collected my luggage and packages, and approached the waiting Intourist representative with a question.

"Excuse me, I've brought two packages with me. One of them — this one — I'm going to dispose of in Samarkand but the other I'm taking with me on to Tbilisi, so I'd like to leave it in your office."

She was tall and thin. She wore dark mascara, heavily pasted on. Her hair was red. Obviously she was a Russian, not a native of this region, an Uzbek or a Tadzhik. Naturally she was a loyal citizen. An informer.

"What is in the package, then?"

"Books and magazines. I'm here to lecture at Alisher Navoi University. The Ministry of Education has approved my trip. The people at the university have already been informed by cable from the Ministry. I imagine they're waiting for me. I wanted to ask you about that too — how to make contact with the Department of Languages, I mean."

"Yes, in good time. But this package, it contains, then, only books and magazines? Are these in Russian?"

"No. In English."

"Would these writings be interesting to Russians?"

"I hope so. Otherwise I've carried them four thousand miles for nothing."

I wasn't sure exactly what materials were inside the packages and I could safely assume that all Intourist officials were informers, and this began to make me feel uneasy.

"Well, I myself would be very interested to see what professors at our university would like to read. Would you mind opening this package for me?"

"I'd be happy to open it. I'm sure you'll be interested."

She set her fists on her hips and waited for the package to be opened. Then she became active as a rodent. She turned the package upside down and dumped the books and magazines onto the table.

To my horror, on the very top of the pile fell a copy of the *Atlantic Monthly*. On the cover was a caricatured drawing of a big, wealthy-looking Russian bureaucrat shoving a sexy-looking blonde into a black Chaika limousine while saying to his uniformed chauffeur, "Take me to the dacha, comrade!" Across the top the title of Hedrick Smith's lead article was printed: HOW THE SOVIET ELITE LIVES IT UP.

Quickly I picked up a hard-backed book.

"I'd be delighted to make you a gift of a book," I said. "I'm sure you read English. Here is a novel."

She looked as if she were standing in a jewelry store, alone, with all the cases open.

Without blinking, she reached over and took two books.

"How good of you to bring books to our people. Comrade Lenin says that a book is like a little fire."

That ended her interest in me. But I assumed she'd spotted the *Atlantic* cover and that I could expect further surveillance.

Later I walked from my new hotel to the ancient spice bazaar. For over two thousand years, foreigners — Alexander the Great, the Arabs, and Genghis Khan — had sacked Samarkand for its spices and its women. Here, Tamerlane plotted his conquests. Here, too, the philosopher Avicenna speculated about the nature of things, and the poet Omar Khayyam composed his melancholy quatrains. I just wanted to take a walk.

The bazaar hadn't changed since ancient times. Striped watermelons, bunches of fennel, enormous ginger roots, cabbages, red grapes, and crates of strawberries were piled in profusion in wooden bins. Bearded men wearing long black robes and fezzes atop their shaved heads lounged under thatched roofs, bags of spices opened before them. Old women sat on the ground hawking small decorated gourds filled with green tobacco snuff. In the center of the bazaar a stone platform was raised about twenty feet above ground level and on top of that was a pavilion from which drifted the fragrances of wood smoke mixed with food.

I was being followed by a Tadzhik with a white beard and mustache, wearing a long black and yellow caftan; and I felt as if I had been caught up in a B movie of Sinbad's adventures. "So," I thought, "I am suspected of subversion — because of those damn magazines. And here in Samarkand, thousands of miles away from the Embassy, anything could happen."

On top of the pavilion a young Uzbek was searing cubed meat in a black iron caldron set on a blazing fire. The Tadzhik followed me cautiously. I paid a rouble for a bowl of meat and rice and at the other end of the platform got a pot of tea for six kopecks. I pretended to sit and eat and pushed the greasy food around while I watched the black and yellow caftan circle around me like a shark. I assumed that the fellow wasn't a thief, just a KGB agent doing his job, and so I had nothing to fear. I never minded having agents around — they were as good as bodyguards.

Then, when I pushed the bowl aside and walked away from the table I saw how wrong I had been. I heard a clatter in back of me and swung around. No sooner had I vacated my place than the Tadzhik made a dive for it — really like a shark now. Immediately he gobbled up the food I had left.

So, after all, he was just a hungry worker who had seen many tourists leave their food uneaten. He had no interest in me at all. Now that he had taken possession of my meal and my tea he glared at me boldly, as if to say, "Well, you kept me waiting long enough! Must you stare at me in your nosy tourist's way?" And in my fear and egotism I had supposed him to be an agent spying on me. After only five months in the Soviet Union I had begun, like everyone else, to feel myself a criminal.

2

The sun was just rising over the mountains in Tbilisi as the plane touched down, but a woman from Intourist greeted me as soon as I stepped off the plane.

"I am Marika Mesknishvili. I am assigned to aid you during your stay in our city. This is my great pleasure. Follow me."

"My bags?"

"Zviad is collecting them. Don't concern yourself, please."

Zviad turned out to be the driver of the invariable black Volga. When we reached the car he already had my bag and bundle inside the open trunk. Each had a chalk line drawn across it.

"Will you please verify that these are yours?"

"Yes," I said, "those are mine."

Zviad slammed the trunk lid. Marika opened the back door for me, and she herself slid in the front next to the driver. The tires spun and squealed and sent a cloud of Georgian dust behind us as we leaped out of the parking lot and flew along a speedway pointed toward the center of town, like a dark arrow shot at the heart of the morning.

Marika turned around in her seat. She talked as fast as Zviad drove.

"Isn't it wonderful? This is our newest expressway, built at a cost of six million four hundred and eight roubles over a three-year period. Based on the most modern principles of turnpike planning and construction. Road building is continuously undertaken in our country as part of our Soviet modernization program.

"Observe the countryside please. We Georgians call our country Sakartvelo, Land of the Georgians. The lovely fertile valleys of our land, only the smallest part of which unfortunately you will see, lie in Transcaucasia, between the mountain ranges of the Bolshoi Kavkaz and the Maly Kavkaz. The Georgian Soviet Socialist Republic covers an area of close to seventy thousand square kilometers and has a population of four point six eight six million.

"In nineteen fifty-eight our fair city of Tbilisi celebrated its one thousand five-hundreth anniversary as the capital of the country. Prior to that our capital was Mtskheta. You must visit Mtskheta while you are here. Sir,

Mtskheta is a veritable museum. I myself will take you there. Once a fortified city of wonderful proportions located at the very confluence of the Aragvi and the Kura rivers, it was an ancient center of religion, as well as a military stronghold, and there are wonderful fortified churches there. The Jvan monastery, high above our Military Road, and the Svetitskhoveli Cathedral built by the architect Arsakidze in the eleventh century, are the most inspiring buildings. But nearby is also our Zemo-Avchala Hydroelectric Power Station. It is dedicated to Lenin, of course. The monument to Lenin is well worth a visit."

When she took a breath she started on another track: "Nature has generously endowed Georgia with vast natural resources and unusually diverse landscapes."

At this point I began to lose my mental grip on her travelogue. Phrases like "per hectare," "annual rainfall," "the highest percentage," and "kilowatt hours" formed little bumps in the smooth roadway of her practiced talk. All I really yearned for was a nap of an hour or two.

But the management of the Hotel Iveria was not quite ready to oblige me. We screeched to a halt at the door before 7 A.M. The lobby was silent. The registration desk did not open until eight. A grizzled old porter, dressed in a dark brown bellboy's suit and looking like a Philip Morris advertisement, took my bag and package under his care while Marika took me to breakfast. Obviously she had no intention of allowing me out of her sight.

"Please tell me what it is you care to do in Tbilisi? Certainly, you would want to see our Museum of Fine Arts, the gold treasures of Georgian antiquity. Also, you must ride the funicular to the top of Mount Mtatsminda. Nebekhi Castle — yes, you must see that. Sioni Cathedral — of course. The Anchiskhati Church — without a doubt. Ah, yes, we shall certainly also make a stop at the ancient St. David Monastery, wherein is a veritable pan-

theon of the great writers of Georgia, such as Ilya Chav-
chavadze and Vazha Bshavila. You, a professor of literature, have read these great men, of course?" She spoke
like a woman checking off a shopping list.

"Yes," I lied. Already I was befuddled by the Georgian
names.

"Isn't there an opera company in the city?" I asked.

"Opera and ballet, naturally. We practice every art.
The walls of our Paliashvilli Opera and Ballet Theater have
been shaken by the mighty bass of Chaliapin and retain
the echoes of the glorious voice of Nezhdanova. Haven't
you also heard of Vano Sarajishvili, the 'Georgian
Nightingale'?"

For a moment, she looked a little bewildered. The bat-
teries of her internal tape recorder seemed to be running
down. Then she said quickly, "However, unfortunately,
our theater has been incinerated and is now under extensive repair."

"The opera house has been burned down? How did it
happen?"

"No one knows. Perhaps the wiring was defective."

"In any event," I said, "I must not make any plans
without consulting my hosts at the university and the Institute of Languages."

"That is the case, naturally. I simply wish to make you
understand, I am ready to accompany you wherever you
go, so long as you remain in our city, which will be — if I
am not mistaken — two nights."

When the registration desk opened, the clerk collected
my passport and handed me a cardboard chit on which
she wrote my room number: 711.

"Seventh floor," she said. "Please hand this slip when
given key by woman on floor. Your bags will be brought.
You may proceed."

As soon as I put my head inside the door, I realized that this was going to be a bad morning. The room was just wide enough to squeeze a fold-out couch along the walls on each side. Between the couches were tables, chairs, lamps, and other furnishings piled end to end. I could hardly edge myself into the room. I went into the bathroom. The fixtures were rusted, the walls were grimy. The toilet didn't flush. Socialism was fine. Socialism should be forgiven everything — but unflushable toilets were inexcusable no matter what their politics.

The ancient bellboy appeared at my heels struggling with my bags and those of a Russian who was moving into the room opposite mine. I stopped him at the entrance.

"Please bring my bags back downstairs," I told the old fellow, who tried to push his way into the room and back me into a corner with my own luggage. I left him in the room. He was probably debating whether I had the authority to give him any commands whatsoever.

"The room is in terrible shape," I explained to the woman at the registration desk.

"But *that* is your room," she said as if it had been left to me in someone's will. "It is *yours*. Don't you see that it has been assigned to you? That *must* be your room."

I took the only possible line of argument.

"I refuse to believe that the Soviet Socialist Republic of Georgia would wish a visitor to spend a night in such poor lodgings."

She looked thoroughly bored by this claim. The elevator doors opened and the old boy appeared, still toting my possessions. He looked fiercely at me.

"Wait here a moment," she said. She abruptly left me and after a moment's conference with the bellboy she left the lobby.

Upon her return she said curtly, "We have no other rooms."

"I insist on having a first-class room. I have paid first-class rates."

"Please listen to me. We *are* going to give you another room. But we have no other rooms *now*. You must wait an hour."

"Fine," I said, with my best show of decisive exasperation, "then I shall return in an hour."

She went back to reading the *Tbilisi Leninist News*.

I decided to take an hour's walk around the city. But no sooner did I step out of the Iveria's entrance when Marika came clattering up behind me.

"Ah, I see that you wish to take an outing in our city. Shall we take the car?"

"Not at the moment. I'm just going to take a short walk in the city."

"Let me remind you that you have a City Tour included in your Intourist first-class arrangements."

"Now, however, I wish only to walk."

"Then — she brightened — "I am only too delighted to accompany you."

She led me to the left. "Here we are walking along Rustaveli Avenue, named after the great Georgian national poet, Shoto Rustaveli, the author of *The Knight in Panther's Skin*. Please turn about now and look at our hotel. It is twenty-two stories, our first high-rise building. Do you like the color? It is faced with bluish-green Tedzami tuff. As we continue on we shall come to the famous Rustaveli Theater. Also the opera theater, under restoration. Its style is pseudo-Mooresque."

She rambled on as we walked, so anxious to get her tour said, and so full of anxiety that I might turn into a side street of no historic interest, that she described buildings long before we reached them — as if it were more important to give her speech than actually to see these supposedly wonderful sights.

"Before you the prospect of the avenue is enriched by the graceful architecture of our Institute of Marxism-Leninism. On your left hand you will soon see the Kashveti Temple, an exact duplicate of the famous Samtavisi Temple of Kartli. Opposite this is our imposing House of Government and just beyond that in a minute you will see the Palace of Pioneers."

"Does it have an art exhibit?" I asked maliciously for my own benefit.

"I think not. But let me call your attention to the Janashia State Archeological and Ethnographic Museum on this side of the street."

"Marika," I said, "these are charming buildings, really fascinating. But if you'll allow me a moment, I'd prefer to stroll in a purely meditative fashion." I searched for some polite way to beg her to be silent. "Let us enjoy in silent admiration the warmth and placidity of this fine Tbilisi morning."

"An excellent notion," she said. "You have an appreciation of our city's beauty that is almost entirely dead in this world except among Georgians, don't you think? Yes, it is a warm morning. At this time of the year, in the month of May, our mean temperature is eighteen degrees centigrade. Our average rainfall for the month is in excess . . ."

So she talked on for the next hour until she left me again at the entrance to the hotel and went to sit in the Volga with Zviad.

The clerk stood up as soon as I entered the lobby and held out a piece of cardboard.

"As you see," she said, "we make good on our word. You have a different room. Room six eleven."

This room looked exactly the same as the room above it,

terribly cluttered with worn, greasy furniture. I had hardly stepped into the room when the grizzled, muttering porter pushed his way in with my bags.

"Bring these back downstairs," I told him. "This is no better. It won't do at all."

He made grinding noises in the back of his throat. Then, he raised one finger as a signal for me to wait. He rushed into the bathroom. I heard the whoosh and gurgle of the commode operating. He came out nodding his head vigorously.

"It won't do," I said in English.

I hurried by him so quickly that I almost bumped into a man unlocking the door opposite mine. It was the same fellow they had been moving in on the floor above an hour earlier.

I put the key on the registration desk. The woman was absorbed in checking lists of figures.

"I want to see the manager."

No answer.

"Will you call the manager for me?"

No answer — and no probability of an answer. Her whole being had turned to stone. Had Stalin himself stood before her she might not have budged. Only a .45 to the temple could have moved her.

I walked into the manager's office on my own.

A tall, rather pleasant-looking Russian in his thirties rose from behind his desk.

"Are you the manager?"

"Yes." He smiled.

"I've come to complain about my room, and I want to go to a different hotel."

"Why, what is wrong with your room, please?"

"It's simply not a first-class room, and my arrangements with Intourist in Moscow are for first-class."

"Yes, let me see." He scanned a sheet which resembled a bill of lading. "Here is your name. It is this hotel they have assigned you to. This *is* a first-class hotel. I see you have paid for first-class. This is your hotel."

"This is *not* a first-class hotel. The room is too small. The furniture is worn. The stuffing is coming out. The floors are dirty. The toilet doesn't flush!"

He didn't blink.

"There *is* a deluxe hotel in Tbilisi. But I see that you did not pay for *de luxe*. Our hotel has been registered as a first-class hotel."

"I am willing to concede that the lobby is a first-class lobby. The restaurant is a first-class restaurant. The hard-currency bar, I will assume, is a first-class hard-currency bar. But I am not intending to sleep in the lobby or the restaurant. I do not propose to flush the foreign-currency bar. My room is not a first-class room! I want to go to another hotel."

"There is no other first-class hotel. This is your hotel."

"Then I will not stay in Tbilisi. I'll leave here after my lecture this afternoon."

"Leave here? But where will you go?"

"The hotel brochure states that cars may be rented here."

"Certainly, through Avis International."

"Then I shall rent a car and drive to Yerevan."

"What will you do in Yerevan?"

"Climb Mount Ararat. Like Noah. I'll climb Mount Ararat."

"But" — he studied his manifold again — "you have a visa only for Tbilisi, certainly only for the Republic of Georgia. Such an excursion would require you to secure a visa for the Armenian Autonomous Republic. That is impossible."

He scolded me: "Do you expect just to wander about the countryside? You have a visa for Tbilisi. Everyone must be registered. Everyone must be looked after. It is impossible to run a country in any other fashion. A child would see that. I am told, though in truth I cannot credit it, that in your country people just travel anywhere, without domestic visas, and settle down wherever they wish, and never register with the City Soviets or the Police. Well, then, how would anyone find such a person? It's completely unthinkable!"

"All right. My air ticket calls for me to go to Moscow through Sochi. I'll leave for Sochi tonight and stay there."

"But how do we know there is a hotel room for you in Sochi? It would be a shame to send a distinguished American to Sochi at the beginning of the busy season. There is probably no place. One must make a reservation for Sochi no later than three weeks in advance. Besides, your visa calls for a stopover in Sochi, not overnight residence."

"All right, then," I said decisively, "rather than stay here I'll return to Moscow by the next flight."

"But" — he smiled serenely — "you are booked through Sochi. Today's flight via Sochi is surely filled. Tomorrow's flight is also booked in advance. *Your* flight is the day after tomorrow, and your reservation is confirmed. It cannot be changed."

"Then I must have a first-class room."

Since he had won on every front, he now said grandly, "Dear visitor, you shall have a first-class room. I will see to it myself."

An hour later the manager himself led me into Room 511, an exact duplicate of the ones above it.

"Are the listening devices installed in only one column of rooms?" I asked politely.

"I beg your pardon?" was all the answer I got.

There wasn't the slightest point in making any further

complaints. Four eleven and three eleven would be just the same.

"This is fine. Thanks," I said to the ancient bellboy, who dropped my bags and stamped out of the room.

Before I left Moscow Bob Miller had done me another favor besides giving me closed packages that contained the satiric *Atlantic* cover — and, as it turned out, a *Reader's Digest* with an anti-Soviet diatribe by Solzhenitsyn. He gave me a typed-list of Georgians to take with me.

"It occurs to me," Miller said, "that it would be helpful to you to have a list of a few people in Tbilisi with whom we've had some sort of prior contact. I've never been to Georgia myself — though I want to go and may even be able to arrange to meet you there — but several people connected with the Embassy have been there in the past. Just recently, when I was cleaning out files I came across some misplaced papers of a guy who was here before I arrived, Roger Hellman's his name, and I noticed that he was in Tbilisi several times. He made many contacts too; the names are in his file. Mostly academics, I guess. He gave away lots of books — the storehouse records show that. Probably teachers of English. They'll come to your lectures, and you'll want to be familiar with the names in advance. That would be a very good gesture. I'll have my secretary type up a list for you."

Now that I was in Georgia I fished the list out of my bag and tried to memorize the difficult names: Gregori Beliashvili, Nathela Gachechiladze . . . impossible names.

That afternoon the lecture went well. More than two hundred people attended. The Georgians were *au courant,* they asked good questions, and they were very pleasant. I began to feel in a sunny mood again.

The Chair of Languages held a nice reception for me with tea, spiced sausages, cheese pastries, corn bread, olives, and bunches of aromatic grasses. I did my best to catch the names of the guests, but so far as I could tell none of those Roger Hellman had contacted had been invited to the reception.

Two young scholars outlasted all the others. The more they thrust themselves forward, the more the others fell back.

"You don't know how wonderful it is to have you here. We dream of American literature," one said enthusiastically.

"Yes, you don't believe us, we sound as if we are exaggerating — but our pleasure is genuine," the other added. "How unfortunate if we should have to break up this conversation now, when we have so much yet to ask you."

"Is it possible that we can continue our talk at dinner? For us it would be an unrivaled pleasure, a great honor," his companion interposed.

"I'd like that, yes," I said.

"Why don't we drive you back to your hotel, then? Rest an hour or two while I shop for whatever poor scraps of food I can find," the taller man said. "Then we will pick you up at seven o'clock."

The taller man's name was Niko Mezrulvili, and the other, younger man, Georgi Toradze. They both dressed well, as much in an American fashion as possible. Both wore sports coats, and Niko sported a black turtleneck. His dark hair was curly and flowed over his collar. He wouldn't have been out of place on the Via Veneto. Georgi was more boyish, less flamboyant and theatrical, but also more serious and intense and shy.

We walked outside. To my astonishment Georgi owned a new red Zhiguli, the Soviet-made Fiat 124. He maneuvered the sedan delicately through the traffic, while Niko made lots of apologies in advance for the poor dinner he would set before me. Back at the hotel I slept fitfully. Earlier, when I had walked with Marika on Rustaveli Avenue , I had seen a series of blown-up photographs of Stalin and his generals in a store window. Now, in my dreams these jiggled like circus posters twitching on the tail of a kite. I got the photographs mixed up in my dreams with the list of Roger Hellman's contacts and I kept scanning the list. Neither Niko nor Georgi was on it. But their faces blended into the iron faces of the generals.

3

As a matter of coincidence, when Niko and Georgi and Georgi's wife Isolda picked mc up, the conversation soon did get around to Stalin.

"First," Niko said, "we are going to take you for a drive to the top of the mountain overlooking Tbilisi, though unfortunately this excursion will probably only increase your appetite and make my poor dinner seem even worse. But perhaps you will remember us for our hospitality, at least."

When we reached the crest and parked, a black Volga with two men sitting in it was parked there. We walked to the edge of the hills.

"KGB," Niko whispered. "They check to see who comes here. Maybe it's a crime for a Georgian to come up here now. Maybe looking at Tbilisi's lights is a crime. They'd hang monitoring devices on the trees if they could. But that is difficult. So they have to send agents themselves up here to spy on us. Don't you know that this is the land of Stalin?''

"I did see a picture of Stalin in a window today," I said, "the first I've seen in the Soviet Union."

"In Moscow he doesn't exist, not officially that is. But could Stalin die? Could a man who slept on an iron bed die? Could a man who slept with his boots on be dead? I don't think so. Yes, he's still with us. In Georgia he's very much with us."

"Niko," Georgi said, "the agents over there are taking down our license number. Probably we should leave."

Isolda nodded her head.

"Let them call me up!" Niko hissed. "KGB have called me up before. Last year they called me up. They say to me, 'Mezrulvili, why do you talk to journalists?' Professor Martin, do you know the correspondent for the *Chicago Tribune*? And do you know Mr. Fred Friendly? I met them in Moscow and they traveled down here to talk to me about conditions.

"So the KGB man says to me, 'Why do you talk to journalists?'

" 'What do you mean journalists?' I ask.

" 'You talked to the writer for the Chicago paper. You also spent two evenings with the journalist Fred Friendly. That's what we mean.'

" 'Excuse me, I forgot they were journalists. They're my friends. *My friends*. Do you understand what friends are? Do you know what that means?' I ask them. 'Even Comrade Stalin allowed my stepfather to talk to friends, though he was confined to his own house. But now, is it no longer permitted to have friends?'

" 'But Mr. Mezrulvili, a loyal Soviet should not have friends among American journalists,' they tell me.

" 'I'm sorry, *I'm sorry*,' I cry to them. 'From now on I shall ask you before I speak to anyone. I shall say to Mr.

Friendly, "I'm sorry, my democratic government does not allow me to talk to you. You tell lies. You say we are not free. We are perfectly free. That is why I am not allowed to talk to you!' Is that what I should say?' I ask the KGB. " 'Niko, loyal Niko,' my agent tells me. 'Won't you let *me* be a friend to you? Try not to be sarcastic. Your stepfather was sarcastic. Do you remember what happened to him?' "

Georgi whispered, "His stepfather was in prison for a long time and then was exiled to his dacha until he died. A great philosopher, a founder of the university, one of our chief academicians. His books were destroyed. He couldn't publish anything for his last thirty years."

" 'Yes,' " Niko continued his story, "I tell him, 'I remember what happened to him. Stalin put him in prison because he was a philosopher. Naturally, being a philosopher is a crime. But I just talk to friends.'

" 'Think of what you are saying,' this KGB fellow tells me. 'Try to get yourself under control. Surely you do not wish to make trouble for yourself. Listen to what I'm saying to you. This is good advice.' "

All during this time Niko took obvious delight in playing both parts — the sly KGB agent, a smooth talker with a mailed fist; and himself, the literature teacher who was outwardly belligerent but secretly terrified. He acted it all out. He gripped my hand, threw his arms to the sky, rolled his eyes, and clutched my shoulders with his two hands.

Isolda said, "Georgi is right. We shouldn't stay too long in such obvious view as this, especially with agents watching us."

Niko hit his palms to his head in exaggerated exasperation. "All right. All right. Maybe the KGB will come tomorrow to see me again. For now, look at how beautiful the lights of Tbilisi are."

Isolda came and stood next to me. "When we were students in the university we used to come up here and say, 'This is like California. It's just as if we were on the top of the Hollywood Hills.' What we meant was, we wished we were in America. But we love Georgia, the real Georgia, you know."

We drove down. I brought out some American cigarettes.

"Ah, Marlboro, what a treat. We know all the American cigarettes. We see them advertised in the magazines," Georgi said, accepting one.

Niko said, "Perhaps it's a crime to smoke Marlboros. Do you think that I should call up the KGB and ask them?"

"Is it like California at all?" the woman asked.

"It is. Quite a lot."

"I'm glad."

Niko's apartment building was in the old section of the city. It was dilapidated, the walls were stained, the floors were filthy. We climbed up two flights of stairs.

The door was painted and paneled, just an ordinary door, except that it was studded with locks. Niko pulled out a big ring of keys, as if he were opening a dungeon or treasure room, and proceeded to unlock an intricate series of dead-bolts, spring locks, and combination locks.

When at last the door sprung open upon a little entry hall, I saw that there were indeed treasures inside, surprising things.

On the wall directly opposite the door was a large map of the United States. Niko walked to the table beneath the map, picked up the telephone, turned a switch on its bottom, and put the receiver into the drawer. Quickly, we passed into the living room. It was sheerly an American apartment. American posters and pictures, carefully removed from magazines, covered the walls. In the very center was the famous full-face photograph of Marilyn

Monroe, lips parted, vulnerable. Everything else seemed to radiate from this — a Woodstock poster, a photo of Greta Garbo, a reproduction of a Wyeth barn, a picture of Norman Mailer chatting with Andy Warhol, a blowup of Balanchine working with young dancers in New York, a still of Woody Allen in *Love and Death,* the *Life* color reproduction of Marilyn's last nude photograph, Sinatra, three photographs of Faye Dunaway, one of Ali McGraw, a front page of *Rolling Stone.* There was much else. I couldn't take it all in at once.

The room was only about six feet wide and fifteen feet long. Along the left wall was a sofa and a cocktail table with a kitchen chair at each end. Hardly a foot of space was left to walk in so we had to proceed Indian file between the table and the bookcase. Along the wall beyond the couch was a sideboard completely covered by the paraphernalia of a stereo set with matched components and a rack of long-playing records. In the center of the room was a rectangular pedestal table surrounded by chairs. The four of us seemed almost to fill every inch of unoccupied space.

"Sit down, sit down, sit down," Niko sang, as he disappeared through one of the doors.

"Come over here on the divan," Isolda urged me.

Georgi called, "Niko, if I can give you any assistance . . ."

He came bubbling out, like the froth on a wave.

"There's room for only one in the kitchen. Here though, you must open these bottles of champagne. Do that for me, Georgi dear."

He rushed out again. The next instant his head popped back through the doorway.

"We must have a record! I must pick it out. Wait a moment."

He went out and hustled back in with a dish of cold

beans and bread, which he dropped on the cocktail table without stopping as if he sped along on roller skates.

He swept past us to the record rack and began to pull albums out.

"Armstrong — no. Benny Goodman at Carnegie Hall. Do you *love* Goodman? *Music for Lovers,* selected and conducted by Jackie Gleason. Hmmm. Shirley Bassey." In a stylized blues accent, he sang a few lines from "Killing Me Softly". . . "Telling my whole life with his words . . ."

"Yes, shall we hear it? You don't like her, perhaps. What about this one? — Maureen McGovern: 'We shall never meet like this again . . . ' Have you seen *The Towering Inferno*? Is it wonderful? Ah, Faye Dunaway, Faye Dunaway . . ." He danced over to her pictures on the wall. "I love her. Isn't she grand? — isn't she beautiful? — doesn't her face tear your heart out? — aren't her bones incredible? Faye . . ." he crooned once more — " 'We shall never meet like this again . . .' "

He skated back to the albums. "How about this: *Goldfinger? Live and Let Die.* Shall we have it? Isolda, darling, put it on. I trust you. I love your husband — but I trust you."

He started toward the door, then whirled around. "Georgi, *do* pour the champagne. It's getting warm. What will our guest think? — serving him warm champagne. What will he say? 'Those Georgians are strange fellows. They forget about the meal. They serve warm champagne. They are country fellows, they get too excited, they behave like children.' Hurry, Georgi, pour the champagne. What are you waiting for?"

"But Niko, you haven't told me where the glasses are."

"Glasses! How stupid I am!"

He dashed off and was back almost at once, his two

hands and his arms filled with glasses. We had to help him put them down.

"I shouldn't own so many glasses," he said. "No Georgian is allowed to own more than one glass, just one glass to drink out of."

He began to play-act again.

"Did I shut the telephone off? Isolda, turn up the record. The KGB will know that I have — how many? — one, two, three . . . *nine* glasses. *Treason!* Tomorrow my agent will call me up and say, 'Niko, this is the last straw. You have nine glasses. It is capitalistic. Think of your position.' But I have an answer. I'll say to him, 'But, darling, I use only one for myself. The others are for entertaining my Russian friends.' 'In that case, it's all right,' he'll say. Bah!

"'Niko,' they call me. Can you believe it? 'Niko' — just as if to say, 'Boy.' 'Come here, boy' — 'Fetch, boy' — just the way you'd call a puppy-dog. 'Take this bone, boy.' 'Be satisfied we let you live, boy.'

"Can only a Russian be a man? I'm forty-three. My father was allowed to marry when he was twenty-two. That was in the old days, before the Revolution. He was a Party member for a while. Then he made a remark in private about Comrade Stalin. That automatically made him a Menshevik. He disappeared before he was forty-three. I'm not allowed to marry. How could a 'boy' get married? We do what they tell us. Georgi, are you a 'boy'?"

"You forget, Niko, I *am* married."

"You're right, Georgians should get married. Then they begin to feel like men, eh? Does he act like a man, Isolda?"

"Niko, why don't you let me help you in the kitchen?" she asked.

"Do I talk too much?" He bowed with mock solemnity.

"It's because I'm ashamed of our dinner. What can I do, though? A *boy* is not allowed to buy food such as men in the Party get. That's the way it is."

Isolda remarked to me when he disappeared, "He's very excited to have you here, you see."

Georgi poured the champagne into three glasses.

"I won't take anything, since I'm driving," Georgi explained. "Drink, drink, don't wait for Niko. He won't settle down for a half hour yet."

Isolda clinked glasses with me, as Niko ran back in with more appetizers. "To our host," I said, raising my glass to him.

"Pardon me," he said in a clowning voice, "but I am nothing. Mr. Brezhnev is our host. Everything we have, all that we are, all that we hope to be is in the hands of our dear white Ukrainian father in the Kremlin. I am nothing."

He held a large glass bowl in his hands as he talked, but until he put it on the table I didn't see what it contained.

"We do have something," he said, "some little things, a few luxuries."

"But where did you get such a lot of fresh caviar?" Isolda asked.

"We have our secrets. Don't you see, Professor, Georgia is a country of thieves and smugglers. What else can we be? All the food we produce goes to Moscow. It must be. Our masters need it, the Russians need it. They have everything in Moscow. We have nothing. They're like locusts. We raise up a crop — whoosh, it's gone. But they're men. We're just thieves. If we want anything we have to steal it. We have to steal our own food back. Maybe we steal the Russians' food sometimes, I can't say. I think that this caviar, in any event, Isolda, came across the Black Sea from Iran yesterday. When the vessel docked in Poti, lo and behold, the caviar on it was nowhere to be seen. Today the Minister of the Interior in Moscow was intending to feed it to his cat. 'Poor pussy,' he is moaning, 'I have no treat for you today.' Somehow, though, this caviar made its way into my kitchen. Let us enjoy our luck!"

The large bowl was completely filled. There must have been at least five hundred dollars' worth of caviar there, even at hard currency prices in the Beriozka stores for foreigners.

"But how shall we eat it?" Isolda inquired.

"Spoons, spoons — where are the spoons? Wait a second, drink champagne, it's Georgian champagne. The only way to eat caviar is to *eat* it! — with champagne, of course!"

He dug a teaspoon into the center of the bowl and brought up a great mound of tiny black eggs. Like a father feeding a child he held it out toward my mouth, and I took it.

"Bravo," he cried. "Now — like this."

He took a spoonful between his own lips with a great smack. At once he snatched his glass of champagne and took a big gulp, motioning for me to do the same and to hold the wine in my mouth.

It made the most delicious sensation. The champagne bubbles lifted the light eggs off my tongue, breaking them away a few at a time, as waves suck away sand castles. The fish eggs seemed almost alive as they danced in the vibrant wine. It tasted as if a thousand microscopic fish were darting wildly about inside my cheeks.

Georgi and Isolda were imitating us now and the four of us sat looking at each other happily, unable to say a word. Their eyes were sparkling. I supposed mine were the same.

"Eat, eat, don't worry about me," Niko urged, as he swallowed his mouthful and sped off.

"Oh," he wailed as he went, "there's so little, so little, so little. Luckily, my sister stopped in a few hours ago, and I set her to work. Together, well, we did something. Have more champagne. We must finish the caviar or tomorrow the KGB will use it as evidence against me. 'Boy, you are eating the caviar meant for Choo-Choo, the Minister's cat. It is a great crime.' Eat! Destroy the evidence!"

He was like a circus. Had the room been big enough, I think he would have done handstands and somersaults.

"Do you go to Balanchine's ballet?" Isolda asked. "Do you like him? He's Georgian. Did you know that?"

"Then, that's why he has such a sense of style," I said, hoping to make a graceful compliment.

"We think that the only interesting ballet in the world is in America," Georgi added. "The Alvin Ailey and the Joffrey. The Bolshoi creaks with age. It's nothing — just ghosts, robots."

"And the theaters in New York," Isolda continued. "La Mama. The Phoenix. The Long Wharf in New Haven."

Meanwhile Niko bustled back and forth between the dining room table and the kitchen, bringing in various kinds of cold salads.

"Now what record will you have? *Hello, Dolly!* — with Pearl Bailey, Pearlie Mae? Bob Goulet and Carol Lawrence? Barbra Streisand!"

Niko imitated Streisand's exaggerated accents and sang a line from "Footsteps, in the Corners of My Mind," with theatrical gestures.

"Let's have Streisand! All right?

"Now, come to the table. Sit there. No, wait. I forgot, I have wine and grape vodka, both homemade at my mother's dacha. She's still exiled there, you know. No one tells her she can't go off. Maybe she could. Maybe, now that my stepfather Javakhishvili is dead, she could just move back to the city. No one tells her anything. Maybe she'd leave her prison. She might live in Tbilisi for six months. No one seems to care. But then one day, out of the blue, a knock might come on the door. 'You know very well, my good woman, that when you and your husband were exiled to the dacha it was forever. Why are you causing us trouble?' Then they'd move her to a camp somewhere. You've read *Gulag?*"

"Yes, some."

"It's all true. Today it is worse than ever. The whole country is a prison camp. Just to live here is to be in prison."

"Wait," Georgi said. "Bring the dinner, Niko."

"And the wine!" I urged.

We had stuffed cabbage and sauerkraut with sausages, khachapuri cheese bread, onions, carrots, tomatoes, and pickles. Soon Georgi wanted to open another bottle of champagne.

"Quick, drink up this champagne," Niko said. "Georgi, I told you to open champagne, it is true. But why didn't you ask *me* to show you how? We'll open another — in the fashion of the Georgian officers in the Soviet Air Force. First drain your glasses!

"Now, I take this knife — it must be sharp and it must have a heavy blade . . ."

With his left hand he grasped the bottle around the label, carefully pointing it away from the table while he tested the knife's edge on the hair of his left arm.

"Fine! Now" — he raised the knife — "one, two, three" — and he brought it down sharply on the neck. Suddenly there was a pop and the bottle foamed and bubbled over. Quickly, he poured some into our glasses. "Drink! It's like iced fire when it's opened this way."

He held the bottle for us to see. It was sliced smoothly

across the neck at a sharp angle. From the far corner he retrieved the cork, which was still embedded in the top of the neck.

"Hit it at the smallest part of the neck, and the knife will go through it like butter, the wine's gases will take the top right off."

"Let me try it," Georgi asked when the bottle was finished.

Niko laid his hand on Georgi's sleeve.

"I forgot to say that only a pilot can achieve it. I'm afraid *you'll* have to do it in the ordinary way."

He turned to me. "You just don't understand what this means to us. Let the KGB call us up tomorrow. Mr. Friendly didn't understand the significance of such a meeting either. 'It's wonderful to talk to an American,' I told him. I knew what he was thinking, that I was exaggerating, flattering him. When I told him later that the police called me because I talked to him, he said, 'You shouldn't take risks. We shouldn't have talked.'

"I said, 'What do we *have* but risks? If I *can't* talk to you I *am* dead. They can't keep me from talking.' But he didn't want to get involved. He wouldn't come back to visit me again. I know what he was thinking. He didn't want to be responsible for my death. Americans don't like to be responsible, they think that it is important for us to live — even if it's in chains. They don't want to be blamed for our deaths."

"We just want to see how you act, hear how you talk, how a free man behaves," Georgi said to me.

"Yes," his wife continued. "We *need* you, just as an example, a proof that there is some alternative, something else beside the Soviets."

"We *love* you," Niko said, reaching over to hold my arm. "We don't know you, but we love you. Why? Because we're slaves and you're free. We're slaves, slaves. You don't understand."

"This is boring for you," Isolda delicately said. "You sit and look at us and listen and yet say nothing."

"You don't need to talk. You're free to talk if you wish," Georgi said. "Us — they can make us talk whenever they wish. There are ways."

"Yes, we bore you," Niko chimed in. "But we love you. You are free and so you don't know you are free. We're slaves. It is a thing we know."

By this time the four of us had finished the Marlboros and I brought out a pack of Pall Mall 100s. I was smoking because the cigarettes kept me awake.

"But they're English cigarettes, aren't they?" Isolda asked.

"No, American," Georgi said. "I smoked them when I was in Egypt."

"You were in Egypt?" I asked.

"Yes, last year," Isolda answered. "I couldn't go with him, of course."

"What did you work at in Egypt, Georgi?"

"Translations. Many translators are needed there. The Russians are translating everything the Americans write, and making recordings of the American telephone conversations, naturally."

"This business of travel — to Egypt — to anywhere," Niko interrupted, "it's a little taste of freedom they give us, a bribe. Like saying, 'Be good and we'll let you out again sometime.' But it also lets us see with our eyes how things are elsewhere."

"It's an excellent way to accumulate certificate roubles, too," Georgi said. "Within two years I was able to buy my car."

"We bore you," Niko said. "Why don't you eat?"

"But," I said, "you yourself eat hardly anything."

"I'm too nervous. I'm your slave. I'm ready to perform any service for you. But we have nothing."

"In Moscow there are plenty of jokes about how much the Georgians have. The Muscovites call you capitalists."

"Moscow has everything. They take everything that's ours. Now they want to take our language away. Everything else may be taken from us. But when they try to take our language away, we'll fight."

"Didn't you know that the Communist Party offices here were bombed?" Isolda asked.

"And, of course, someone set fire to the opera house last year. Why do we need an opera house? To hear Tchaikovsky? To listen to Glinka? Our masters want us to sing in Russian. They sing everything in their gross language. Imagine singing *Carmen* in Russian? *Un Ballo in Maschera* in Russian! It's barbaric."

"Yes, they teach us Russian in school," Georgi continued. "We have to subscribe to *Pravda* and *Izvestia*. Why do we need these papers? — to wrap up fish? We're supposed to speak Russian. The Russians can't speak Georgian. It's too difficult for them. 'Such impossible sounds,' they wail. It gives them headaches."

"But you're free, you don't understand us," Niko said. "You'd like to help us. That's the way Americans are. But you can do nothing. You'd like to make contact with dissidents. But it's impossible. Who placed the bomb in Party headquarters? Who left a fire bomb in the proproom in the Paliashvili opera house? You'd like to help us to be free. But you can do nothing."

Georgi asked, "Aren't you acquainted with Raisa Orlova Koplev and her husband Lev? They're famous dissidents. They are the very ones, you know, responsible for smuggling Solzhenitsyn's manuscripts out into the west. These are the only kind of Russians worth knowing — those who know what it means to fight for freedom and to suffer."

"We have our fighters too," Niko said. "The Georgians have always been fighters. Probably you have heard that the Russians rounded up dissidents in Georgia. Perhaps you may even have heard one or two of their names mentioned, like Nathela Gachechiladze, Oisif Iankoshvili, Gregori Beliashvili. . . . Haven't you heard these names?"

I *did* know these names. All were on Roger Hellman's list, a list that was in my suitcase at this very moment. I almost held my breath.

"No. I've never heard those names at all."

"We thought perhaps your friend at the Embassy — what *is* his name, Isolda? — I think it is Robert Hillman — may have mentioned such fighters of Tbilisi to you. Don't you know that he came down to our city many times and spoke to many people here?"

"But I never met Hellman at all. He had been replaced months before I arrived in Moscow."

"You never met him, then?" Georgi asked dubiously.

"Never once."

"Well, we were wrong in thinking so," Niko said. "What does it matter? You think us children, anyway."

"What happened to those three you mentioned?"

"Who can be sure? Certainly they must be alive. You know how it is," Isolda answered.

Niko turned to the phonograph. "I forgot about Peggy Lee. Here's a record by Peggy."

"Dance with me," Isolda said, taking my hand and leading me into the vestibule. She put her arms around me. Like most Russian women she was not limp exactly, but soft. Dancing with her was a pleasure.

After a few songs Georgi came to dance with his wife. Niko handed me a brimming glass of champagne. From the dancing my head was in a whirl. He had dozens of questions about America and I answered them as best as I could. When I looked at my watch I saw that time had passed quickly. Already it was one o'clock in the morning.

Isolda came back with Georgi and took my hand again. This time we danced to an old Andy Williams record. We danced for a long time. Isolda cupped her two hands on the back of my neck.

My head had cleared but I felt stupid and tired. When the record was over we sat down and I said to Georgi, "I'd like to go back to the hotel. I'm awfully tired — exhausted. I hardly got any sleep last night."

"We bore you," Niko said.

As a matter of fact, he was beginning to bore me. But I simply reiterated my desire to go back to the hotel.

We walked outside and stood at the car, talking. Niko insisted on riding with us back to my hotel.

"But you'll be awake for the rest of the night cleaning up the mess we made," I pointed out.

"What does it matter? This is a special night, a great night for me."

"Let him come along," Georgi urged, "or he'll never let us leave."

Before we had proceeded two blocks, Niko directed Georgi to make a turn and to take us to the top of the mountain again.

A few hundred feet before we reached the crest Georgi turned the car lights off.

"There's no point in attracting attention," he explained.

We parked the Zhiguli and walked up some stone steps to a pavilion belonging to the funicular railway. We looked over the city. Georgi had insisted on staying with the car and Niko went back to keep him company.

Isolda was standing on my right side. She twined her arm in mine and leaned her head on my shoulder in such a little-girlish, natural way that she made me feel very tender toward her.

"Tomorrow night," she whispered, "Georgi has classes to prepare. He *must* stay home. But I know he would insist that I accompany you — well, wherever you wish me to take you. 'We love you,' as Niko says. Yes, certainly we all love you. It would be an honor — if you wanted me, I mean." She twisted toward me, pressing her breasts hard against my arm, and reached across my body to touch my left cheek with her fingertips.

From the direction of the car came a scuffle of voices.

"We'd better go and see," I said.

A policeman was arguing in Russian with Georgi and Niko when we came up to the car.

"It is true that this is a city park," the policeman said. "True, too, that no law is in the books against driving up here at night. But the question is: why would you come up here in the dark of the night if you didn't have something to hide? My instructions are to assume that anyone who does so is planning some illegal act."

Georgi inched over and whispered in my ear; "Please don't say anything. This is a mix-up. We wouldn't want him to know we have an American up here. Just keep quiet."

Isolda on the other side of me, twined both her arms around my right arm and held on tight.

"And, therefore," the watchman continued, "I advise you to leave this area immediately before I am obliged to act upon my assumption."

"You see how it is," Georgi moaned as he negotiated the curves down the hill, "it is not our own country anymore."

Niko added: "Who needs a demonstration of that? We

are simply slaves. Who could doubt it? You'd like to help us — but you can't. You're an American — you love freedom."

"But what can you do?" Isolda breathed.

"Why not meet us when we come to Moscow?" Niko suggested. "Let us meet at the Koplevs'. Do you know where their place is?"

"I've never been there. No."

"They live on Krasnoarmaskaya Ulitsa, number one, the first floor. I'll write it down for you."

He scribbled in a little notebook. "Oh, yes, it's near Metro Aeroport, not a long walk from the station. We'll be there in a week. Do meet us there, will you? Call them up." He mentioned their telephone number which I wrote on the slip he handed me.

"We'll be at your lecture tomorrow," they all said at the door of the hotel.

The night guard regarded us sullenly. He opened the door only enough for me to squeeze through, as if to show that he regarded arrival at one's hotel at 2:45 A.M. a deep impropriety.

I walked up to the fifth floor. The *dezhurnaya* was stretched out on one of the vinyl-covered couches facing the elevators. There was no need to wake her: the top drawer of the desk had been pulled out — possibly by another night owl — and I picked up my key and walked silently down the hall.

Just a step before my door I realized I should have made some noise earlier. The door opposite mine was wide open. Sitting on a wooden chair a few feet back from the entry was the same man whom I had seen moved into 712 and 612. Now he sat asleep in the doorway of room 512. Without intending to, I had come up to the door so quietly that I must have seemed to him, in his weariness, an illusion that had glided into his vision the way a wallpaper pattern begins to move if you stare at it long enough. He was awake but he didn't react at all to my appearance. His eyes were like pewter buttons. Was it possible to sleep, I wondered, with one's eyes open?

Then he did react — in the most unexpected way. He didn't start or flinch at all. His eyes simply clicked into focus and he stared at me for a few seconds without moving a hair.

He got up stiffly from his chair and walked to the doorway and stood before me. Sadly he shook his head from side to side, as if to say, "So, because I cannot complete my day's report until I note the time of your return, you keep me waiting for you until almost three in the morning. And besides depriving me of my rest, you insult me in my profession by creeping up on me like a thief."

Slowly he drew a notepad from his inside jacket pocket and turned the pages until he got to the last entry. He unscrewed the top of his pen and in heavy black ink wrote and underlined: "2:50 A.M." He made no attempt to conceal this notation: he wanted me to feel his exasperation with me; he must have hoped I would see how unfair to him I had been. Finally, moving only one arm while he continued to stare at me, he reached out, found the door, and shut it between us.

That was the last time I saw him. But the next day when I walked through the lobby on my way to breakfast, Marika was waiting for me. She took me to breakfast, escorted me to the university for my lecture, and remained to hear it. My three friends of the previous evening were not there, to my relief. Afterward she insisted on taking me to Mtskheta. She allowed me to wander alone about the ruined Jvari Temple. For a long time I lay in the grass in the shadow of the dome and watched the clouds move. Probably I slept a little, but if so, the passage

from wakefulness to sleep and back again occurred with
the same liquid ease with which the clouds scudded
across the sky.

Tbilisi was dark by the time we got back to the Iveria.
Marika left me at the elevator, promising to be waiting in
the lobby at five the next morning, when I would have to
leave for the airport. Along with my key I was handed a
package.

When I untied the string I found a note inside. "We are
sorry to have missed the pleasure of seeing you again
today. Here, as a special reminder of Georgia, are some
Georgian *churchkhelas,* made by dipping walnuts strung
on a thread into grape juice and flour. Rely on our love.
We'll see you in Moscow in a week. With respect, Niko."

4

A few days after my return I went to the Embassy to
pick up my mail and I ran into Lynn Noah, the head of the
cultural section.

"Well, how was it? Did you have a pleasant trip?" he
asked in his slightly stiff but pleasant fashion. Noah was a
China expert, perhaps a little misplaced in Moscow, but
with a charming wife.

"Fine. Samarkand was marvelous. So was Georgia
really. But I had a lot of company in Tbilisi."

"I don't understand. A lot of company?"

"Which reminds me," I continued. "Mr. Miller very
kindly gave me some books and magazines to take along."
I told him about what surprising items had tumbled out of
the package in Samarkand.

"Of course," Noah said, "they *should* have been looked

at more thoroughly before being wrapped up. But so many of our magazines have something in them the Soviets might consider offensive."

I went on and sketched out the scrutiny my every move had gotten in Tbilisi.

"I see," he said and thought for a while. "The trouble was Hellman. You know, he made several trips to Georgia."

"Yes, Miller gave me a list from Hellman's old files of people he had met."

"I guess Bob didn't quite understand about Roger. I'll talk to him. It's unfortunate, of course, that you got caught up in a series of accidents that had nothing to do with you. I realize now that you are the first American we've sent down since Hellman was there. He went down and distributed American novels and contacted lots of intellectuals in the institutes for humanities and foreign languages. Well, to put it simply, I suppose the authorities in Georgia may have thought that he was — I don't say he was — attempting to contact and aid people who were at least suspected of holding dissident views. I'm not — repeat, *not* — saying that Hellman was a" — here Noah paused and drew cryptic scrawls in the air with his forefinger that I could scarcely read backward and merely guessed to be "CIA" — "but in any event the Soviets are very touchy in Georgia. We've heard of lots of protests around Tbilisi. It's explosive there now, and the Russians thought that Hellman contributed to the trouble. Through channels, in any event, we were asked to replace him — rather than have him expelled."

"So you sent me down there — with subversive literature — with a typed-up list in my suitcase of those people Hellman had met, probably all revolutionaries. Naturally the KGB informers would have found the list when they searched my suitcase, as they always do. It must have seemed obvious to them that I was his replacement in whatever they believed his mission had been. I am given a list of people who, whether they're dissidents or not, are at least suspected of being troublemakers. And you don't even give me one word of warning."

"Perhaps it *was* careless," Noah conceded tentatively. "But isn't it better that you knew nothing? The fact that you were completely innocent kept you out of trouble."

"Innocent, yes. But I had plenty of chances to make a mistake. Better say lucky."

5

Two days later when I answered the telephone I recognized Niko's voice.

"We've just come up — yes, the three of us — for a flying visit. Tomorrow evening we have a chance to go to Raisa Koplev's. She's dying to meet you. I'll get a taxi and pick you up."

"All right," I said at once.

"How did you enjoy the *churchkhelas,* then?"

"I ate one on the plane going back, and I gave the other to a Georgian student of mine."

"The Russians think that these confections are some variety of fruit. They think they grow on trees. When they visit Tbilisi, they ask to see the *churchkhelas* trees. But this is no time for criticizing Russians. All people who love freedom must join together. I am told that several prominent people will be visiting Rai. To whet your appetite, let me just name one: Nadezhda Yakovlevna Mandelstam will be present."

"I never expected to meet her before my departure. This will be a great pleasure."

"When do you leave Russia, by the way?"

"Not until the middle of June, after the diplomas are given out at the university."

"Not for about three weeks, then?"

"Yes."

We arranged a time to meet on the next day and exactly on the hour Niko rang me from the lobby.

"Will you come up?" I asked.

He managed to convey a sense of urgency. "No, join me as quickly as you can. I have a taxi. Georgi and Isolda are waiting at Rai's apartment for us."

When I stepped outside Building B, Niko was leaning over by the driver's side talking to him through the slightly opened window. All official taxis in Moscow are painted the same sickly shade of green, and I was rather surprised to see that Niko had made the mistake of arriving in a black Volga.

Quickly we drove north. As we turned left at the river I pointed out the dacha once occupied by Josef Stalin.

Niko chattered inconsequentially, full of surprise that I had never met the Koplevs.

A block before we reached our destination Niko circumspectly ordered the driver to let us out, as if we were engaged on a secret mission whose danger I should feel. We walked to a massive postwar building where, he said, the Koplevs had their apartment. Stores occupied the first floor entirely. To visit Lev Koplev — the model for Rubin in *First Circle* — and Nadezhda Mandelstam in an apartment situated above a furniture store and a dairy seemed ludicrous.

A young woman opened the door. Her blond hair was cut in bangs in imitation of the poet Bella Akhmadulina.

"Niko," she said, "it's fine to see you."

"Let me present Professor Martin to you. This is Natalya Gorbanyevsky. She is our finest young woman poet. I say this with certitude."

"I'm very happy to see an American here. Come, you must meet Rai."

The poet took my arm and led me to a pleasant-looking middle-aged woman. "Here is Dr. Martin, whom Niko brought, Rai. Raisa Orlova Koplev."

She held out a strong hand to me. "I've heard of your books on American writers. I hope you've read some Russian literature worthy of your notice. If not, let me assure you, there are a number of dissident writers to whom I would be happy to introduce you. But you've already met them on your own, eh?"

The apartment was plain and drab. It walls were covered with a heavy material, embossed and painted mustard brown. The furniture was scarred and moth-eaten.

"To tell the truth," I said, "I've been kept so busy preparing lectures that I haven't had time or occasion to meet many people outside the university."

"That's most unfortunate," she said wearily. "But please believe me, here, in this apartment, we can speak freely — and we do. Notice the walls: that is stamped tin which covers them. Impossible to bug through that. At no time, moreover, is this apartment left unattended: we keep watch to be sure that no listening devices are planted here. The windows are double-paned. We like our music — as you notice — good and loud. We take precautions. You are among friends."

She said to the woman poet; "Please take Dr. Martin into the 'throne room.' That is what we call our poor alcove when Nadezhda Yakovlevna Mandelstam occupies it. She's incredible, you know. She really is our queen. I think you'll find your Georgian friends in her court just now. I'll join you there in a few moments. I have a few questions concerning recent American literature which I hope you may answer for me."

There were probably four or five little rooms in the apartment. But they were all so clogged with stuff that distinctions between rooms originally intended for different purposes had been lost. In one tiny room a dining table and some chairs were pushed against the wall; in another, a day bed, night stand, and dresser were placed. But in all the rooms, books and newspapers and manuscripts, boxes of pencils, blank paper, sketches, paintings, magazines, teacups and plates, bouquets of dried flowers, maps, rolled-up posters, pots of ivy, and other paraphernalia were stuffed and piled and squeezed, until each room resembled all the others.

As she led me along the entry hall, pausing here and there to emphasize a point in conversation, Miss Gorbanyevsky spoke about modern American writers whom she admired. She mentioned Lowell and Mailer. She seemed to know that I had written a little book on Lowell.

"I'm sure you recall Lowell's imitations of Yevtushenko and Voznesensky," Natalya Gorbanyevsky said. "How do they seem to you?"

"I think they must be very good."

"Certainly they are better than the originals, believe me. Lowell is a clever fellow. He knows how to make a thing appealing. He'd be a good propagandist. He deceives himself. They're just not as good as he makes them out."

"But they've written fine things, don't you think?"

"They've written what you've wanted to hear. They are allowed to appear rebellious because they are so good at deceiving you."

"And Lowell's translation of Mandelstam?"

"Less good than the original, of course. The others are idea-men, advertising men. But Osip Mandelstam — his language was unexcelled — perfect. Besides he was a man of courage. What an example of courage he is to us all!"

She paused only a flicker and then added, "That's all I wanted to say to you. Beware of imitations. And one more thing: courage is not easy, even for a Mandelstam."

A door at the end of the hallway opened and Isolda stepped through it. She seized my hand.

"How good that you could meet us here! It's a long way from Tbilisi."

"I was truly sorry," I said, "not to have seen you again — you especially — before leaving the city."

"I see you're talking to our famous poet," Isolda said. "Perhaps someday, Natalya, you will be a visiting professor in the United States and can to talk to Professor Martin there, in his university in California."

"But I," Natalya said with a gasp, "I could never leave the Russian soil."

"Let me bring our guest to meet Nadezhda Yakovlevna. Then I'll return to you," Isolda said to her. She took me through a door into a sleeping alcove separated from the larger room by an Indian print curtain. The alcove was poorly lighted by a shaded wall fixture and a single candle burning before a large icon in one corner. Three men stood up. A frail old woman lounged on a sofa bed. A knitted afghan, unraveling at one end, was wrapped about the lower half of her body. She was obviously the center of attention. Georgi came over.

"Please," he said, "allow me. This is Professor Martin, about whom I have been speaking. Foremost among our distinguished company is our incomparable Nadezhda Ya-kovlevna Mandelstam."

The lady lowered her eyelids and wrinkled the corners of her mouth.

"And here is Yergeny Barabanov, our art historian, who

is quite out of favor with the authorities for the part he played in publishing *From Under the Boulders* with Solzhenitsyn. And here, also, is Anatoli Marchenko. He too is a dissident whose name you may recognize."

Both men glanced at me as we were introduced, then dropped their eyes to the floor. But Madame Mandelstam beckoned to me.

"What do you think of Solzhenitsyn?" she inquired in a surprisingly vigorous and melodious voice, when I came to the side of her lounge.

"He's a brave man, I think."

"A good answer. Yes, he is brave. But not a great writer, don't you agree? What good will his bravery do him now? His sort of courage was only necessary when assassination or death in the camps threatened him. Now what will he do — go to live in Hollywood? Write for the movies? Narrate travelogues about Russia for your television stations?"

"I'm surprised to hear you speak so strongly against him."

"Not against him. Against his departure. He should have died before agreeing to leave. He could have done more for our movement by dying than by living and writing his one book over and over again. He was single-minded, a monk, a hermit. But he *could* have died. What a furor it would have caused!

"*My* husband went to the camps. He had much to write yet. *He* was a man of genius. Your friend Mr. Toradze here has generously called me incomparable. But I am nothing. Do you know my books, *Hope Against Hope* and *Hope Abandoned?* I am really telling the story of a great man, my husband, much greater than the army of weak-kneed rebels who criticize the system like little sparrows pecking at a marble statue.

"To be sure," she added graciously, "there are a few

exceptions. Yevgeny here — he lost his job, he lost a great deal. Officially he doesn't exist. But, if he steps out of line — even by being in this room listening to an old lady ramble . . . and Anatoli — he is a saint, aren't you, Anatoli? He's been to the camps. He knows what suffering is. Even now, he isn't permitted to be in Moscow. But in this place, outside the city's outer circle, and just for an afternoon's visit, well, the authorities will wink . . . so long as he makes no trouble."

"No one could aspire to the courage of your husband," Marchenko whispered hoarsely.

"Mr. Martin," Barabanov said, as if he feared to say even this much, "I've read some of your essays. I can't agree with all you say. But you've kept your integrity, at least."

"Now boys, leave me alone with our guest," Mrs. Mandelstam said, waving them into the next room. They left. Only Georgi hovered in the background.

"Yes, my husband was a special man. Killed just for writing a poem about Stalin! Even now only a few of his poems have been published. I am afraid to release the rest for publication in any part of the world.

"But I have scholars helping me. I get the poems out, don't ask me how. They can't murder those writings. They make their way. I am not worried about them.

"On another occasion I might have asked you to copy out some of Osip's verses and scatter them through your own papers as you depart our country. I could dictate them to you, I have them memorized. But I have something much more important to ask of you.

"My husband must live not only in his work, but also in his spirit — a spirit of defiance of the state that represses and tries to destroy the soul and hope of man. That is why we must do everything possible to unify the dissident forces in our country.

"What a hell it is here. Fighters for freedom in Odessa have no way of joining with their counterparts in Riga. Those in Bratsk never meet those in Perm. The dissidents of Kharkov — what do they know of those in Kirghizia? The KGB are everywhere, more than ever. Now it's war to the death. Few can be trusted.

"That is precisely why this apartment, Raisa Orlova's apartment, is so crucial to everything. Here everyone is trusted. Here dissidents from every part of our country meet and make contact. Here the revolution grows.

"For instance, our dear friends, Georgi and his wife Isolda, and Niko Mezrulvili are fighting, as my husband did, for freedom. Yet — just to speak of their cases for a moment — they've both been out of the country and they can't find a way to join with the underground movement in Georgia. Georgia is very far from here, as you know. And the Georgians are suspicious of outsiders.

"Here is where we need your help. Won't you help to put them in contact with the dissident movement in Georgia? Surely your predecessor, Mr. Hellman, passed on information that would be of some use."

"But I don't know what you mean."

"Names, places — that sort of thing. If only Mr. Toradze had *some* information he would be able to become a part of the fight for freedom. He'd find the leaders."

"I'm sure he would. He's very clever," I said as I smiled sweetly at Georgi. "But I really don't know anything."

"Did you ever hear my husband's poem? —

In bitter May, month of delusions,
break, as nature breaks the ropes
of ice that chained the trees,
break your heart, your fears
your whole being,
and be as defiant as truth.

Won't you help us all, Professor Martin, by helping our friends? Think about it." She lifted her fine hand to me to be held and kissed.

"Yes, leave me now. I must talk to Georgi, ask a special question of him. Go and have a drink. Talk to Raisa Orlova. Then come back to me."

I thanked her and went through the curtain. Outside, Isolda took my arm.

"Come over and say a few words to Lev Koplev, Raisa's husband. He's a great Brecht scholar, you know, besides being Solzhenitsyn's friend."

To my surprise she led me to a man whom I recognized. He was engaged in conversation with Niko.

"It's my pleasure to introduce Professor Martin to you, Lev Koplev."

I looked hard at him.

"This is certainly an unexpected pleasure," he said. "Niko only now told me that you were visiting Nadezhda Yakovlevna, Professor. I hope it was a pleasant meeting."

"Perfectly. So, you are a scholar of German culture?"

"Yes." He spoke a little nervously. "Why don't you let me get you a drink. Some juice perhaps?"

Niko said, "Surely Jay would prefer something tastier — a little vodka or some brandy."

"I really would prefer juice, you know."

"Let me bring it to you," the man introduced to me as Koplev said.

Raisa Orlova, who had come in from another room, offered me a plate with some bread and sliced meat on it.

"Lev recently said to me how grateful we are for your presence in Moscow. We don't go out in public, you understand, or we would have come to some of your lectures. To have Americans here, speaking in public — it can't help but foster still greater freedom. This is the very reason why I have chosen American literature as my special field. Even to write of an American book can be a revolutionary act. You — you are our hope incarnate."

I took the juice offered to me and busied myself eating and drinking while listening to the rebellious chatter of the others.

"I'm afraid that I have lectures to prepare tonight," I remarked as I wiped my fingers. "But I told Mrs. Mandelstam that I would come back and say a few words to her before I left. Mr. Koplev, will you come with me and make sure she's finished her conversation before I go in? You'll do that for me, won't you?"

I drew him with me, separating him from the others.

"I'd really like to have a long conversation with you about Brecht sometime," I said, loud enough for the others to hear.

Then as low as I could whisper I added, "Tomorrow afternoon — around two — at the cafeteria?"

"Certainly," he answered loudly. "Yes, such a talk would be a pleasure for me too. I'm grateful to you."

With one hand he pushed the curtain aside.

"Do go in," he said.

"Well, Professor," Mrs. Mandelstam said, "have you considered how you wish to aid our cause? Let me tell you a parable. Once there was a young king who possessed many jewels. He divided them between his two sons. One son guarded his treasure diligently. He devoted his life to standing guard over it, and it is said that he lived to a very old age. He was a famous, wealthy man while he lived. The other son behaved in the opposite fashion. No sooner did he receive his inheritance than he began to give it to the needy. To one and all he gave freely, so that soon his vault was empty. He died a pauper, unnoticed, buried in an unmarked grave. But when these two princes were dead, the miserly man of wealth was forgotten immediately, while the generous pauper became famous in every part of the world. As you perceive, the first son is the 'loyal' Soviet citizen, afraid to talk, to join with others, to expose himself. The other son is like my husband, like Osip Mandelstam, giving away everything, even his life, dying an anonymous death in an unknown labor camp. The question for any man is — isn't it? — what kind of fortune he has and whether he will not use it for the benefit of others. What do you choose?"

Her voice had risen dramatically and, for a woman who pretended to be frail, she gestured and moved vigorously. At her last words she rose and stood erect before me, tottering. Georgi, who had remained standing at the foot of her bed, regarded me intently.

"I'm sorry to say, however, that I have nothing to give."

"Then — " Instead of finishing her sentence, she turned her face away and waved her hand in dismissal.

"Niko," I said when I came out, "there's no need, really, to drive me back to the city. I know precisely where the Metro is, and I prefer the walk."

Niko became entirely indifferent. "As you wish," he muttered and drank off his vodka.

I said goodbye to them all, but every person there seemed tired, like ballerinas after the final curtain of *Swan Lake,* hardly interested in my own departure or even in each other.

"Thank you for your hospitality in allowing me to visit your home, Mr. Koplev," I said to the man who showed me to the door.

"I'm sorry you could not stay longer."

"Personally, I'm glad."

"I see what you mean," he said and closed the door.

Actually I did want to walk. This part of Leningrad Prospekt was a mixed residential and shopping area. Shining like beacons in the darkness, the twin glass towers of the Hotel Aeroflot and the Ministry of Civil Aviation dominated the skyline. Below them the avenue widened; a landscaped parkway ran down its center. If I walked far enough toward the city the avenue would eventually become Gorky Street and lead to Mayakovsky Square and the Hotel Peking.

This was the approach to Moscow by which Hitler's troops intended to take the city. His armies had been stopped by Moscow's tanks just a few miles to the north. Along the same avenue Napoleon had left Moscow, after resting at the Petrovsky Palace just a few blocks away. The imperial armies had come and gone: they destroyed some things, but they had certainly left few traces.

I walked as far as the gigantic Dynamo Soccer field and found the Metro station. Before descending into it, for a few moments I looked at the great empty shell of the stadium. All the cheering was over. Not an echo remained, only a few scraps of uncollected debris from the last match.

6

Despite what I had told my Georgian friends, I had reservations for a compartment in the Polish car on the train to Warsaw for the very next day.

Tatjana knew my plans, for I had called to ask her to arrange for a taxi to the station. She was bubbling over at her success in her exams and already planning a paper that she had been invited to deliver at a conference in the Gorky Institute. Actually, ever since our excursion to Abramtsevo I had seen very little of Tatjana. Officially she was busy at her studies, but I figured that she may have been directed to stay away from me for reasons I could only guess at. And so I made no demands on her. But she declared her intention to ride to the station with me; and so I asked her to have the car come at two-thirty, which would give us an hour to say our last goodbyes.

I liked Marya better than anyone else in Moscow and naturally I planned to spend the last of my "Moscow Nights" with her.

Even ten days in advance I hadn't been able to secure a reservation for two at the downstairs restaurant in the Hotel Peking — some sort of congress or other was occupying the hotel. So much for the legendary Friendship Salad!

But as it turned out Marya had her own special ideas about how we must spend our last hours together. She made it a little secret drama and gave me a number on Tsvetnoi Boulevard where I should meet her at six-thirty.

As I walked down the street, even from a considerable distance I could pick her out of the crowds in her loose, light blue jersey dress. A breeze pressed it against her body and flared it out behind her. The sun flashed for an instant on a blue and gold silk scarf that I had gotten from Paris for her. I knew she'd be wearing it in her favorite manner, around her neck like a western bandanna. But she held herself in such a special way that even had I never before seen the dress or the scarf I would have instantly recognized her from far away. Somehow she always seemed to be both calm and expectant, at rest and tense, like a stringed instrument. That was it — she was quiet and vibrant at the same moment.

I came up to her and we embraced very fleetingly. She made a soft murmuring, humming noise in my ear and when our faces drew apart she was smiling as if it were her birthday.

"You look wonderful," I said.

"Well, I feel Parisian tonight," she answered, referring

to the bright Yves St. Laurent scarf. "How do you like my
choice?" She pointed to the building where we stood.
Family groups were streaming into the entrance.

The word over the door wasn't in my vocabulary but
there was no doubt where we were.

"Never, never, never," I said, "did I imagine that I'd
spend my last evening in Moscow at the circus. It's
perfect!"

"Yes, come on, then," she said, taking my arm and
holding it tightly, as she always did, "I have the tickets.
It's my *treat*" — she used the English word, sounding for
all the world like a high school girl out on a Coca-Cola
date.

It *was* perfect. We had the best seats — best for us,
that is, since we were in the last row and there were plenty
of empty spaces in front of us. We said silly things to each
other and other things that we meant seriously, but we
mixed them with our comedy and made them seem less
serious for the moment. Somehow, because we were at
the circus we found we could say anything — not just because no one would overhear us there, but because it was
the finest place in the world to say goodbye to someone
you cared about and were leaving forever.

I told her a long, tediously funny story about a party
where I had accepted a challenge to eat the most blini
with sprats — sprats from the Black Sea, sprats from the
Caspian Sea, sprats with lemon, sprats with oil — each
worse tasting than the previous kind. And she told me a
much funnier story about the adventures that a friend of
hers had had while smuggling a truckload of prerevolu-
tionary oriental carpets out of Russia.

We talked about Sartre and Marcel Marceau, and
Marya improvised a very amusing theory, which she called
the "Theory of the Mistake."

"Take us," she said, "we were not meant to meet: Mistake Number One. Or to sleep together: Number Two. And Mistakes Three and Four and a hundred, up to . . . say, countless mistakes. Here, in the Soviet Union, our machines are perfect, our computers never make a mistake, the Party is flawless. But we, so long as *we* continue to make mistakes, we are authentic — or, at least full of errors — which is to say, still human. Maybe my theory itself is mistaken — if so, all the better!''

After intermission all the acts involved dressed-up clownish bears — bears on bicycles, bears in wheelbarrows, bears in barrels, bears dancing with bears, bears fighting and bears kissing. We cheered the bears and ate each other's ice cream and held hands.

In our own way we did say goodbye there in the back row of the circus while the Russian bears did their stunts. By the time we walked out toward Marya's Metro stop nothing more needed to be said.

If I had asked her to come back to my apartment to spend the night she would have come, of course; but I understood that her choice had been right and I merely drew her into the shadows beside the entrance to the Metro and we held each other for a moment.

"Call me, then, before you leave, won't you?" she asked as she skipped off prettily into the light of the entryway. "I plan to stay home with a cold tomorrow."

The door swung closed behind her. It's the worst thing about doors, that they're always closing.

XI
Exit, Pursued by a Bear

My last night in Moscow was filled with bears. For some reason which I could no longer remember when I awoke, in my dreams I was determined to search behind every scrap of drapery in Moscow and a bear was hiding behind each curtain. In the middle of the night I woke up and drank the last bit of lemon vodka in the apartment, but it did no good. My dreams of bears continued when I went back to sleep. The problem was, I guess, that I still had to ask Lev Dahl one more question before I left.

In the morning I called Tatjana Efimovna and asked her to have the taxi arrive an hour earlier than we had planned. Then I called Marya.

"*Do svidaniya,*" I said when I heard her voice, "I hope your cold will be better soon."

"Your accent is still terrible," she replied.

"And you have the nicest accent in Moscow, so it's the pupil who must be to blame."

"Yes, he is. Jay, darling, you'll never know how much I liked you, deeply liked you. But" — she added quickly — "I think I'll always be a mystery to you — like Malevsky."

When we finished talking I packed my bag and ate a chocolate bar and read a translation of *The Knight in Panther's Skin* while I waited for Tatjana. We drove to the Byelorussian Station, where I removed my bags from the trunk and brought them to the waiting room. I asked Tatjana, as a last favor, to watch over them for a short time. I had kept the car and when we arrived at the Hotel Peking, I tipped the driver again to wait outside.

Lev Alexandrovich Dahl came to my table soon after I sat down in the cafeteria.

"I was watching for your arrival across the street in the shadows of the pillars of the Concert Hall," he said.

Gingerly he changed the subject. "Won't it ever warm up? You've seen a real Moscow winter. But you've seen no spring at all. Perhaps spring will still come in before you leave."

"I'm leaving today, by the four o'clock train to Warsaw."

"But that Georgian, the Mezrulvili fellow, thinks you are staying another three weeks. I heard him tell the others so after you left the apartment. I think that they plan to try something else on you. They're sure you're a CIA agent and that eventually you'll trust them with names of dissidents. They are really very desperate. And very naive."

"I don't suppose you'd call and tell them, after I leave you, that I am taking the overnight train?"

"You know I can't. Obviously, I would find it impossible to extricate myself if I informed on you. I'm completely stalled in every way."

"I count on that, naturally. But tell me, shall I call you Mr. Koplev? Lev Koplev or Lev Dahl? How did you become an expert on Bertolt Brecht and German culture overnight? What a surprise it was to see you impersonating Koplev. Never mind. What I really want to know — and it's *all* I want to know — is whether the others were all actors too, all of them? And did you hire them all, just like making up a variety show?"

"It was, in any event," he said, "a show that fell flat on

its face. Still, Martin, you were a wonderful audience. You were fine. You acted your own part and, like a good, polite audience, applauded just as if you had been taken in all the time. At least you spared the actors, you fooled the players by pretending to believe them. And you saved me."

"And you must still satisfy my curiosity, one last time."

"Actually I can't answer your question about *all* the actors in the drama. Some mystery must remain. I'll tell you all I can. You'll have to accept what I tell you. If you are really leaving today, you haven't time to give me a third degree, you know. That takes days — and a rubber hose. So you'll have to accept what I tell you.

"Your Georgian friends are convinced that you are a clever agent. If they had asked me — if they had known enough *to* ask me — I would have told them you are a charming fellow, a writer, a critic — nothing else. But they never asked me. They believed that you held the key to solving all the problems that faced them with the dissident movement in Tbilisi. They were in a tough spot. The opera house was burned, the C.P. offices were bombed, fires were started in the basement of the City Soviets building. These things scared them. They had to locate the rebels — or lose their own jobs.

"They were worried, and they were, of course, stupid. From the time the Ministry of Culture informed the Tbilisi KGB that a person connected with American literature was coming to lecture at the Institute, they assumed they would soon have Hellman's replacement in their clutches. They were probably jumping with joy: a solution seemed to have fallen out of the sky. They formed what they thought was a clever ruse, to befriend you — you, a simple American — and get your secrets.

"You look at those fellows and you can almost see the wheels spinning behind their glazed-over eyes. Hellman had certainly made important contacts with the dissident leaders. He made lots of trouble, or got it started. Then he got out in plenty of time. When the bombing trouble started and they realized that he had not come to Tbilisi merely to show slides and give books away, he was relaxing at his desk in the Embassy, quite safe.

"Soviets use the same plans, and make the same mistakes, over and over. And so they assumed you would act the same way Hellman did. In any event, they believed that you were a new Hellman, a new bear performing old tricks.

"I listened to them talk you over after you left the apartment. So, you refused to accept a hotel room — two or three rooms? — that were filled with electronic surveillance devices? They said that somehow you spotted the bugging instantly. You insisted on changing rooms. You destroyed subversive literature in your room instead of giving it away. These things all gave them further reason to think that you must be a master spy. Once they had that idea fixed in their heads, anyway, everything you did seemed to confirm their suspicions. If you had done the opposite it would have been the same.

"To get your secrets they would have tried anything. They thought they *were* trying everything. They did their best. The woman — "

"Was she, Isolda, really Toradze's wife?"

"Of course not. But she would certainly have slept with you if that would have done the trick. So would Toradze, for that matter, if he had found you inclined that way."

"And they were KGB?"

"Yes and no. Party members certainly. Niko may have been a real agent. The other two? — maybe administrators in the Institute, lecturers, translators. After all, they had to be fairly well informed on the arts, they had to deck

out an American apartment. Homesickness and champagne often mix together. Especially for Americans.
You're such a shallow nation, aren't you? The easiest way
to gain the confidence of an American is to tell him you
love his country — that's the very thing that would raise
the suspicions of the citizens of every other nation.

"Be that as it may. They did everything they could.
They watched you like buzzards. They had one triumph — a great one, which only made them all the more
ferocious to have you reveal everything. Apparently they
found a list of dissidents when they searched your luggage. They knew these must be dissidents because only a
few days previously they had caught three of the people on
the list planting plastic bombs in the Palace of Pioneers.
That list confirmed all their suspicions. They didn't even
stop to ask how someone they believed to be so clever
could be so stupid as to carry typed lists of dissidents
around. So, they rounded up the people on the list and
they were busy with them — grilling them — until you
left. They couldn't get back to you. They lost you.

"But they had provided for that. Indeed they had even
concluded that you would be more comfortable and more
easily cajoled into revealing something to them on your
home ground, in Moscow. They had planted the germ of
meeting you in a famous dissident's apartment, where
you'd feel free. They had to create a dissidents' meeting
to tempt you, just the way they created an American
apartment to make you nostalgic and talkative. This is
where I came in.

"I will confess that I have arranged a few such charades
in the past. It is a special kind of entertainment, isn't it? It
looks hard, but think about it and you'll see that so long as
the conversation remains general it's not difficult to im-
personate any famous person. I did hire a few people to

play the parts. As you suggested, it is not very different from putting on a variety show. Indeed, I believe I once mentioned to you the name of Anna Merchuli, the old actress who gives a dramatic performance about meeting Chaliapin.

"She played Nadezhda Mandelstam. Wasn't she perfect? Didn't she do it well? Naturally, I wasn't there to hear her — but later she herself told me that to speak to you as she did, to sing her song of freedom as it were, almost moved her to tears at the very end. I understand she even improvised some Mandelstam-like verses on the spot. Yes, her own invention. But she got carried away and forgot herself — she ignored the fact, which everyone knows, that Nadezhda Mandelstam is infirm, and leaped up before you. Actually, she also forgot that her broken hip wasn't mended completely, she got so involved in her part. Now she's back in the hospital. She always plays her parts with real conviction.

"I got Natasha Ulyanova, the xylophone performer, to play Raisa. Actually, the two of us really were married at one time. And I played Koplev — an excellent role for a man of culture.

"But our Georgian KGB had neglected to say who it was we were supposed to perform for. There was nothing unusual about that. Why should actors know the names of their audience? To play our roles satisfactorily is all even the KGB can ask.

"So when I came into the room and saw you, I almost fainted. I wished I *could* have fainted, I felt so completely chilled — right to the bone. But I was in a sweat also. After the trouble I had gotten in over not reporting your contacts with Andrei Nikolaivich I would have been a dead man if you had sauntered over to me and asked bluntly, 'What's going on here, Dahl?' On the other hand, once you addressed me as Koplev, pretending not to recognize me, if our acquaintance had later slipped out, it would have seemed all too obvious that we were in cahoots."

"And the others who were there? Who were they?"

"That's the mystery I leave for you. *I* didn't hire them. The Georgian agents arranged that. All I *can* tell you is that the woman was indeed Natalya Gorbanyevsky. She has a child to raise. Compromises may be required of her sometimes. Once she wrote astonishing lyrics. In her youth she *was* daring — a Valkyrie.

"Oh, by the way, I believe that the apartment may have really belonged to Lev and Raisa Koplev. Probably they were brought into Moscow for questioning while we used their place.

"About the two other men, I'm not sure. Maybe they were informers — maybe the real thing. But they *were* very quiet. They asked permission to go soon after you did, and they left quietly, without goodbyes, as soon as permitted. Perhaps they were authentic personages — playing the roles of themselves. Most of us play a part these days. And at the end of everything is mystery.

"You are a mystery to our friends, in any event. By now you are a legend in Georgia. Probably they'll make a movie about how they caught you. The Georgians love motion pictures. After a while that's how they'll believe it happened; they'll believe they did catch you. Georgians are that way.

"They made only one mistake, a common one here. They assumed you were guilty."

"They made another," I said, "believing that I told the truth when they asked about my departure. They could have checked. I've had my tickets for over a week."

"That was the fault of their pride. Like children wearing dress-ups, they never imagined that you could see completely through their disguises. They never supposed you'd lie about a simple thing like that."

I got up to go. "I'm not sure I should shake hands with you," I remarked sternly, "when I'm still not certain that you weren't the one who informed on Andrei."

"Or, perhaps, I was the one to save you. But," he smiled and put out his hand, "since your train leaves in less than forty minutes — "

"Yes, I must accept the mystery."

"And that's to accept, perhaps, everything, just everything. And isn't *that* why you really came here?"

"The mystery," I said, and shook his hand.

When I was halfway across the room to the door, I heard him call out, "Martin!" I turned around swiftly.

He still sat at the table, grinning. Then he made a fist, with the thumb pointing up to the sky, and he jerked his hand and thumb upward.

Just like Tyrone Power in *Dawn Patrol*, I thought — acting to the last.

I got back to the station shortly before three o'clock and found Tatjana waiting patiently, consuming a sweet roll with *pivo* — beer.

"I want to tell you before you leave," she said, "that my plan has been changed. I've been promised a job."

"In Moscow, you mean?"

"Yes, it's a dream. I'm to work in the U.S.A. Institute as soon as my examinations are finished.

"On literature? To work on literature?" The U.S.A. Institute seemed like a strange place for anyone but a political scientist.

"Well, yes and no. I'm to read the productions of your liberationists and assess the revolutionary potential of women in America."

"Our student revolutionaries disappointed you, I know. Perhaps our women will do better."

She changed the subject slightly. "I know that you spoke to Alexander Golyarchik at the Institute on my behalf. It was very important to me in getting accepted."

"I simply told him you were the cleverest person in Moscow. I'm sure I had no influence at all; but I am surprised that you heard about our conversation, especially since it was held in the apartment of the Embassy's Air Force attaché."

"Alexander Ivanovich himself told me about it. He's charming, isn't he? And very powerful. And he looks like Jack London. I have you to thank, I'm sure, for scattering the seed that started everything moving there."

"I have you to thank, too, for several fine excursions — and good advice — and particularly for that wonderful day at Abramtsevo."

"I've disposed of them all, you know, all the supplies I traded for that day. You wouldn't believe the demand in Moscow."

"And I've sent my two portraits back in the mail."

"You won't have any trouble at the border, I'm sure."

"Not unless the guards are worried about the notebook I've kept during this trip."

"Train travelers are seldom bothered. I know you'll be all right."

"And so will you," I said. "I'm confident that within a few years you'll be part of a big cultural delegation to the United States or else get a fellowship to study at Columbia or Stanford. I've no doubt we'll meet again — and I promise to take you on a tour of Hollywood."

Tatjana's eyes had a rare, faraway look for an instant. I knew she was estimating the probabilities of what I had suggested. I had really meant it too, and her calculations must have come out on the positive side of her imaginative scales, for she smiled and said, "Yes, and to a California swap-meet."

We walked toward the Polish car, which was now available for boarding.

When we reached the steps, she hesitated for a moment, the only time I ever saw her embarrassed, and then she reached into her bag and pulled a big Zenit camera out of it and asked the steward of the sleeping car to take our photograph together.

"It's all right?" she said, a little dubiously, as she posed herself next to me. "You don't mind?"

"Not if you'll send me a copy," I whispered, trying to keep my mouth unmoving for the photo. Tatjana stood very straight in front of the camera.

"I'll go into your compartment with you," she remarked after she collected her camera. "Just for a minute."

Inside we sat on the seat that I would later make into a bed.

"First, we'll kiss like Americans," she said. "And now, like Soviets, say farewell. Be quiet, sit still for a moment, without talking, simply thinking of each other. It's like the prayers that Russians used to say for departing travelers. It's what we do instead of prayers."

After a minute she was satisfied with this ritual. "Well, that's it," she said and jumped up decisively. "Oh," she said, diving into her bag again and producing a carefully wrapped parcel, "this is from Elena — she says you will need it on the trip."

When she left a moment later I looked out my window and, as she passed it below me on the platform, she gave me a little wave and a quick blink of her big eyes and then swept on to her other errands.

I unwrapped Elena's bon voyage package and placed its contents on the window table — a thick slice of sausage, a can of Vietnamese pineapple, a roll, and a cough medicine bottle filled with brandy. My last Russian meal. I knew that tomorrow in Warsaw I'd be feasting on the best duck in the world at the Kamienne Schodki, but Elena's simple offering drove even that prospect out of my mind.

The train sped south across the glittering Moskva, now festooned with bunting and plowed by gay excursion boats. Then we turned west and eventually the night came on.

I opened my notebook. Tucked in the back were shreds of paper and cards and envelopes on which I had scribbled the history of my encounters.

If I were to write about my life in Russia, how would I choose among all my experiences? Would there be a place to give an account of my day at Abramtsevo or the even earlier and funnier trip when Tatjana and I went to the Russian Hut in search of a bear meat dinner? How would I work in the episode in which a drunken MGU professor of classics cornered me in a steambath and made me listen to a two-hour diatribe against Aram Khatchaturian's ballet *Spartak*? How much could I tell about my close call in Tbilisi? As I read through my notes I saw that much of what I had recorded consisted of fragments that led nowhere: seeing wedding parties drive up to Red Square to leave a bridal offering of flowers near Lenin's tomb, like bouquets on the Blessed Mother's altar; hearing a rock band in Krasnodar play "Go Down, Moses" and "No One Can Take My Freedom Away"; drinking a glass of tea on the top tier of GUM, the great department store on Red Square, and feeding crumbs to the sparrows that had lived for generations inside the vast store; giving coins to the maimed beggars sprawled in the snow outside St. Nicholas' Church in Lenigrad.

I arranged my notes on the dark leather seat until they looked like stars in a distant galaxy. Then, suddenly tired of the whole subject, I switched off the light and sat quietly by the window, thinking of the people in Moscow that I missed already. Tatjana was right — it was like praying.

Long into the night I sat by the window, until the stars pierced the deep Russian sky everywhere I could see.

I meditated on the stars and thought of all the episodes of my life in Russia, the people I had met during these months, saints and sinners and spies and fly-by-nights, and my unnamed, unknown cohorts in the Hotel Peking in the heart of Moscow, the center of all mystery.

I remembered the last questions that my Russian language tutor in the United States had asked. I had no relatives in Russia, I was not Jewish, I knew no dissidents. Perhaps, however, I *had* become a disloyal citizen. Yet not, I told myself, an enemy of the people.

I remembered that whenever I went to the opera or ballet at the Palace of Congress, during intermission I would see several old gentlemen whose broad chests were covered with medals and awards, dozens of them. Heroes of the state invariably wore blue suits so that the red ribbons and the gold medals would show to best advantage.

The stars arranged against the night looked like a heraldic crest of medallions.

I felt myself nodding, and wisps of dreams blended with the dark shapes outside the window. The train's rocking motion, as always, made me feel sleepy and floated me on a thick warm river. "You'll never know how much I liked you," I heard Marya say — or was it Tatjana? What was Andrei whispering? His words and his luminous face were swept away on the quick-running flood.

All my friends were lost to me now.

Yet not lost. However they changed, they would remain the same for me, just as Tatjana and I would stay forever fixed in her snapshot, two antique lovers in a paper miniature.

My notes jiggled on the dark seat as the train rocked. I had made them haphazardly, accidentally. Now I must make something of them, a legend which would match my life in Russia and make my friends and enemies and lovers move and speak once more.

Even when I fell asleep I continued to see my notes. They took life and shape, like shirts drying on a clothesline tossed by a wind. They waved their arms at me in a gay, ghostly dance.

As I slept, the train passed across the border into Poland. I slept and dreamed backward into my legendary Russian life.